DEMOCRACY, LIBERALISM, AND WAR

CRITICAL SECURITY STUDIES

Ken Booth, SERIES EDITOR
UNIVERSITY OF WALES, ABERYSTWYTH

DEMOCRACY, LIBERALISM, AND WAR

Rethinking the Democratic Peace Debate

EDITED BY
Tarak Barkawi
Mark Laffey

LYNNE
RIENNER
PUBLISHERS

BOULDER
LONDON

Research for this project was supported by the
Social Science Research Council.

Published in the United States of America in 2001 by
Lynne Rienner Publishers, Inc.
1800 30th Street, Boulder, Colorado 80301
www.rienner.com

and in the United Kingdom by
Lynne Rienner Publishers, Inc.
3 Henrietta Street, Covent Garden, London WC2E 8LU

Library of Congress Cataloging-in-Publication Data
Democracy, liberalism, and war : rethinking the democratic peace debate /
    edited by Tarak Barkawi and Mark Laffey.
        p. cm.
    Includes bibliographical references and index.
    ISBN 1-55587-955-1 (alk. paper)
    1. Democracy. 2. Liberalism. 3. War. I. Barkawi, Tarak.
II. Laffey, Mark.
JC421.D46344 2001
327.1'72—dc21   2001019384

British Cataloguing in Publication Data
A Cataloguing in Publication record for this book
is available from the British Library.

Printed and bound in the United States of America

        The paper used in this publication meets the requirements
  ∞   of the American National Standard for Permanence of
        Paper for Printed Library Materials Z39.48-1984.

    5 4 3 2 1

Contents

Acknowledgments

We have incurred many debts in producing this volume. Bud Duvall first suggested that we needed to generate new scholarship on the "democratic peace," rather than simply collect existing critiques in a textbook as we had originally intended. We thank Bud for that initial impetus and for his intellectual and professional guidance over many years. We are grateful to the Committee on International Peace and Security of the Social Science Research Council (SSRC) for providing funds for the workshop, held in Minneapolis in 1998, at which earlier versions of most of these chapters were presented. We also thank the College of Liberal Arts of the University of Minnesota for providing additional funds. The workshop and subsequent revisions of the chapters benefited immensely from the participation of Ido Oren and John Owen. Thanks also to Shampa Biswas, Bud Duvall, and Jutta Weldes, who acted as discussants.

From an early stage of the project, Keith Krause, Robert Latham, and Martin Shaw offered enthusiastic support and practical advice. We are especially grateful to Robert and the SSRC for helping us to obtain funding to present the project at Columbia, Aberystwyth, and the School of Oriental and African Studies. Thanks are due to the audiences at those institutions for their stimulating questions and critical commentary, from which we learned a great deal.

Some of the chapters in this book were presented in earlier versions at the International Studies Association meeting held in Los Angeles in 2000. Thanks to Mick Mann, Bruce Cumings, and Tim Kubik for taking time out of their busy schedules to participate in the session and to Mick Cox, who proved a fine discussant. We thank Walter Carlsnaes, John MacMillan, and two anonymous reviewers—one of whom implied that we are communists—for their comments on an earlier version of the introduction. Finally, we thank Richard Purslow and Shena Redmond of Lynne Rienner Publishers—the volume is better for their help.

This project has been a long time coming to fruition since we first began talking about it in Liquor Lyle's and the 400 Bar in Minneapolis. Those closest to us—Susie and Jutta—have contributed to it in innumerable ways. They have our heartfelt thanks, for we never would have gotten here without them.

—*T. B.*
M. L.

1

Introduction:
The International Relations of
Democracy, Liberalism, and War

Tarak Barkawi and Mark Laffey

The only worthwhile answers are those that blow up the questions.
                                        —Susan Sontag

In the closing years of the twentieth century, world politics was marked by celebrations of democracy and the global spread of liberal institutions such as market economies, free trade, multiparty electoral systems, and human rights. As well as promising prosperity, for many these developments offered hope that a solution to the problem of war was at hand. In Western policymaking circles it became commonplace to link liberal institutions in economy and politics to peaceful interstate relations (Clinton, 1994). Even if they continued to use force in their relations with nonliberal states, liberal states were far less likely to wage war on one another. Scholars claimed to provide rigorous and scientific support for the purported relationship between democracy and peace. They argued that a zone of peace had developed among liberal democratic states, confirming long-held assumptions regarding the peaceful propensities of republics (Kant, 1991 [1796]; Oneal and Russett, 1997).

While the pacific benefits of liberal democracy were being trumpeted, world politics continued to be marked by extreme divides of wealth and power as well as the continuation of violent conflict. If international life had become more peaceful and prosperous in the Western heartlands of the zone of peace, it remained impoverished and conflict-ridden in much of the zone of war outside. For proponents of the "democratic peace" (DP), the solution is simple: the further spread of liberal institutions throughout the

1

world, a solution that has been taken up in practice. A wide variety of governmental and nongovernmental organizations now promote democratic and liberal institutions across the world (e.g., Dobbs, 2000; Robinson, 1996b).

This volume challenges the received international wisdom about democracy, liberalism, and war. The now extensive literature on the DP is concerned with a single hypothesis regarding the impact of liberal democracy on interstate peace. Such a narrow focus blinds inquiry to the multiple relations between and among democracy, liberalism, and war in the modern world. The zones of peace and war are not separate and discrete phenomena explained by the presence or absence of liberal institutions within states but effects of mutually constitutive international political, social, and economic relations. The DP, with its transhistorical causal law based on fixed definitions of democracy and war and a nation-state ontology of the international, is far too simplistic a frame from which to analyze the various historical and contemporary configurations of democracy, liberalism, and war. This volume places the empirical pattern identified by the DP—of peace between liberal democratic states—in international and historical context. In doing so, it reveals the *multiple* relations among democracy, liberalism, and the use of force; identifies transformations in the character of war and the state elided by the DP; and shows how claims for the pacific nature of liberal democracy are Eurocentric and depend on bad history and historical forgetting. Attention to international and historical context is crucial to any understanding of the place of democracy, liberalism, and war in world politics.

In addition to introducing the volume, this chapter outlines what it means to place the DP in historical and international context. The next section briefly discusses the differences between the perspective taken in most of the DP literature, both among critics and proponents, and that taken in this volume. It then illustrates how attention to context transforms our understanding of states, of war and the use of force, and of democracy and liberalism.

FROM THE DEMOCRATIC PEACE
TO THE INTERNATIONAL RELATIONS OF
DEMOCRACY, LIBERALISM, AND WAR

According to proponents of the DP proposition, one variable condition (status as a liberal democratic state) has a powerful causal impact on another (peace, that is, the absence of war among such states). This impact is evidenced in a pattern of very strong empirical regularity identified in statistical tests (e.g., Ray, 1995). All that remains in doubt, in this view, is the causal mechanism itself—that is, a theoretic explanation for the causal relationship (Bueno de Mesquita et al., 1999; Morgan, 1993; Russett, 1993:

chapter 2). Emerging in response to the statistical discovery of the existence of interstate peace among liberal democracies, a growing qualitative literature, building on the seminal work of Michael Doyle, seeks to identify the causal mechanisms and processes responsible (e.g., Doyle, 1983; Owen, 1994; Elman, 1997, 1999). In essence, the claim now being made is that the character of international politics itself, long premised on the ever-present possibility of war, has undergone fundamental transformation in some parts of the world. At the same time, and despite the contemporary rhetoric of globalization, the underlying context of international politics is assumed to have remained fundamentally the same. In the literature on the DP, that context is conceived as one of relations between and among territorial and sovereign states. The great bulk of analysis both for and against the DP proposition takes for granted that the basic unit of analysis is the sovereign territorial state and its relations with other states. The DP is a peace between and among liberal democratic *states* (Doyle, 1986; Maoz and Russett, 1992, 1993; Gowa, 1999). The prescription for more peaceful interstate relations, then, is to "just add liberal democracy" (Morgan and Schwebach, 1992).

The DP debates are premised on ahistorical assumptions of embedded statism and are caught in the territorial trap (Agnew, 1994). They assume across historical eras the centrality of both the sovereign territorial state and the anarchic character of the international system to analysis of the DP. Sovereignty, territoriality, and states are important to an understanding of world politics. But social and political processes not limited by sovereign state borders such as globalization (Held et al., 1999), the internationalization of capital (Jenkins, 1987), and modernity (Chapter 9, this volume)— to cite only three examples—are equally crucial to the analysis of international relations. Such historical processes of global social change are productive of the international context in which relations between states take place; they are in fact constitutive of international orders and the entities, such as liberal democratic states, that populate them (Ruggie, 1993; Scholte, 1993). Analysis of the diverse historical contexts of relations between and among liberalism, democracy, and war is necessary if we are to understand their changing role in the international system. Indeed, such analysis forces recognition of the ways in which democracy, liberalism, and war—in their relations with one another and with other social phenomena such as capitalism and sovereign statehood—are intimately bound up with "the international" (Halliday, 1994: chapter 1).

Assumptions of embedded statism also enable the tendency in the DP literature to divide the world, both conceptually and empirically, in two. Scholars and policymakers routinely speak of "two worlds," a putative zone of peace located predominantly among Northern states and a zone of war located in the South (van Creveld, 1991; Goldgeier and McFaul, 1992; for an empirical critique, see Kacowicz, 1998). Where the former is characterized by Lockean and Kantian logics of rivalry and friendship, the latter remains caught in a Hobbesian logic of war (Wendt, 1999). Dividing the world in two implicitly denies the existence of sustained and systematic relations between the two zones. But the emergence of a liberal peace in the North is inextricably implicated in the emergence of a nonliberal zone of war elsewhere (e.g., Barkawi and Laffey, 1999). There is only one world, not two (or three; Ahmad, 1994 [1992]; Pletsch, 1981). The bifurcated division of the world found in the DP debates reproduces older discourses of North-South relations: the claim that there is a democratic peace rests on a Eurocentric conception of modernity. This is evident in the teleology implicit in the hierarchy between the two zones. The zone of peace shows to the zone of war its future—if it embraces liberal democracy—whereas the zone of war shows to the zone of peace its own recent past. Only national development along liberal democratic and free market lines can admit Southern states to the zone of peace and prosperity.

In its present form, the DP literature offers a poor vantage point from which to analyze the nature and meaning of the zones of peace and war because of the extraordinarily limited terms within which the debate is conducted. The fixation on a one-way causal hypothesis regarding the impact of liberal democracy on peace is far too narrow an ambit. Indicative of this narrowness is the failure adequately to critique the basic theoretic terms through which the DP proposition is constructed and the fact of democratic peace produced. It is a truism that the meaning of terms such as *democracy* and *war* is essentially contested in both political life and social scientific inquiry. The assumed centrality of the sovereign state to analysis of world politics is also subject to questioning by scholars and nonscholars alike. And yet, a few significant exceptions aside (e.g., Latham, 1997; MacMillan, 1995), across the range of proponents and critics of the DP little dispute exists over the meaning of democracy—liberal or market democracy; the definition of interstate war—that of the Correlates of War project (CoW); or the main unit of analysis—the sovereign territorial state. The only relationship analyzed in almost the entirety of the literature, quantitative and qualitative alike, is the purported causal relation between liberal democracy and interstate peace. Such limited theoretic terms shared among critics and proponents of the DP produce a relative blindness to the multiple relations among liberalism, democracy, and war evident to students of modern history and politics. Adequate analysis demands attention to this broader universe.

In pursuit of this objective, the chapters in this volume rethink the foundations of the DP debates by reconsidering the terms through which those debates are conducted. They do so by placing democracy, liberalism, and war in historical and international context and by refusing to assume in advance which are the most significant causal relations, their direction, or their consequences. Such a shift in focus generates significant insights into the relations between liberal democracy and interstate war as understood in the DP debates, but that is not our primary goal. Relocating the international and historical contexts of democracy, liberalism, and war leads to a research agenda centered not on the question of why liberal democratic states seldom use force in their relations with one another but instead organized around *the international relations of democracy, liberalism, and war.* That agenda begins by critically interrogating the terms framing it: the state, force and war, liberalism, and democracy.

States in Context

In the DP literature a commitment to the sovereign state structures analysis of the relations among democracy, liberalism, and war in fundamental ways. The conceptions of democracy and war that inform the DP hypothesis presuppose the territorial state: "democracy" refers to a particular set of electoral institutions and political and civil rights within the boundaries of a sovereign state, and "war" refers to interstate relations (Russett, 1993: 11–16). Variation in the frequency and spatial distribution of war between states is attributed to the liberal democratic character of a state's internal politics and to the norms that emerge to govern relations between such states in an anarchic interstate system. Where the internal politics of states are not liberal democratic, it is assumed that interstate relations continue to be governed by realpolitik and hence that the likelihood of interstate war is not reduced. The sovereign territorial state sits at the core of the DP debates.

Beginning with the sovereign territorial state motivates the focus on interstate dyads evident in the DP literature and means that explanation can move in only two directions: either inward to domestic society or outward to the international system, conceived as the space in which states interact. Assumptions of the state as a sovereign entity and the location of state-society relations within a territorially defined totality reinforce the presumption of anarchy in interstate relations and the turn to classical realist models of geopolitical relations. In common with realist accounts of the international, this state of affairs is assumed to have lasted for a very long time. The DP hypothesis is explicitly transhistorical in nature, purporting to apply since at least 1816 and in some views extending back to the city-states of ancient Greece (Bremmer, 1993; Maoz and Abdolali, 1989; Weart, 1998). The theoretic terms used to construct this proposition are considered analytically and empirically valid for all of this period. A state is a state is a state, whether in the fourth century B.C., at the beginning of the nineteenth century, or at the end of the twentieth century. Particularly questionable is the tendency unreflectively to date the DP from 1815, in accord with the conventions of the CoW data set. Historical periodizations require substantive justification. It is unclear why 1815 is significant for analysis of relations between liberal democratic states other than that this date conveniently avoids the war of 1812–1814 between the world's two leading liberal powers.[1]

The sovereign territorial state is the wrong place from which to begin analysis, as reflection on the history of the state and the international system shows. For 250 of the past 300 years the dominant political form in the international system has been not the territorial state but the imperial state and the empire (Shaw, 1997b: 499; see also Doyle, 1986; Petras and Morley, 1981). In analysis of imperial states and empires, both formal and informal, it is not analytically justifiable to draw a rigid boundary between a peaceful and prosperous metropole and a strife-torn and exploited periphery, as each is intimately bound up with the other (e.g., Kolko, 1988). Moreover, even at their height empires typically do not display either the centralization of authority or the hard territorial boundaries taken for granted in discussions of the territorial state. For states that are or have been both imperial and liberal, such as Belgium, Britain, France, Holland, and the United States (see Doyle, 1996: table 1), analysis of the relations among liberal democracy and war cannot simply stipulate that the character of relations between territory, population, and rule takes the form of sovereign statehood (Chapter 6, this volume). Relations between the formal apparatus of the "home" state within an imperial state or empire (e.g., Britain) and the populations and territories, both at home (e.g., in Wales, Scotland, Ireland, and England) and abroad (e.g., in Australia, Egypt, Kenya, and India), over which rule is exercised are multiple and diverse. Typically, rule through liberal institutions was limited to the home territories and established settler colonies, while the empire was governed autocratically or indirectly through local potentates. In the contemporary era, similarly diverse relations among rule, territory, and populations are easily identified. Rule of the periphery by the core is now often exercised through international bodies such as the International Monetary Fund, World Bank, and the World Trade Organization that are not democratically organized and have no sovereign power in the Westphalian sense (Cox, 1981; Peck and Tickell, 1994).

The changing nature of the state evident in the imperial history of international relations renders assumptions based on embedded statism profoundly problematic. The DP debates assume that states have remained essentially the same, most importantly with respect to their capacity to wage war independently over the period of the DP. But even along this core dimension of state power—force—states are not the same in all times and places. This is readily apparent in the changing international organization of force. For example, over the course of the twentieth century, the norm for Western liberal democracies was alliance warfare or preparation for it

(McNeill, 1982: chapters 9–10). This led to increasing transnational military organization and coordination with respect to operations, training, logistics, and weapons procurement. These processes were evident in World Wars I and II and accelerated with the founding of the North Atlantic Treaty Organization (NATO) in 1949. The question of why NATO members, who constitute a significant percentage of the population of the zone of peace, have not waged war against one another is largely nonsensical. The militaries of these states were integrated to a significant degree, especially in respect to command and control, and the processes of strategic decision-making have been centered in Washington, symbolized by the fact that a U.S. general has always been the supreme commander. Indeed, the largest armed forces aside from the U.S. military, those of the former West Germany, lacked an independent national command structure during the Cold War (Bundesminister der Verteidigung, 1985: 73, section 160).[2] In these and other ways, West Germany was rendered (like Japan, where similar relations were evident) a semisovereign, externally penetrated polity (Deudney and Ikenberry, 1999).

A focus on force as one of the state's defining characteristics thus reveals that the state has undergone significant transformations. A stipulated conception of the state obscures its shifting nature, over time and across different international systems. To understand the relations among democracy, liberalism, force, and war—and the social and political dynamics that shape such relations—attention must be paid to historical transformations in the nature of the state and the state system. Aside from the path-breaking work of Robert Latham (1997), little attention is given to these developments in the DP debates.

Liberal democratic institutions and their effects on war and the use of force are poorly understood if interpreted through the figure of the sovereign and territorial state. The social and political processes productive of a historically evolving international system, and the role of liberalism and democracy in it, do not come in sovereign territorial boxes. As John Agnew and Stuart Corbridge argue, "The territorial state has been 'prior' to and a 'container' of society only under specific conditions" (1995: 94). By fixing the essential territorial character of the liberal democratic state, as in statistical analyses and historical studies that assume states have been essentially the same since 1816, the history of political and social relations, of those relations constitutive of states and the international systems they are embedded within, is "stripped of explanatory force" (Maclean, 1984: 137; Thorne, 1988). We are then literally unable to conceive of explanation in anything other than the state-centric terms that shape almost all extant analyses of the relations among democracy, liberalism, and war. In an era characterized by increased awareness of the global forces shaping social and political life, this is a curiously ahistorical and geographically naive

assumption. The relations among state, society, and territory vary historically and across the international system and are shaped by larger processes
of global social change—processes obscured by analytic commitments to
embedded statism (Chapter 9, this volume).

Mention of "larger processes of global social change" that transcend
and transform the territorial state inevitably implicates our argument in ongoing debates about globalization (McMichael, 2000; Scholte, 2000). These
debates are centrally concerned with the ways in which the international
system and the entities within it are shaped by global forces and processes
not readily understood in terms of states and their relations with one another. The dynamics of such processes and relations cannot be reduced to
relations between states, sovereign or otherwise, or those between North
and South, or to relations between domestic and international spheres; and
causation cannot be located exclusively in one or the other. Typically, the
causal dynamics of these relations and processes are multiple and codeter-
mining. They are properly international and must be analyzed as such.
Globalization and the social forces associated with it are central to our conception of a changing international system, of the historical context of relations in world politics.

Much recent discussion of globalization emphasizes the myriad ways
in which the world is becoming one place and typically constructs this as a
post–World War II phenomenon (Ohmae, 1990; cf. P. Smith, 1997). In contrast, we take a longer view of the timeframe appropriate to an understanding of global social change, including globalization (Arrighi, 1999). The
presentist bias evident in the globalization debates overlooks the different
forms taken by global social change over time and obscures the ways in
which what is now referred to as globalization emerged out of earlier forms
of global social change associated with Western imperialism, the internationalization of capital, the spread of bureaucratic forms of social organization, and modernity more generally. Relations of hierarchy between core
and periphery are often reinforced rather than erased by processes of globalization, such as those evident in the ongoing restructuring of the international economic order, for example, or in the promotion of neoliberal forms
of governance and economic development (Raghavan, 1990; C. Thomas,
1999). This undermines claims that globalization is an entirely novel phenomenon or that it produces an increasingly homogenized world.

There is a widespread tendency to assume that states and globalization
stand in opposition to each other and to see globalization in economistic or
cultural terms alone. The role of force and state power in globalization is often
overlooked (Panitch, 1996). But force has been and continues to be integral
to the processes of transformation glossed under the rubric of globalization,
both within states (Chapter 8, this volume) and between them (Andreas,
2000). Globalization was made possible by Western colonial expansion,

which faced armed resistance at nearly every turn. Similar patterns are evident in the contemporary era. The operations of Western multinational corporations (MNCs) in the Third World often face resistance ranging from nonviolent demonstrations to banditry and insurgency. Much like the old imperial trading companies, MNCs have consequently made arrangements for their own security—raising security forces, seeking protection from those of the host government, or even subsidizing elements of the host government's military.[3] The patterns of continuity between contemporary globalization and older, allegedly extinct relations of imperial power projection are sometimes strikingly evident. Militarized "humanitarian intervention" in the former Yugoslavia has resulted, in Kosovo and Bosnia, in colonies ruled by the international community in which elections that do not result in the right choice are subverted at will by Western officials.[4] Such practices, intimately bound up with globalization, reproduce discernibly imperial relations of hierarchy and subordination.

Once proponents of the DP define the basic ontology of the international in terms of sovereign territorial states, the major dimensions along which variation can take place are the presence or absence of liberal democracy (Is this state a liberal democracy?) and war (Is this state at war?). Stipulated definitions of democracy and war mean it makes little difference whether analysis takes a statistical or a qualitative form. Such questions deny the historicity of the international system and of the theoretical terms that enable the DP proposition. This is apparent if we consider the historically changing character of war and the use of force.

Contexts of Force and War

War, or organized violence between political entities, is an institution subject to historical transformation. Limited clashes for limited gain between the small professional armies of old-regime Europe gave way in the Napoleonic era to the continental campaigns of massed national armies. Throughout the eighteenth and nineteenth centuries, expansion into the non-European world led to continual armed conflict, or "small wars," often waged through proxies or with foreign-raised, colonial troops. Within Europe, the rise of mass society, of the industrial capacity to arm, equip, and transport armies of millions, and of professional general staffs monopolizing knowledge of the means and purposes of war created the possibility for a new form of industrialized "total war." Unleashed in the first half of the twentieth century, this form of war twice transformed European politics and society in ways far too numerous to catalog. The popular costs of war became so great that absolute war aims were necessary, and war assumed the face of a deadly contest between ideologies. The advent of nuclear weaponry, however, rapidly made the prospect of further total wars suicidal, and the Cold War era began. Armed conflict between great powers once again became limited and chiefly took the form of struggle between their respective clients in a periphery caught up in the upheavals of decolonization. With the collapse of the Soviet challenge to Western liberal and capitalist hegemony and the rise of information technologies, war underwent further transformation. Cyberwarfare makes possible deterritorialized forms of attack and, for the first time since the early days of revolutionary guerrilla warfare, promises a significant increase in the power of counterhegemonic forces. Relying principally on air power, Western powers turned to "peace enforcement" and "humanitarian war" to effect their purposes through armed force in the Gulf and the Balkans.

Against these many transformations in the nature of war, in the international organization of force, of relations between war and society, and of the purposes for which war is fought, the DP is based on a single, static definition of "interstate war": violent conflict between sovereign states resulting in at least 1,000 battle deaths, although some authors use a lower threshold of 200 deaths (Small and Singer, 1982; Weart, 1998). This definition is the main indicator of war used in constructing the DP hypothesis; if no violent conflict that meets these criteria is occurring, states are considered to be at peace.[5] Establishing an empirical pattern across historical eras, as in the DP, requires a fixed definition of war. Such a definition is necessarily based on an image of war derived from a particular historical context, of European power politics in a system of sovereign states. As a consequence, it is insensitive to the character of war waged *outside* that context, an insensitivity well illustrated by Spencer Weart's offhand remark regarding the Central Intelligency Agency's (CIA's) invasion of Guatemala in 1954: "Anyone who insists on putting a conflict like this in the category of 'war' would have to invent some other term to describe . . . horrific full-scale international warfare" (1998: 220–221). The emphasis on "scale" is evident in the logical error built into the CoW approach, which bases its definition of war in part on a threshold of military casualties, a measure of intensity, rather than a substantive conception of what kind of a relation war *is* in a modern context—one in which force is used to achieve political purposes. Naturally, how force is organized and used is shaped by historical and international context. Analysis must therefore be sensitive to the particular social and strategic terrain upon which political authorities and their military forces operate. The fact that the CIA used force in 1954 like a "light, handy rapier" should not be allowed, by definitional fiat, to obscure the fact that the United States waged a war against Guatemala (Karl von Clausewitz, quoted in McClintock, 1992: ix).

More than simply matters of scale is involved. Sovereignty is fundamental to CoW's typology of war. Wars are categorized on the basis of their relation to sovereign borders, with the chief distinction that between intrastate and interstate wars (Small and Singer, 1982; cf. Wayman, Singer, and Sarkees, 1996). Such categories assume what should be empirically investigated: that historically wars and armed forces have had fixed and regular relations with sovereign statehood. They also assume that sovereign statehood remains a substantively unchanging institution. Neither of these assumptions can withstand even cursory historical scrutiny (on sovereignty, see Biersteker and Weber, 1996; D. Williams, 2000). For example, CoW stipulates that for a state to be considered at war, its own national armed forces must actively engage in combat and suffer casualties (Small and Singer, 1982: 218–219). In this way an entire history of war by proxy, of the use of clients and foreign-raised forces, is obscured. CoW classifies events in Guatemala in 1954 as a civil war—an internal conflict between two *Guatemalan* factions (Small and Singer, 1982: 324). The role of the United States in actively producing and supporting one of those factions is rendered invisible (Chapter 6, this volume). Equally, the significance of the long-term integration of Western militaries, evident in the contemporary organization of NATO, for how we understand the modern state is invisible. Against the embedded statism of the DP debates, integration of the means of exercising violence means the state in its classical Weberian conception is no longer national but international (Shaw, 1997b). Warfare—and the changing character of relations among war, armed force, and society—contributes to the making and unmaking of international orders and political forms. Stipulated definitions based on numbers of national military deaths and the diplomatic recognition of sovereignty are simply unable to comprehend the place of war in the history of international relations (e.g., Weltman, 1995).

Wars occur in definite historical contexts that shape their conduct and consequences for other social relations and processes, such as democracy or sovereign statehood. Clausewitz (1976), for example, was acutely aware that the French Revolution had unleashed new social forces that dramatically altered the face of war in his time, and so his analysis focused on relations among "the people" conceived as a nation, sovereign political authority, and the military. Martin van Creveld (1991) has usefully termed Clausewitz's approach "trinitarian": war is waged by entities composed of a government, a people, and a military contained behind sovereign borders and is a means by which such entities secure their interests and protect the good life made possible by settled, territorial rule. It speaks to the power of Clausewitz's analysis that his account of war in trinitarian context provided a useful, if partial, guide for understanding *European* war right through the total wars of the twentieth century. His insistence that war is an act of force with no logical limit and that the passions of the people had become harnessed to the military power of states prefigured both the destructiveness of modern war and the ways in which the good life within states was increasingly shaped by the demands of war preparation and war waging. It would be a fundamental mistake, however, to assume that trinitarian war provides an adequate guide to the nature of war across historical and geographical contexts; even European states conducted war outside Europe in very different ways. This is the error proponents of the DP make in using CoW's category of interstate war as the main indicator of war between democracies.

The core difficulty with fixing the meaning of war is that analysis is rendered insensitive to historical transformations in the nature of war and to the implications of these transformations for Western democracies (Chapter 9, this volume). For example, beginning in the mid–nineteenth century, war was progressively industrialized and totalized. During World Wars of the first half of the twentieth century, the bureaucratization and industrialization of warfare arguably transformed the Western state into a "single national firm for waging war" (McNeill, 1982: 317). Conceptions of the nation were harnessed directly to total war through the mass conscription of citizen armies (Hobsbawm, 1990; Mann, 1988: chapter 6). Historically static definitions of war render the totalization of modern conventional warfare marginal to analysis, despite its significance for the kinds of political, social, and economic institutions that characterize contemporary Western liberal democracies (e.g., Shaw, 1988; Sparrow, 1996; Tilly, 1992). The merging of industry, technology, and bureaucracy into an apparatus for waging war contributed directly to the militarization of society (Gillis, 1989; Shaw, 1991) and the consolidation of authority within the executive. Additionally, large-scale modern conventional warfare is of necessity alliance warfare and entails a meshing of the military and industrial complexes of allies. Alliance cooperation in World War II laid the groundwork for the integration of Western militaries that was so much a feature of both the Cold War and post–Cold War eras. Military integration worked to undermine the ability of citizens in North Atlantic democracies to determine the policies pursued in their name, as, for example, in the case of nuclear deployments in Western Europe. In these and other ways, the totalization of war has broad implications not only for what war is and how it is conducted but also for the social institutions and practices of democracy.

The implications of the changing organization of force for democracy are evident in the development of nuclear weaponry. One feature of the embedded statism in the DP debates is the unexamined assumption that liberal democratic militaries are fully controlled by civilian executive authority (Chapter 5, this volume). Yet the history of nuclear weapons acquisition, targeting, and operational planning in the United States suggests strongly that the executive and its strategic advisers failed to exercise control over the military bureaucracies (D. Rosenberg, 1983; Sagan, 1993). Not only did placing nuclear forces on high alert challenge the war powers of both the Congress and the president, but if the president had sought a nuclear option from his military advisers he would have been constrained fundamentally by the military's assumptions and planning regarding the size, nature, and targeting of any nuclear strike (Bundy, 1988; Eden, forthcoming). Such constraints resulted in part from the technical complexity of nuclear operational planning, but they also reflected assumptions about the nature of the Cold War and the Soviet opponent built into the military's planning—assumptions that would not necessarily be shared by a civilian executive authority seeking to avert the catastrophe involved in *any* use of nuclear force (Barkawi, 1998; Bundy, 1988: 589–607). Luckily, this "gap" in civilian control was never put to a major test, but it nonetheless demonstrates the need for historically sensitive analysis of shifts in the nature of armed force and its relation to democracy. There can be no assumption, as CoW makes, that a context of trinitarian war is appropriate for analysis of warfare across historical, social, and strategic contexts. Nor can one assume, as proponents of the DP do, that the militaries of democratic states are not international actors in their own right, able to shape and influence events both at home and abroad—often in ways contrary to the wishes of citizens and political authorities. Obviously, this last point raises serious questions about how liberal democracy is presumed to work in the DP literature.

States and warfare are perennial, if historically variable, features of world politics; liberalism and democracy are not. Indeed, whether as central and defining or merely marginal features of particular states and international orders, liberalism and democracy are the exception rather than the rule. We thus consider these elements of the DP proposition last.

Contexts of Liberalism and Democracy

The DP debates adopt an essentially liberal definition of their independent variable, democracy, which is defined as an institutional ensemble consisting of competitive multiparty elections, a representative legislature, a broad franchise among citizens who share a bundle of liberal civil and political rights—including the right to own private property—and a market economy in which most investment decisions rest in private hands (e.g., Doyle, 1996: 5–6, and table 1, note a).[6] Defining democracy in liberal terms, collapsing the distinctions between democracy and liberalism, is unsurprising given that liberalism is the dominant ideology of the modern state in the contemporary West. But democracy and liberalism are distinct and by no means necessarily compatible (Chapter 8, this volume). Historically, democracy and liberalism have taken different forms and meant different things to different people, with different implications for institutional forms and the relative power of publics and elites. A fixed definition of democracy or liberalism will reflect a particular historical moment; a particular set of social, political, economic, and social circumstances; and a particular understanding of what being democratic or liberal entails. Struggles over the meanings of democracy, liberalism, and their institutional forms comprise much of the political history of the Western liberal democracies, a history obscured by the stipulated institutional or procedural definition used in the DP debates.

Reflecting on the contested and malleable nature of democracy revealed by its histories, as well as the sheer complexity of modern polities, John Dryzek (1996) argues that democracy should be understood as a project, as the product of political struggle over the degree to which publics can participate in and shape the conditions of their lives.[7] Democracy is about *popular rule*. Liberalism, in contrast, is about the construction of a particular kind of *social order*, organized around the individual and his or her rights. There is no necessary connection between a particular set of institutions—domestic or international, liberal or otherwise—and democracy; even the existence of an opposition party is only contingently part of what democracy means (Cruise O'Brien, 1999). Like Clausewitz's conception of war, Dryzek's view of democracy as a project directs attention to the ways in which it is shaped by political and historical context. It opens up the question of why democracy has come to be understood in particular ways and the consequences for institutions, practices, and state action. Seeing democracy as a project, as the contested product of political struggle over the contours of rule by "the people," however defined (Chapter 4, this volume), enables the drawing of distinctions between different kinds of democracy linked to the particular social relations out of which they emerge. Analysis is sensitive to the particular social and political terrain on which democratic projects are pursued. By contrast, the statistical proofs of the DP necessarily involve fixing the meaning of democracy in ways that reflect a particular context, that of North American social science and the politics of North Atlantic democracies (Oren, 1995). That understanding informs nonquantitative analyses as well (e.g., Owen, 1997; Elman, 1999).

Efforts to analyze democracy and liberalism in context are further hampered by a commitment in the DP debates to empiricism in the service of scientific rigor. Indeed, the contemporary appeal of the DP proposition owes much to its distinctive blend of liberalism and empiricism. The discovery of the DP in statistical analyses requires that democracy—and by implication, how it functions and its effects on states' decisions to use force—be defined across historical periods. This is so despite the explicit recognition that as a result of shifts in the franchise, for example, democracy has changed over time. A liberal conception of democracy is assumed to be applicable to the entire period of the DP. If this were not the case, statistical comparison of cases from, for example, the nineteenth, twentieth, and twenty-first centuries would be invalid. Such an assumption explicitly denies the significance of changing institutional forms, and hence of historical context, for the nature and meaning of democracy. To the extent that changes in the meaning and institutional forms of democracy are acknowledged, they are seen primarily as matters of coding; implicitly, the more democracy changes, the more it stays the same. This ignores the fact that whether or not a particular polity is democratic cannot be determined simply by pointing to the presence or absence of a particular set of institutions (Chapter 3, this volume). Democracy means different things in different times and places and can be pursued through a variety of institutional forms; determining whether some set of arrangements is democratic is inherently a *political* question (Taylor, 1985). Taken together, the liberalism and empiricism structuring the DP debate lead to modes of analysis that fetishize liberal democracy, its mechanisms, and its effects.

Fetishizing democracy is problematic for analysis, because in addition to ignoring the significant changes democracy has undergone historically, it directs attention away from broader processes of social change and their consequences for both what democracy is and how it works. Changes in the nature of liberal democracy itself undermine the assumption that it is either liberal institutions or a set of norms attributable to the social relations they inform that account for the reduced likelihood of democratic states to use force in their relations. Shifting institutional forms and diverse and changing relations with other social institutions and practices mean that democracy—liberal or not—relates to state power in different ways. For instance, over the past two centuries the rise of mass societies and the bureaucratization of politics profoundly transformed liberal democracy (Arblaster, 1984; Chapters 4 and 5, this volume). Liberal democracy in its contemporary form emerges out of these and other diverse processes as a liberal solution to the problem of popular rule: it is a form of elite democracy (M. Weber, 1978: appendix 2; Crozier, Huntington, and Watanuki, 1975). The DP debates ignore the significance of such changes (cf. Robinson, 1996b).

Mass societies developed across the international system alongside the global spread of industrial forms of production, prompted in part by the introduction of large-scale industrial processes that required concentration of populations in urban locations (e.g., Barraclough, 1967: chapter 5). The mobilization of popular masses in anticolonial movements was also important. The increasingly urban character of politics contributed to the rise of vast, impersonal, and ideologically malleable publics. These developments contributed to the centrality of ideology and nationalism in twentieth-century politics and shaped the ability of states to contemplate the use of force and the forms of warfare in which they engaged (Mann, 1996). Ongoing struggle over the meaning and extent of democracy was also conditioned by the variable willingness of the middle class to ally with the new urban working class against entrenched interests and in support of efforts to extend the franchise and the reach of popular rule into the "private" sphere of economic relations (Rueschemeyer, Stephens, and Stephens, 1992). For liberals, popular democracy was anathema and threatened rule of the rich by the poor, who far outnumbered them. Struggle over the proper extent of popular rule over private matters contributed, like the requirements of modern warfare, to the massive expansion of the state apparatus. Mass politics also transformed the state. Both democratic and nondemocratic political systems became dominated by party machines articulated with the highly developed systems of administration and enforcement characteristic of the modern state (e.g., Lindbloom, 1977; Zolo, 1992). In the contemporary period, these transformations continue as democratic and nondemocratic states are reworked in neoliberal ways (e.g., Gill, 2000; Kelsey, 1997).

Despite the implications of these and related shifts for both democracy and *liberal* assumptions about the character of Western states (e.g., Held, 1987), in the DP debates these polities are defined in terms of essentialized and ahistorical understandings of market democracy. As a result, attention to historical shifts in the nature of democracy, in how it works and the implications for the use of force, is rendered marginal to analysis.

These tendencies in the DP literature and their consequences are also apparent in the historically oriented work of analysts such as Michael Doyle (1986, 1996), John Owen (1994, 1997), and John MacMillan (1995, 1996). In contrast to the empiricism evident especially in the statistical literature, these scholars have produced studies of the democratic or, more correctly, the liberal peace sensitive to historical context and make more guarded claims regarding the impact of liberalism on peace. As a result, their accounts of such causation are empirically more plausible than those found elsewhere in this literature, but the manner in which they use "liberal" as a category of analysis remains problematic. Even in the hands of these scholars, the nomenclature of "liberal state" is fundamentally misleading. The institutions and agents identified as liberal in these analyses are not, from a historical sociological point of view, wholly or exclusively liberal; they are also bureaucratic, capitalist, postcolonial, masculine, imperialist, and so on. Liberal states such as Japan, Britain, or the United States are complex and multifaceted social formations; understanding them as liberal reduces this complexity to a single dimension and works against identifying the ways in which liberalism is implicated in a particular context. For example, if liberal conceptions of democracy reflect and enable relations of class power and patriarchy (e.g., Macpherson, 1973; Elshtain, 1993), this ought to raise doubts about the role of liberalism in producing peaceful norms of conflict management that can then be projected into the international system (e.g., Adler, 1997). The violent history of labor and gender relations within liberal democratic states, invisible in the DP debates, suggests a more complex relationship among liberalism, democracy, and social order—peaceful or otherwise.

Ironically, essentializing the liberal character of such polities and attributing forces for peace to liberalism and those for the use of force to other social forces (e.g., Owen, 1997) lead to neglect of the role liberalism and democracy actually play within these formations and across the international system as a whole. In contrast, it is precisely the placing of liberalism and democracy in *international* context that this volume seeks to achieve.

PUTTING THE DEMOCRATIC PEACE IN MOTION

Questioning the assumed centrality of the sovereign territorial state to analysis of world politics, refusing to define war solely in terms of CoW's categories, and rejecting reified understandings of liberal democracy open up a view of the international relations of liberalism, democracy, force, and war different from that found in the DP debates. Doing so enables us to put these categories in motion and to see their different historical configurations. Different forms of democracy, liberalism, and war are linked to the particular social contexts out of which they emerge and reflect the relations of power found there—of capital and labor, for example, or of core and periphery. Democratic projects and war and the use of force are shaped by local and international relations of power (Chapters 7 and 8, this volume). Processes such as bureaucratization and the rise of mass societies or colonization and decolonization are not restricted to particular states but develop across the international system as a whole, producing diverse consequences for particular expressions of democracy and liberalism and for the circumstances under which states and others use force. These processes transform both the nature of the entities in the international system and the relations between them. To repeat, the dynamics of these processes are international; they must be analyzed as such. Shifting the angle of vision in this way throws new light on the international relations of democracy, liberalism, and war. By way of illustration, we sketch one possible line of inquiry here.

It is worth recalling that democracy became one of the organizing principles of core states during the creation of a global system of empires, forged and maintained by colonial wars. Global processes of colonization and decolonization had a direct impact on the development of democracy as a form of social and political organization, both in former colonial territories and in metropolitan states. Imperial power was pitted against local communities and peoples defending or seeking forms of rule often more democratic than those imposed on them. The emergence in former colonies of modern forms of political and social organization is unintelligible apart from the experience of colonization and decolonization. Mass parties in one-party systems and authoritarian forms of state were often the side effects of organizational imperatives stemming from the prosecution of anti-colonial or anti-imperial war (e.g., Ho Chi Minh's Vietnam, Fidel Castro's

Cuba, or Nicaragua under the Sandinistas). Forms of organization adopted in the context of struggle structured postcolonial politics and society in profound ways (Ahmad, 1995). Significantly, one-party systems were often articulated as "democratic." If democracy is about rule by the people, there is nothing inherently undemocratic in rule being carried out by a single party. What is important, at least rhetorically, is the relationship between "the people" and the party as a vehicle through which "the people," viewed as a collective subject rather than an aggregation of rights-bearing individuals, struggle and exercise rule (cf. Held, 1995: 12–14). States and people fashion democratic claims and institutions according to their histories and position within a changing international system.

Wars of decolonization shaped the colonizers too, contributing to social and political upheaval in Britain and the United States and to political transformation in France and Portugal. Resistance to imperialism in the periphery led to transformation in the core. Projection of force abroad had direct consequences in the United States for the practice and meaning of democracy and its relation to war (Chapters 6 and 7, this volume). New forms of military manipulation of the media were developed in the wake of the Vietnam War, forms designed to limit the kind of criticism that plagued the U.S. military in Vietnam and to build "support for the troops" in future conflicts (Klare, 1991, 1995). The defeat in Vietnam had consequences for democracy elsewhere as well. U.S. efforts to militarize its Third World allies were stepped up, as specified in the Nixon Doctrine, in order to shift the burdens of containment strategy onto clients. This had dramatically negative consequences for democracy in places like Chile and Central America, for example. Defeat in Vietnam also prompted the United States to rethink the employment of its own forces, as in the Weinburger Doctrine, which sought to use them only in situations of overwhelming superiority and with adequate public support. To maintain this support, considerable effort was put into minimizing U.S. casualties, as evidenced in the preference for air power in post–Cold War conflicts. As a result, the nature of war changed, both for the U.S. public and for the objects of U.S. military action. For the vast majority of the U.S. civilian population, war took on the character of a "spectator sport" (Mann, 1988: 183 ff) in which nationalist, militarist, and xenophobic sentiments could be safely expressed. Meanwhile, the Iraqi and Serb civilian populations were subjected to prolonged aerial bombardment designed to minimize Western military casualties.

The DP debates raise important questions about the ways in which liberalism, democracy, and war contribute to the production of peaceful worlds. These questions cannot be adequately addressed within the limits of the debates as currently defined. Democracy and war are not separate and discrete variables mediated by the sovereign territorial state but inextricably intertwined social relations, over time shaping and reshaping each other and the state in the context of larger processes of global social change. Locating democracy, liberalism, and war in historical processes of global social change and throwing doubt on the embedded statism that structures these debates opens up a research agenda centered not on the question of why democratic states rarely use force in their relations with one another but instead organized around the international relations of liberalism, democracy, and war.

That agenda must begin by critically interrogating the terms framing it. Equating Kant's republican constitutions with "representative democracy" (Russett, Oneal, and Davis, 1998: 441), for example, or attributing the DP to the internationalization of a "civic culture" (Adler, 1997: 347) betrays a deeply unreflexive attitude toward analysis. None of the terms that enable the democratic peace proposition can be taken for granted. Instead, analysis must question the primacy of sovereign boundaries and historicize rather than stipulate the meaning of democracy, liberalism, and war. Instead of fetishizing liberal democratic norms and institutions, it must attend to the multiple meanings of liberalism and its relations with other social processes. And instead of assuming that democracy and liberalism are forces for peace, analysis must attend to the ways in which they promote the use of force. The ultimate aim of this volume, then, is not simply to critique the democratic peace but to draw attention away from the investigation of a single hypothesis. Redirecting scholarly attention to the wider universe of relations among democracy, liberalism, and war opens up new space for investigation of their role in the making of peaceful and not-so-peaceful worlds.

OUTLINE OF THE VOLUME

Taken together, the chapters in this volume challenge conventional approaches to analysis of the DP in two ways: they *historicize* and *contextualize* the terms of the debate. The variable nature of democracy, liberalism, and war and their impact on one another mean that analysis must be sensitive to historical location and social context. Of course, this does not mean that analysis cannot or should not identify patterns and regularities. But such patterns and regularities will not take the form of a transhistorical, one-way causal hypothesis regarding relations between liberal democratic sovereign states. Placing democracy and force, liberalism and war in their multiple contexts highlights the context-dependent nature of their forms, meanings, and effects and necessitates attention to co- and multiple determinations. The chapters in this volume identify a set of historically and politically significant relations between democracy and force, liberalism and war, thereby generating new hypotheses and questions for research. They provide new ways of thinking beyond the boundaries of an increasingly stale and disciplinary debate between realists and liberals in which the assumptions shared by critics and proponents alike far outweigh the differences that divide them.

The volume opens with chapters by David Blaney and Himadeep Muppidi, each of whom takes the DP debates outside of their founding context of relations among liberal democratic states in the North Atlantic, casting their taken-for-granted assumptions in a sharply different light. The DP explicitly theorizes the extension of various domestic relations into the international realm, destabilizing the boundaries between inside and outside usually taken for granted in democratic theory. Reading the DP as a contribution to *world* democratic theory, Blaney argues that the limits of liberal democracy as democratic practice, in particular its inability to tolerate non-liberals, undermine claims that the extension of liberal democracy into the international realm produces peace. On the contrary, the extension of liberal democracy entails a process of othering that produces conflict and war. Blaney instead calls for the development of a more genuinely democratic world project, beyond the antinomies of realism and liberalism. In a related argument, Muppidi's constructivist view of democracy and peace in postcolonial South Asia makes clear that most analyses of the DP rest on the generalization of unexamined assumptions about the centrality of democracy to state identity and practice peculiar to the West (cf. Chapter 8, this volume). Focusing on India, the world's largest democracy and hitherto all but invisible in the DP literature, Muppidi shows how the variable effects of democracy on interstate relations depend on the meanings attributed to it. In India, democracy is less central to state identity than it is in the West. This highlights the limits of analyses premised on an essentialized understanding of liberal democracy and casts further doubt on efforts to produce peace by promoting liberal democracy beyond the North Atlantic.

Stipulated conceptions of liberal democracy in the DP debates have blinded scholars to the complexity of the history of liberalism and democracy and to the shifting relations between democracy and force. The next two chapters highlight the consequences for analysis: historical forgetting and bad history. Focusing on ethnic wars, Michael Mann challenges the liberal view that ethnic cleansing is launched by authoritarian rather than elected and quasi-democratic regimes. This false assumption is derived from liberalism's misperception of itself and a failure to engage its own history. Especially in colonial settings, for example, mass ethnic killing was directly linked to popular democracy and often targeted indigenous communities more democratic than those of the settlers. This, notes Mann, is the reverse of liberal theory. Closer attention to historical context reveals a more complex and less savory relation between democracy and the use of force than that assumed in the DP debates. In a related analysis, Tim Kubik challenges the assumption that civilian political authority in democratic states exercises effective control over the military. Modern militaries have little in common with the republican citizens' militia Kant thought crucial to perpetual peace, enjoying greater autonomy and reducing the costs of war for the bulk of the population. But scholars have ignored the military by treating it as a variable entirely dependent on the domestic political structures and norms of the liberal democratic state. Kubik challenges this assumption through an analysis of the modernization processes of the German military in the early twentieth century, a modernization more akin to those in liberal democratic states than the DP debates assume. Perhaps surprisingly, historiographical debates about German militarism and modernity force us to rethink taken-for-granted assumptions about the relations between democracies and their militaries.

The next three chapters focus on the heartland of the DP: the United States and the Cold War international order. Situating warfare during the Cold War in historical context, Tarak Barkawi addresses a core lacuna in the DP debates: How is it that the chief liberal power during the Cold War, the United States, waged antidemocratic wars in the periphery? Rather than evade this question by definitional fiat, as do proponents of the DP, Barkawi shows how the strategic context of the Cold War in the Third World led to new forms of war waging, forms that fall outside the statist categories of the DP and that worked to undermine important features of U.S. democracy, such as the legislative control of war powers. Similar themes emerge in Bruce Cumings's chapter. Focusing on the dynamics of modernization, democratization, and warfare in East Asia, he shows that the nation-state ontology of the international presupposed by the DP debates is fundamentally misleading in analysis of the relations between democracy and war. Instead, Cumings emphasizes the ways in which regional orders were inserted into a U.S.-dominated world order. Against the Eurocentric assumptions that inform the DP debates, he also shows that democracy developed through indigenous processes in South Korea and in opposition to U.S. security structures. The U.S. projection of force abroad emerges as a significant factor in shaping the character of democracy at home too. The development (or not) of democracy, both in East Asia and in the United States, cannot be understood in terms of a nation-state ontology of the international. Mark Rupert's chapter further develops this argument about relations between the Cold War international order and democracy. Like Blaney, he points out that coding liberal states as "democratic" directs attention away from the limits of the forms of democracy found in the West. By subsuming capitalism under the category of liberalism, the DP debates ignore the question of whether and how capitalist economies can be said to be democratic. Market democracies, it turns out, are not very democratic at all. Focusing on the continued use of state powers of coercion in labor relations inside liberal democracies, Rupert raises the issue of whether the kind of market democracy the West promotes abroad and at home can be said to be democratic in any significant sense.

These chapters unsettle taken-for-granted assumptions about relations among democracy, liberalism, and war. Martin Shaw and Raymond Duvall and Jutta Weldes sum up the themes of the volume and offer suggestions for future research. Looking at the development of the international system as a whole, Shaw identifies the limits of nation-state ontologies of the international by looking at the development of relations of state power in the modern period. Those relations do not map onto the sovereign territorial division of the globe. Shaw identifies the emergence, transformation, and contemporary decline of forms of state usually understood as national and their gradual transcendence by international forms of state power. This, he argues, is a pivotal change in the modern era and is at the root of the emergence of a zone of peace in the international system. In the final chapter, Duvall and Weldes outline a new critical research agenda for the analysis of the international relations of democracy, liberalism, and war. Organized violence, its causes, and effects are of continuing concern in the contemporary world, and the relations between violence and other kinds of social organization merit serious study. But in its present form, the DP literature is not much help, however real the empirical pattern to which it points. Calling on scholars to abandon their fixation on "a simple bivariate empirical pattern of dubious transhistorical significance," Duvall and Weldes argue instead for greater attention to "the historical systematic contexts that provide the conditions of possibility for the empirical pattern, as well as to the multiple and complex other ways in which liberalism, democracy, war, and peace are interrelated and codetermined." An agenda organized around constitutive rather than causal questions, they argue, directs fresh attention to established concerns, about the DP's claim to explain the world, for example. But it also opens up new lines of inquiry, not least about the ways in which the DP as a set of knowledge claims and policies intervenes in the world. Future research into the international relations of democracy, liberalism, and war must begin by highlighting the role of the DP in reproducing a world characterized by extreme divides of wealth and power, and the continuation of violence directed at nonliberal others.

NOTES

This chapter draws on Barkawi and Laffey (1999).

1. According to Bruce Russett (1993: 16), "The war of 1812 is easy to dismiss simply because it precedes the beginning date—1815—of the best-known compilation of all wars" (Small and Singer, 1982). He goes on to note that there were very few democracies in the international system at the time and adds that Britain did not

fit his criteria either of suffrage or of a fully responsible executive. For a discussion of the War of 1812, see Owen (1997).

2. The Bundeswehr was organized as an army in an alliance, not as a force for independent power projection. All operational units were under NATO command. The top German general was not a commander in chief but an inspector general. There was no joint or combined headquarters from which air, sea, and land operations could be controlled. See Bundesminister der Verteidigung (1985) and van Orden (1991: 354).

3. For example, British Petroleum (BP) recently financed a Columbian army brigade to guard its facilities against guerrilla attacks. The brigade employed terror against local villagers protesting degradation of their farmland caused by BP operations (Gillard et al., 1998).

4. See "Doing Democracy a Disservice: 1998 Elections in Bosnia and Herzegovina," IGC Balkans Report No. 42, September 9, 1998, www.crisisweb.org; visited January 15, 2001; see also Dobbs (2000).

5. But see the material cited in Barkawi (Chapter 6 in this volume), especially n. 1.

6. Compare the different definitions offered by Bruce Russett and John Owen. Russett (1993, chapter 1) excludes civil liberties and "free-market economic liberties," focusing instead on polyarchy as the key variable; cf. Robinson (1996b). In contrast, Owen stresses liberal ideology: "I define liberal democracies as those states that are dominated by liberal ideology, and that feature, in both law and practice, free discussion and regular competitive elections" (1994: 102). In this view, democratic states can be liberal or illiberal.

7. That project is defined in terms of scope—the range of social domains to which democracy is considered applicable; franchise—the number and character of those who can participate in deliberations about a domain; and authenticity—whether the deliberations take place in a clear, nontechnical language (Dryzek, 1996: 4–6; cf. Held, 1995, part 3).

2

Realist Spaces/ Liberal Bellicosities: Reading the Democratic Peace as World Democratic Theory

David L. Blaney

The observation that democracies do not go to war with each other has spawned a vast literature, composed mainly of definitional debate, competing empirical tests, and alternative formulations of causal mechanisms (Chan, 1997). My interest, however, is in a generally unintended dimension of the democratic peace (DP) discussions: as a contribution to democratic theory. The use of the term "contribution" should not be misread to signal that the DP thesis settles some important questions in democratic theory, as in various triumphal readings of the end of the Cold War (Fukuyama, 1989; Pye, 1990). My point is quite the opposite. Reading the DP thesis as political theory has the effect of unsettling much of liberal democratic discourse by (1) pointing to the instability of the distinction between the inside and outside of the political community and (2) suggesting the limits of liberal democracy as democratic practice. These might be seen as surprising claims since the DP literature is appropriately criticized for taking for granted, perhaps legitimating, a narrow and ethnocentric reading of the democratic tradition (Brown, 1992; Tanji and Lawson, 1997).

My argument depends on two interlinked themes. First, the DP literature theorizes (albeit thinly) the extension of "domestic" social relations, political institutions, and cultural norms into the sphere of international relations. A less thin theorization of this process suggests that DP theory implicitly destabilizes the boundary between political community and anarchy on which territorially settled democratic practices rest. This theoretical movement is clearer in a reading of Kant and various commentaries on the contemporary relevance of his "Perpetual Peace" (1970). Such a destabilization opens the question of the possible and appropriate sites of democratic political community. The general outline of this argument should be familiar, as it draws on R.B.J. Walker's and William Connolly's analyses of the spatial dimensions of the modern political imagination.

Second, DP theorists admit that conflict and war continue between liberal and nonliberal states. A few highlight this as a specific problem for liberal states. But most, rather than search for the political resources that might generate liberal/nonliberal coexistence, embrace a process (or ideal) of cultural assimilation by nonliberal societies—an assisted, often coerced liberalization of the nonliberal zones. Extending the logic of the DP thesis that "domestic" processes and norms shape international behavior, I explore this failure to live peacefully with nonliberal societies as a difficulty with the norms and processes of liberal democracy itself. In fact, the bellicosity of liberal states appears domestically as a systematic intolerance of the non- or less-than-liberal other within liberal norms and practices. Liberalism's "internal" problem with the other, parallel to the first theme, is a source of much political controversy and demands creative democratic theorizing.

Taken together, these two arguments focus our attention on the limits of our conventional liberal democratic political imagination as a source of political theorizing and raise the possibility of a world democratic project, the contours of which are far from apparent and barely theorized.

The project of reading the DP literature as a particular, if problematic, political theory is likely to be greeted with suspicion. I imagine resistance, on the one hand, from democratic peace "theorists," who (with some apologies to Michael Doyle) claim solely to inhabit the world of a positive social science of international relations. By setting aside the distinction between political science and political philosophy that frames the DP literature, I thereby plunge these scholars into a mostly unfamiliar world of explicit political and ethical debate. On the other hand, democratic theorists have claimed possession of political and ethical debate yet held virtually unquestioningly to the very boundary between political community and international relations that DP theory implicitly challenges (some remarkable exceptions include Held, 1995, and Gilbert, 1999). But to relocate the democratic project as a (nascent) world project is not to dismiss completely the traditions of democratic thought. It is rather to embrace them in a way that places democratic theorizing and debate within a global discursive space of multiple and multilayered traditions of political and ethical interpretation. I turn to this issue at the end of the chapter.

FROM INSIDE TO OUTSIDE: THE PROBLEMATIC INTERNATIONAL POLITICAL THEORY OF THE DEMOCRATIC PEACE

The DP thesis is usually articulated as a "liberal" answer to realism: the spread of liberal democratic regimes progressively pacifies the propensity to conflict and war claimed by realists as inherent in an anarchical ordering of global political space. Despite this, the conventional formulations of the DP literature are framed within the contours of a realist political imagination, even as they simultaneously destabilize that imagining of political possibilities. This argument is made against the backdrop of a particular reading of the realist political imagination as in part productive of democracy as a territorially based practice.

The Antinomies of the Realist Political Imagination

R.B.J. Walker (1993: 33–34, 37) situates the discussion of political community and democratic possibilities within a peculiarly realist configuration of world politics. For Walker, the realist imagination functions both as a "celebration" of the possibility of political community in the face of the end of the fixities and certainties of a premodern era and as a "warning" about the limits of political identity and community beyond the territorial state (15). More specifically, the principle and practice of sovereignty institutionalize a logic of inclusion and exclusion—inside and outside. Politics and the pursuit of the good life are possible only in particularistic political communities. The possibility of these political communities is international relations: the ethically tragic interaction of particularistic states (62–64). Thus, despite the cosmopolitan pretensions of democracy as a theory of the good life, democratic practices continue to be articulated primarily within the particular forms constrained by a world of territorial states (141–142).

William Connolly (1991) elaborates this point. He argues that the possibilities of territorial democracy and the dangers of international relations are dual elements of an imagining of the political as "an essential symmetry among territory, action, and membership" (463–464). Both international relations and democratic discourse imagine and legitimate a political space within a territorial state, the population of which is constituted as a "people" or "nation." The people are "bound together by a web of shared understandings, identities, debates, and traditions," which make a common moral life simultaneously possible and distinguishable from the moral life lived by those in other states. In the world of democracy/international relations, political and economic institutions are organized to allow the people to shape their own destiny according to their "own deliberations and decisions" and to "enable a plurality of lifestyles to co-exist within the territory of the state" (463).

Both Walker and Connolly note, however, that this political configuration of democracy and realism is unstable. Walker explains that the universalistic ethical claims associated with modern political communities are difficult to contain within the particularistic spaces assigned to them by sovereignty. Rather, the fragmentation of international relations constructs a "longing for reconciliation and integration" expressed in transgressions of the boundary between inside/outside, in the extension of "established principles in a more emancipatory direction" in the name of a "more universally conceived humanity" (Walker, 1993: 17–19). The cosmopolitan pretensions of democracy likewise resist the "realistic appraisal of the limits of democratic practice" entailed in the spatial demarcations of sovereignty by holding on to the (often vague and undertheorized) hope of a genuinely world politics. Thus, within a realist political imaginary, democracy necessarily appears as "an ongoing struggle rather than a finished condition" (Walker, 1993: 141–146). Connolly notes a similar tension and incompleteness in the relation of democracy and the state system in that it "forms the space of democratic liberation and imprisonment." Just as it liberates by providing the location for organized democratic structures, the nation-state also "imprisons because it confines and conceals democratic energies flowing over and through its dikes" (Connolly, 1991: 476).

Against this backdrop, the DP thesis may be read as a political/theoretical intervention—a shift in political imagination that vitiates the clear distinction between political community and international relations even as DP theorists explicitly hold on to the inside/outside framing of political possibilities. In partial contrast, Kant's "Perpetual Peace" provides a more explicit reflection on the site of political community, although, as some contemporary examinations of his work suggest, Kant does not completely transcend the limits of an international political architecture. These commentators complete the movement by embracing a cosmopolitan vision counterposed to the particularities of the state system. I will examine each of these positions in turn.

The Democratic Peace and the Realist Political Imagination

The DP thesis depends on the territorially settled character of liberal democratic practices, as it is the effects and extensions of these practices from the inside to the outside that are said to explain peaceful relations among democratic states. Despite serious questions about the constancy of the notions of liberalism or democracy (Oren, 1995; Ray, 1997: 52–54), the literature generally converges in its description of liberal democracy. Bruce Russett (1990: 124–125; 1993: 31) is exemplary in linking the "powerful norms against the use of lethal force both within democratic states and between them" to the wider matrix of norms and institutions that constitute liberal democracy: the equality of citizens, the right of dissent, and electoral accountability. What is clear, but is made explicit only by Doyle (1983: 207–208), is that the form of equality is "juridical" and that self-rule government must be the government of a sovereign state. Thus importantly, the DP's notion of liberal democracy is also an account of the territorial state, the society it "contains," and the practices of citizenship and electoral accountability within national boundaries.

Although the DP thesis is grounded in the realist configuration of inside/outside, it also moves against it. The "habits and predispositions" formed in a democratic "internal politics" are extended to interactions in the space beyond, pacifying the "outside" of international relations (Russett, 1990: 127). The DP literature generally distinguishes three separable (if interrelated) accounts of this extension of the logic of liberal democracy across the inside/outside divide.

The first, a normative/cultural explanation, involves the claim that the *"culture, perceptions, and practices* that permit compromise and peaceful resolution of conflicts without the threat of violence within come to apply across national boundaries toward other democratic countries" (Russett, 1993: 31). This extension of liberal culture and practices beyond borders constitutes a "transnational democratic culture" within which liberal states and citizens jointly exercise a right of self-determination in a spirit of mutual accommodation (Russett, 1993: 31).

A second, structural/institutional account gives a different stress. Here the institutional constraints of democracy—the need to mobilize popular support—make it less likely that leaders will commit their countries to war. This constraint is explained in part by the reluctance of citizens to bear the costs of war. But it also depends on the relative transparency of democratic processes to those both within and beyond the borders of the state. Democracies not only individually find themselves constrained, but each is aware of the other's constraint, and this joint knowledge becomes the basis for their interactions, as in "security communities" and other forms of international integration (Russett, 1993: 38–39; Starr, 1997: 155–158; Doyle, 1983: 228–230).

Finally, the logic of economic interdependence, in interaction with democratic politics, is said to support a liberal zone of peace. In part, the claim is about the disincentive to military conflict where the mutual benefits of trade are at stake. But this logic depends on an open political process, since citizens will be unwilling to accept the (in this case, opportunity) costs of seeking alternative (and second-best) sources of supply and market outlets (Oneal and Russett, 1997: 270). Further, the kinds of interest group activity (including transnational associations) allowed by liberal societies and the international economic agreements entered into by (optimizing) liberal states foster an ongoing spirit of cooperation (Oneal and Russett, 1997: 270). Doyle (1983: 231–232) describes these as "crosscutting transnational ties that serve as lobbies for mutual accommodation," because "international financiers and transnational, bureaucratic, and domestic organizations create interests in favor of accommodation and have ensured by their variety that no single conflict sours an entire relationship." The literature increasingly refers to these relationships as forms of global governance (Rosenau and Czempiel, 1992).

Although these accounts of the pacificity of liberal democratic relationships should not be taken for granted (see Chapters 4, 6, and 7 in this volume), my point is different and follows from Walker's and Connolly's analyses of the instabilities of the realist imagination. The idea of the settledness of liberal democracy as a territorially bounded practice cannot be sustained where the universalizing project of liberal political and economic practices is also embraced. The DP literature implicitly embraces such a project in terms of a transnational democratic culture, security communities, complex interdependence, and global governance that in part shift our domain of explanation (and politics) from the territorial political community to transnational social and political relations. More strongly, economic interdependence increasingly blurs the distinction between the domestic and the foreign, frustrating a clear and coherent national interest (Keohane and Nye, 1989: 27–35). Indeed, global economic processes move beyond borders, at once partly escaping national democratic regulation, requiring various (often ad hoc and meager) measures of regional or international regulation (Jessop, 1997; Hettne, 1997), and fostering localized resistance (Kothari, 1997). And whether as precondition, concomitant, or consequence of this flow of money, goods, and people, identities appear to be less securely fastened to the nation-state: social life is discussed increasingly as simultaneously global and local, and, consequently, the term "society" is being claimed for the globe (Meyer et al., 1997; Chapter 9, this volume).

Thus, the DP thesis of the pacification of international relations appears also as a political theory of the decline of the symmetry among territory, action, and membership that Connolly notes as the possibility of settled democratic practices. Rather, various movements and groups exert demands that are simultaneously internal and external, seeking to further democracy by pushing beyond the boundaries of settled practices and identities (Connolly, 1991: 479; see also Held, 1995). In such circumstances, the point is not that we are perched on the edge of a world democratic politics; too much about the character of contemporary global processes and institutions weighs against that claim (Pasha and Blaney, 1998). And as Walker (1993: 145) notes,

> The meaning of democracy has become even more obscure and contentious at precisely the moment when democratic breakthroughs are being celebrated so widely. Or, to put this slightly differently, the prospects for an historically specific understanding of democracy seem brighter than ever—to some commentators at least—at precisely the moment when that understanding seems increasingly dissonant with rapid transformations in the structural context in which people struggle to exercise some control over their own lives.

It is the very obscurity and contentiousness of the meaning of democracy in our age that calls us to a reimagination of global political and social space.

Kant, Sovereignty, and Cosmopolitanism

Kant's "Perpetual Peace" and some recent reflections on that work (collected in Bohman and Lutz-Bachmann, 1997) reproduce this theoretical movement and cement this conclusion. Kant's program for a perpetual peace is laid out in three "Definitive Articles" requiring states with republican constitutions to form a federation pledged both to peaceful relations among them and to treat all humans with hospitality. Although his republican vision diverges from contemporary liberalism, a certain resemblance to the claims of DP theorists has tempted these thinkers into a wholesale appropriation of Kant as a theorist of the liberal peace (Onuf, 1998: chapter 9).[1] As in the DP, the logic of political community is extended from the inside to reshape the outside of international relations. Citizens of a republic, who bear the brunt of the cost, will use the relative openness of republican politics to restrain leaders who, feeling little of the required sacrifice, are more likely to be seduced by the glories of war. Republican states, understanding that restraint is necessary to freedom, will commit themselves to mutual self-restraint. And in the spirit of respect for human freedoms, states will welcome foreign visitors with hospitality, allowing relatively unfettered cultural and commercial interactions that support a wider human community (Kant, 1970: 99–108).

Kant's reasoning strikes the familiarly unstable balance between particularistic sovereigns and universal principles characteristic of the realist political imagination. On the one side, the republican idea and form represent a universality crucial to the possibility of a pacific union. The republic is the necessary product of the moral imperative of reconciling political order and the autonomous will of the individual. Parallel to the contemporary liberal vision, the republican form secures the rights of the individual to freedom within a civil legal order that limits that freedom only to the extent required by the freedom of others and the need to regulate conflicts of interest among autonomous, property-owning individuals. Because the laws of a republic embody this commitment to justice and the alternative is a state of lawlessness and social war, we can consider the duty of individuals to be subject to this legal order as a product of their own will or consent, as evidence of a social contract (Kant, 1970: 99–100; Reiss, 1970: 20–25). The state of war existing between states, however, threatens the lives, property, and liberties of citizens, potentially undermining this reconciliation (Kant, 1970: 231; Reiss, 1970: 34). By analogy, Kant's reasoning about the republic would compel actors, whether individuals or republics, toward the establishment of a more encompassing republic (Lutz-Bachmann, 1997: 69–74).

On the other side, Kant accepts the particularity of states and opts instead for a much weaker federation of republics, limiting the application of this analogy. The relations among states are not analogous to a state of war (a "lawless condition"); "as states, they already have a lawful internal constitution, and thus have outgrown the coercive right of others to subject them to a wider legal constitution" (Kant, 1970: 104). A pacific federation appears the proper response, since it does not aim to establish a public power coercive of states. Because the "international right" of sovereignty is imperiled by the exercise of the sovereign right to wage war, reason dictates that states should create a federation through which they pledge to forgo the exercise of that particular right (Kant, 1970: 104–105). In this sense, a pacific union short of a world state is merely the consequence of the exercise of reason. Later in "The Perpetual Peace," Kant extends this argument by discrediting the idea of a world state as too distant from people to command the obedience required of a republic, as a "soulless despotism," liable to decay into "anarchy" (Kant, 1970: 113).

Yet the issue is not quite settled. After dismissing the force of the social contract analogy, Kant almost immediately reinstates its higher moral status, if not its practical force. He writes that the only "rational way in which states coexisting with other states can emerge from the lawless condition of pure warfare" is, by direct analogy to individuals, to establish a public legal order in the form of an "international state, which would necessarily grow until it embraced all the peoples of the earth." The difficulty here is not the ultimate status of "international right" or sovereignty but a practical one: "this is not the will of the nations." That is, states refuse to accept the force of the argument—"the positive idea of a *world republic*." Thus, we must turn to "a negative substitute in the shape of an enduring and gradually expanding *federation*" (Kant, 1970: 105). Here practicality, rather than the dictates of reason, justifies accommodating the sovereignty of states.

Indeed, such practical matters play a crucial role in securing the perpetual peace and, in the end, in displacing the weight of the claim to sovereignty. Given states' unwillingness to part with sovereign rights, why should we think a pacific union is more than, as in the usual charge, an idealist hope? In response, Kant appeals less to the power of reason and more to the force of the "mechanical process of nature" to "guarantee" the perpetual peace. By the process of nature Kant means to suggest that the forces of history direct human evolution, even against the will of humanity, in "conformity with the end which reason directly prescribes to us (i.e., the end of morality)" (Kant, 1970: 108–109).

Again, we are left with an ambiguous result. Although experience of war, as much as or more than the republican idea, drives human beings to form republics, the formation of particularistic republics appears dictated by the contingencies (or wisdom) of nature in the form of the irreducibility of religious and linguistic variety. Thus Kant turns to an additional historical fact: the *spirit of commerce*. Commerce "takes hold of every people," gradually establishing "a universal community" as the condition of a cosmopolitan law (Kant, 1970: 107–108, 114). Thus natural forces forge a wider commercial community that brings the practices of states into closer correspondence with the dictates of moral reason.

Neo-Kantian Cosmopolitanism

Contemporary commentators, by contrast, claim that the forces of history push us far beyond what Kant envisions. Indeed, the state of today's "natural forces" appear as a basis for dismissing Kant's embrace of sovereignty and his rejection of a stronger cosmopolitanism as, in the end, historically contingent rather than dictated by the necessity of universal reason. Jürgen Habermas (1997) argues that with 200 years of hindsight, we now clearly see the principle and practice of sovereignty as an impediment to the realization of human freedom. Not only have global processes rendered claims of the independence of states obsolete, but individuals and groups use new telecommunications technologies to create an emerging global public sphere. In this context the ultimate fate of human rights rests not in the hands of sovereign states but in the prospects for a cosmopolitan democracy. David Held (1997) argues similarly that the disjuncture between the sites of social relations and political accountability has become so large that we can no longer adequately imagine democracy solely in relation to the nation-state. Rather, discussions of democracy must center on the globe as a political domain. James Bohman (1997) and Axel Honneth (1997) give more weight to the diversities that exist in the present and therefore are more circumspect in claiming the immediate relevance of strong cosmopolitan claims, but both point to the growth of a global public sphere in the form of world public opinion (Honneth) or an international civil society (Bohman). And neither interprets current diversity as an impediment in principle to the evolution of a cosmopolitan order, although this order must—as in the republic—organize spaces for social difference and political opposition. In all of this, Kant is seen as at once trapped within his times and prescient of the order logically, if not inevitably, to follow.

I would give a different interpretation. The DP formulation, Kant's "Perpetual Peace," and advocates of a global public sphere together represent recognizable responses to the instabilities of the realist political imagination. In each, we find ethics and the "realities" of international relations counterpoised such that opponents of power politics are faced with the usual prospects. Either they pursue that "illicit" idealist practice of speaking universal truth to the fragmentations of power, or they place hope in the historical vindication of that universality through temporal processes—development or modernization (Walker, 1993: chapters 3, 7). Thus the challenge to the primacy of the sovereign state occurs against the backdrop of inside/outside, encouraging us "to believe that either these patterns are permanent or that they must be erased in favor of some kind of global cosmopolis" (Walker, 1993: 179). If, by contrast, we set aside the certainties of both sovereign political community and its cosmopolitan antidote, we are faced instead with an open question about the possible and appropriate sites of democratic theory and practice.

FROM OUTSIDE TO INSIDE:
THE LIMITS OF LIBERAL DEMOCRATIC DISCOURSE

The claims of a liberal zone of peace or a thicker global cosmopolis face a problem of the "other": the recalcitrant nonliberals of the world. The DP is, unfortunately in the eyes of its proponents, not (yet) universal in practice. Zones of war remain within and among nonliberal states and between liberal and nonliberal states (Doyle, 1983; Russett, 1990; Singer and Wildavsky, 1996; Ray, 1997; Owen, 1997). The "global cosmopolis" is inhibited similarly by national, ethnic, religious, ideological, and economic differences (Habermas, 1997; Honneth, 1997; Held, 1997). Although the issue of the nonliberal other looms large in this literature, it does not seem to prompt serious reflection about the universality or adequacy of liberal democratic theory and practice.

Responses to the "problem" of the nonliberal other tend to shade from a triumphal confidence to the presence of some nagging but mostly unexplored doubt. Nearer the pole of triumphal confidence we find the liberal U.S. apologists and the neo-Kantian critical scholars joined as somewhat strange bedfellows. Although only the neo-Kantians turn their cosmopolitan vision against the inequalities and exclusions of contemporary political orders, both sets of thinkers define the landscape of world politics in terms of an opposition. For the apologists the world is divided between zones of peace, democracy, and wealth and zones of turmoil, authoritarianism, and (optimistically) development (Singer and Wildavsky, 1996: xi, 3). For critical scholars "stable, politically civilized zones" act as "nodal points in a global network of multilateral security arrangements" curbing the violence of the opposed sphere of international relations (Honneth, 1997: 175–176). Although democratic transitions are discussed with a greater assurance of inevitability by apologists, both see the liberal democratic state as the model or "temporal median of the present," and both prescribe action to ease the transition (compare Singer and Wildavsky, 1996: xiii, 11, 47, Habermas, 1997: 131–132, and Honneth, 1997: 162–163; the quotation is from Habermas).

There is also a certain alignment of their vision of international institutions. The apologists favor a heavier hand, recommending that democratic states work to make democracy the primary source of international legitimacy. The point of this policy, they are quick to note, is not exclusion but *eventual* inclusion by encouraging (perhaps imposing) democratic transitions (Singer and Wildavsky, 1996: 107–117; Diamond, 1990: 242). The critical theorists rely more on the impersonal forces of history to erase current differences in regime and view. By creating a sense of "shared risks," a "global public sphere," or a transboundary civil society, historical forces establish the practical foundations on which a global cosmopolitan consensus can be freely and willingly achieved (Habermas, 1997; Bohman, 1997; Honneth, 1997). Even the question of external intervention does not solidly divide the two groups. External military intervention of a patient, carefully considered, and multilateral character is openly embraced by the apologists of U.S. policy (Singer and Wildavsky, 1996: 200–201; see also Ray, 1997: 61–62). Despite the important reservation, following Kant (1970: 106), that civilization or cosmopolitanism cannot be imposed, critical theorists retain some role for intervention (Honneth, 1997). Thus, though the nonliberal other retains a presence in both sets of arguments, the "problem" of nonliberals is treated as historically contingent rather than as a fundamental challenge to an already vindicated liberal democratic/cosmopolitan vision.

For a notably few DP theorists, by contrast, the observation that liberal states continue to wage war against the nonliberals casts a shadow over the achievements of the DP. Doyle (1983: 324–325, 331), Owen (1997: 3, 5, 14, 32), and Russett (1990: 129–132, 142) argue that this feature of the behavior of liberal democratic states is merely the flip side of the DP. If the DP is entailed by a form of mutual legitimation, respect, and prudential behavior among liberal states, nonliberal states are apt to be seen to fall outside of that sphere of special consideration. More strongly, nonliberals tend to be seen as lacking a basic legitimacy in international affairs, traceable to the idea that only liberal democratic domestic arrangements can possibly reflect the consent of the governed and constrain the foreign policy behavior of elites. As Owen puts it, nonliberal states "are viewed *prima-facie* as unreasonable, unpredictable and potentially dangerous" (1994: 95); this liberal vision tells "liberals which foreign states are friends and which are enemies" (1997: 14). Thus nonliberal states are constructed as sites of legitimate intervention for liberal purposes and perhaps as objects of violent moral crusades—both paradigmatic forms of "liberal imprudence" in Doyle's terms, "liberal favoritism" in Owen's, democratic "xenophobia" in Russett's, and liberal bellicosity in mine.

This conclusion prompts some reflection. For Doyle this failure to coexist with nonliberals constitutes a major moral and intellectual challenge (1986: 1163), but he is less than forthcoming about the direction we should take. Russett hopes that the continuing spread of liberal democracy will render the issue moot but worries about the practical problems with transferring liberal models of governance (1990: 132–137). Owen (1997: 22–63) explicitly investigates the logic of such exclusionary thinking (discussed later), but ends with an apology because liberalism is "tolerant relative to its alternatives" (29).

Thus these moments of pause lead none of the three to seriously consider the possibility of defects in liberal democracy itself. Although this is not puzzling at a superficial level—that is not their project—it is more puzzling when placed in relation to the central claim of the DP that international behavior can be understood as an extension of the character of domestic regimes. It seems pertinent to ask: Is the failure of liberal states to coexist with nonliberals in international relations the consequence of some defect in liberal democracy as a form of political community?[2] Seemingly authorized by the DP discourse, this question is effectively ruled out because liberal democracy is not simply taken for granted; it is also legitimated by its claimed contribution to peace in an anarchical world. Yet nonliberals remain a feature of our world, and as long as this is the case the DP project will remain incomplete, and liberal bellicosity will apparently continue as a stain on the legitimacy of liberal democracy.

The Democratic Peace and the "Other"

It appears, however, that the nonliberal is more than an empirical problem for the DP. Rather, the distinction *and* hostility between the liberal and nonliberal is constitutive of the DP project itself. Two authors' work is suggestive. John Owen is explicit in his identification of liberal perceptions of the other as the crucial causal mechanism in producing liberal peace and war (1997: 3–4). He notes that the political and moral visions held by policymakers and the wider public are "always formulated in contrast to an opposite" (1997: 14) and that liberals as a group necessarily form through a process of "exclusion and opposition" (1997: 29). Ido Oren (1995), in response to Owen's 1994 article, makes a somewhat different point. Oren suggests that the DP theorists' deployment of a distinction between "our kind" and others is an artifact of U.S. self-perceptions of friends and enemies. That is, we necessarily think of those with whom we are at peace and those with whom we fight as "our kind" or not, respectively. Although Oren points us back to the logic of power politics, we might as easily read his work as indicating processes of constructing meaning and identity.[3] Owen more clearly recognizes that the DP thesis points to processes of social construction (1997: 232–233), but his stress on the behavioral implications of the perceptions of *preexistent* agents inhibits a deeper confrontation with the politics of the construction of self and other (see Campbell, 1992; Inayatullah and Blaney, 1996). By contrast, Miyume Tanji and Stephanie

Lawson (1997: 151) are explicit in their attempt to expose the process of "othering" at play in the DP literature:

The "answer" to the question of what constitutes "true democracy" is implicit in the model of democracy assumed by the thesis—a model that has been used to demarcate the borders of a democratic community in world politics. Thus, what "democracy" means in the thesis is authoritatively assumed in advance, posited as an unassailable universal, and deployed as the foundation of a moral high ground in the global sphere. Staking claims to the moral high ground on the basis of a vision of "true democracy," however, often serves to intensify hostile attitudes on the part of those who are effectively excluded, or consigned to the category of "the uncivilized." . . . Such practices only rationalize the most repugnant aspects of identity politics. Enemies and friends can be constructed by stressing particular cultural identities that in turn feed into tendencies to dichotomize insiders/outsiders, democratic/non-democratic, tradition/modernity, Asian/ Western, and so forth.

Although some have made more encompassing claims about the source of such processes of "othering" as, for instance, a feature of modernity more broadly (Nandy, 1987; Todorov, 1984), I will explore a (perhaps) narrower claim. That is, I will follow a path already cleared by the DP thesis: a second-image analysis, tracing the bellicosity of liberals toward nonliberals in international relations to its "source" in the exclusionary and intolerant logic of liberal democracy itself. This charge against liberalism is, although controversial, central to contemporary contestations of liberal theory and practice. I draw here on numerous critics, both from within and beyond liberal society, that stand collectively as a serious and sustained indictment of contemporary liberalism.

Liberal Democracy and the Temptation of Liberal Fundamentalism

Liberal democracy is often justified by its (unique) capacity to reconcile legitimate political order with the pluralism born of the liberty of individuals. In John Rawls's famous conception, political order is secured by agreement on the "fundamental terms" or "principles" governing social and political institutions. "Free and rational persons" will necessarily agree to an order that secures "an equal right to the most extensive basic liberty compatible with a similar liberty for others" and a system of "social and economic equalities" that is free of arbitrary exclusions and is to "everyone's advantage" (Rawls, 1971: 11–12, 60–61). The implication drawn is that liberal democracy realizes an impartiality or neutrality in its basic procedures and institutions and therefore could be embraced universally—by any reasonable person, across moral or religious differences (Rawls, 1971: 11–12, 31–32, 251–257).

This claim of neutrality or universality is controversial. Indeed, Rawls himself has come to accept that "justice as fairness" implies a peculiarly liberal political ethos or culture (Rawls, 1989: 240).[4] Nonetheless, Rawls (1988, 1989) insists that liberal norms and procedures constitute a narrow or "thin" political morality that is effectively neutral in that it disallows public action justified in terms of any controversial religious or philosophical doctrine. Although this limits the scope of citizens' demands and circumscribes ways of life, these are the preconditions of political legitimacy in a society of plural moral views and lifestyles.

The fact that liberal democracy constructs a space for certain kinds of pluralism is incontestable. Connolly, however, echoing the concerns of many critics within liberal society, argues that the space of acceptable pluralism is "too stingy, cramped, and defensive" (1995: xii). Specifically, Connolly argues that liberalism is really a form of partisanship on deeply contested political issues—an attempt "to impose a liberal creed upon others in the name of a universal reason, a natural subject of rights, a neutral state, or a fictive contract." Many groups arriving or arising in a liberal society consequently "find some of their key convictions consigned to the "private realm" by secular liberal neutrality" (Connolly 1995: 123–124). Susan Bickford likewise notes that liberal pluralism is sustained in Rawls by imposing a "public identity that is constituted by what enables us to agree," placing "our personal or social identities" beyond political life (1996: 7–8). Yet as Chantal Mouffe (1990, 1992) suggests, democracy has an essential indeterminacy at its foundation; there can be no prepolitical or final resolution of fundamental questions of justice and identity of the kind Rawls and other liberals seek. Claims about the neutrality of liberal procedures and norms (and the identities and exclusions they entail) appear, then, as a form of hegemony. The point here is no more than the flip side of Rawls's claim about liberal neutrality. Where Rawls claims that pluralism requires a liberal morality, circumscribing identity as the fundamental basis of political practice, Connolly, Bickford, and Mouffe expose that this liberal political practice is also a source of exclusion and suppression of identity.

More precisely, liberal norms and procedures presuppose individuals who are able to choose their ends, social ties, and identities. Thus the charge is that a liberal society is hostile to the kinds of belonging and moral encumbrances that come with human sociality, particularly with membership in ethnic, cultural, or religious groups (Sandel, 1984). Even consistent liberal efforts to extend a degree of respect and protection to nonliberal cultural groups must be limited by the ultimate priority of the individual and individual rights in a liberal society (Kymlicka, 1995). In the end, the survival of such groups and practices cannot be guaranteed in a societal space where identities and ends are subject to the vagaries of a liberal cultural marketplace, short of the virtual isolation of that group from the rest of society (Spinner, 1994).

Many would suggest, however, that this exchange does not quite capture the violence toward nonliberals perpetrated by liberal democracy. Bickford explains that the supposedly neutral "public persona" citizens are asked to assume within a liberal democracy is laden with "particular unstated norms in mind" that effectively silence certain voices (1996: 102–103). Gloria Anzaldua (1990) suggests that such norms authorize and marginalize different identities within the personalities of minority citizens (especially women), fragmenting them in ways that can impoverish their capacity to act. Iris Marion Young (1996: 123–124; 1990: 97) similarly argues that even at its best—in the form of a radically deliberative doctrine—liberal democracy is constructed in ways that are exclusionary rather than genuinely universal or culturally neutral. Deliberation is treated as a contest in which formal and general argument is privileged as a weapon. Other modes of communication that employ passion and play are excluded despite their vital role in constituting spaces for communication, suggesting alternative lines of thinking, and fostering processes of learning and transformation. This burden falls especially hard on the less privileged, women, and various ethnic and cultural groups whose ways of speaking and acting fall beyond these limits.

James Tully (1995: 5, 28–31, 41, 52–53) pursues a similar indictment beyond where Young leaves it, taking on directly the assumption of uniform citizenship and a singular and indivisible form of self-rule. This assumption, crucial to the idea of a settled liberal democracy as presumed and defended by Rawls and other liberals, produces constitutional arrangements oppressive of the right of self-rule of various cultures and forms of life, except to the extent that those cultures assimilate themselves to the prescribed norms. The requirement of assimilation prompts widespread opposition and demands for new sorts of political arrangements more respectful of the forms of action, speaking, and social relations necessary to self-rule for these groups. Tully suggests that this, in effect, returns us to a preconstitutional state, that we cannot respond to this oppression without giving up the idea of constitutions as an "unsurpassable form." As in Mouffe, there is an indeterminacy in democratic arrangements; constitutions are simultaneously a foundation and a subject of "democratic discussion and change." Specifically, Tully calls us to find within our liberal democratic traditions of self-rule and equality the possibility of a new form of constitutionalism that accommodates cultural difference. This entails invigorating a "just dialogue" that recognizes the varied "ways of participating" in dialogue or, closer to Young, the many "culturally different ways of giving reasons and defending a claim."

Postcolonial critics of the universal legitimation and imposition of liberal democracy pursue a parallel line of reasoning, although from a position somewhat outside or beyond the liberal tradition. For instance, Bhikhu Parekh (1992, 1997) and Tanji and Lawson (1997) work to expose the cosmopolitan pretensions of liberal democracy by counterpoising liberal culture, exhibiting a priority of the individual and a morality of choice, to an alternative cultural emphasis on the priority of the community and shared values. Tariq Banuri (1990: 77–81), similarly and as if in direct response to Rawls, challenges liberal modernity because it constructs a cultural map that simultaneously separates the impersonal and the personal and privileges the former. The properly modern individual—as observer, agent, and actor—is detached from the community and others. This "impersonal" status and mode of being is taken as the basis for denigrating "personal" ties, obligations, and identities and rendering them politically and socially marginal. Although these two modes of being coexist—in fact, are intertwined—in every society, only liberal thought and society foster this kind of dualism and demand for assimilation of one to the other. Ashis Nandy (1990: 127) likewise argues that the secularism of politics demanded by the liberal version of tolerance turns on a polarization of "civil versus primordial" and "great traditions versus local cultures or little traditions." Secularism, then, is distinctly intolerant of cultures; "it is definitionally ethnophobic and ethnocidal, unless of course those living by cultures are willing to show total subservience to the modern nation-state and become ornaments or adjuncts to modern living" (127).

What is common in these arguments and crucial to my inquiry is the charge that liberal democratic thought and practice foster an overly restrictive logic of inclusion and exclusion within their boundaries. Fred Dallmayr (1996: 24–27, 168–169), drawing on several of these authors, summarizes the claims very nicely. Liberalism's privileging of procedural fairness as a way of promoting "a tolerant juxtaposition of cultures and life-forms" is in fact an embrace of a culture of "mutual disinterest and aloofness" and a relegation of concrete life forms to the status of a privatized "culture." He writes: "Self-other relations, in this case, are curiously split or dichotomized: while sameness or identity is presumed to persist on the level of general principle (stylized as 'reason' or 'human nature'), historical cultures and beliefs are abandoned to rampant heterogeneity (tending toward segregation or ghettoization)" (24). The likely consequence of exporting this model of the individual and society "in the name of liberal neutrality" is "that traditional cultures in developing societies tend to be progressively 'defoliated' or shunted aside into folklore" (27).

These descriptions collectively point to a kind of fundamentalism within liberal thought and practice reminiscent of Tanji and Lawson's discussion of liberal "othering." Connolly (1995, chapter 4) explicitly investigates this temptation to fundamentalism within liberal thought. In his terms, liberal society appears as normalizing, treating "the small set of identities it endorses as if they were intrinsically true." Identities that often grow up in the conditions of a liberal society but differ from this truth are often seen as "fundamental threats, deviations or failures in need of correction, reform, punishment, silencing, or liquidation" (1995: 89).[5] Others draw the implication of this "domestic" political arrangement for interactions in the global domain. Since various forms of cultural resistance greet the liberal democratic imperative (Dallmayr, 1996: 175–176; Tanji and Lawson, 1997: 136–140), the spread of liberal democracy and the concomitant set of human rights appear as the imposition of a Western global design—a "project of global homogenization" (Sheth and Nandy, 1996: 15)—justly labeled neoimperial because of its resemblance to an earlier civilizing mission or standard of civilization (Parekh, 1992: 160; 1997; Gong, 1984: 90–93; Linklater, 1993: 30). More strongly perhaps, John Gray suggests the consequences of a fundamentalist "belief in the universal legitimacy of [liberal] institutions": "Liberal policies animated by such universalist beliefs are bound to treat all other regimes and ways of life as rivals or enemies rather than legitimate alternatives. Liberal morality is not a formula for coexistence among regimes that contain a diversity of ways of life. So long as the world contains a diversity of regimes, it is a prescription for conflict" (1998: 34).

If this understanding of liberal democracy is accurate, it supplies an account of the logic of liberal intolerance or bellicosity undertheorized in the DP literature. And if nonliberals remain a feature of the global landscape (and we have every reason to doubt the universal appeal of liberalism), we can expect the DP debate to continue to evidence a familiar contour. Liberals will continue to bemoan the partial and separate character of the liberal zone of peace, constructing simultaneously nonliberal regions and actors as "naturally" war prone and as targets of a (often overtly violent) process of assimilation of all societies and cultures to a liberal democratic model.

A WORLD DEMOCRATIC PROJECT?

I have suggested that we cannot rest with our conventional political conclusions that circumscribe the territorial state as the exclusive site of democratic theory and practice, that claim liberal democracy as a settled or finished project and a clear support for world peace, and that (implicitly or explicitly) authorize a cosmopolitan vision as an antidote to the particularities of a society of states. The direction we should move as a response to these destabilizations of political orthodoxy, however, is less than clear.

One alternative to the often violent, homogenizing project of the globalization of liberalism is immediately evident: we could imagine the political dynamics of a peace across liberal and nonliberal regimes. Peaceful coexistence among states of varying moral systems and political regimes has been a central feature of numerous investigations and political projects within international relations (see, for example, Bull and Watson, 1984; Chay, 1990; and Walzer, 1994). But the implications of the argument thus far seem actually to point us beyond these investigations, toward a democratization of international society.

To elaborate briefly, the critique of liberalism explored here suggests that liberal society can claim no special privilege or universality—that it is but one method among many incommensurable means of balancing or "resolving" the innumerable competitions and tensions among the goods and values that contribute to human well-being (Gray, 1998). This ontological judgment is interwoven with a certain political stance: "Conflicts between incommensurate ways of life are settled by achieving a *modus vivendi* between them" (Gray, 1998: 32). Andrew Linklater (1993) moves in this direction in his response to the DP claims. He argues that we can avoid the tendency of liberal othering (of either war against or violent assimilation of the nonliberal) by articulating a less exacting standard of international legitimacy as a basis for mutual coexistence. Linklater suggests adopting a principle of "constitutionalism"—requiring civilian rule, minimal use of coercion, and respect for interdependence and international obligations—but not a liberal democratic litmus test (33). Arranging such a modus vivendi, however, seems to require more than Linklater imagines, as is clear if we return to Tully's analysis of negotiating fair constitutional arrangements. Although he moves in Tully's direction in one sense—by remaking the constitution of international politics in a direction of greater tolerance of nonliberal regimes—Linklater fails to address the need for a "just dialogue" as the basis for new (in this case international) constitutional arrangements.[6]

Although we might read Linklater and Tully as both making a call for a more democratic international society and beginning to explore the preconditions of an international democratic political practice, this conclusion appears to entangle us in a series of tensions. Imagining a process that generates modus vivendi among regimes of various types on an ongoing basis seems to contain a democratic bias and to commit us to a standard we had relaxed. Put somewhat differently, by advocating a democratic international system, we presume a democratic imperative as the foundation of an international politics to which we propose our vision as a political option. This difficulty is perhaps unavoidable. As Mouffe noted, the foundations of any political arrangement are themselves political and contestable; therefore, we face perpetually what Connolly (1991: 464–466) calls a "paradox of political founding."

The implication is, in fact, more challenging: the democratic bias of the idea of modus vivendi in part vitiates the boundary between the inside and outside of communities and cultures, potentially destabilizing their dispositions and faiths. A dialogical partner is inevitably exposed to the implicit or explicit criticism of the other and to the proposals for internal reforms (or revisions of identity) this might suggest. More strongly, the generosity toward pluralism implied by an international politics of democratic modus vivendi is a challenge to fundamentalist dispositions that set strict limits on internal pluralism. In this way, a strong democratic vision cannot be limited easily to the organization of mutual coexistence of competing values and visions. Even though we should not presume a cosmopolitan vision, we should recognize that democratic discussions, processes, and movements will occur internally and across boundaries as well, potentially extending the domain of democratic theory and practice.

Does this suggest a world democratic project? The critique of liberal democracy explored here—questioning its territorially settled character and exposing its universalist pretensions and its forms of exclusion and oppression—should prod democratic theorists to a much overdue reimagination of democracy (Sheth and Nandy, 1996: 17). Scholars, pursuing the direction suggested by the neo-Kantians, have begun increasingly to recast the democratic project at least in part as a world democratic project or vision, reimagining global political space in myriad directions (Falk, Johansen, and Kim, 1993; Held, 1995; Wapner, 1996). Instead of pointing to a resolution of questions about the appropriate site of democratic theory and practice, however, this fact entangles us in the difficulties already raised in relation to liberal democracy as a homogenizing project. For any world democratic project, troubling questions remain: Who is the "we" that is the subject of world democracy? And who is authorized to speak on its behalf? Despite the increasingly global character of democratic theorizing and claims, in a world of cultural difference and unsettled territorial demarcations these questions as of yet have no straightforward answers (Walker, 1993: chapter 7; Bader, 1995).

Thus we continue to be torn between visions that defend the realist political imagination and those that transgress it in varying ways and degrees. This richness of possibilities is the stuff of a "just dialogue" of visions and cultures. Negotiating the differing imperatives of these visions is at once the precondition and the substance of a genuinely world politics. To put it differently, this is a dialogue we must enact and in which we are already partly implicated.

NOTES

Earlier drafts of this chapter were presented at the workshop "Democracy, the Use of Force, and Global Social Change," Minneapolis, MN, May 1–3, 1998, and the

PIPES workshop, University of Chicago, January 7, 1998. I wish to thank the participants in both workshops as well as Shampa Biswas, Terry Boychuk, Kurt Burch, Chuck Green, Sung Ho Kim, Naeem Inayatullah, Jennifer Mitzen, Nick Onuf, and Duncan Snidal for careful readings and thoughtful comments.

1. Nicholas Onuf (1998: 241, 53–55) argues that this is a misrecognition, noting that Kant (as a republican rather than a liberal) placed greater emphasis on duties than rights and on the common good than democratic participation. Chris Brown (1992) makes this point and adds that Kant's notion of costs to actors is direct (excluding notions of opportunity costs), and his appreciation of the mutual benefits of trade does not incorporate the idea of comparative advantage articulated only after his time. Tim Kubik (Chapter 5, this volume) similarly contrasts Kant's (republican) assumption of warrior citizenship with the professional armies of today's liberal societies.

2. Some have objected that it is not pertinent at all, that, to paraphrase, one does not naturally question the good kids on the playground (those who do not fight among themselves and fight with others less). Rather, one would immediately look to the bad kids (those who do fight among themselves and with the good kids as well) for an explanation of playground fights. Although this objection is appealing on its face, my argument about the DP undercuts it. My claim is that the very distinction between "good" and "bad" kids reflects the conception of the good kids and that this normative construction is implicated in the conflicts between the groups thereby constituted. The construction of the situation by the group constituted as bad kids may be suspect as well, often inverting the original claim instead of moving beyond it, but that is not the concern of this chapter.

3. This conclusion is not surprising given Friedrich Kratochwil and John Ruggie's (1986) demonstration that engagement with a world of norms, expectations, and shared understandings entails a shift in our ontological and epistemological moorings in an interpretive direction.

4. Other liberal theorists, like Michael Walzer, have been less obscure, claiming that liberalism is "a certain way of drawing the map of the social and political world" (Walzer, 1984: 315). Consistent with this, both Rawls (1993) and Walzer (1994) are clear that this conception of justice and the institutions and procedures it entails cannot be readily extended beyond already liberal societies. Indeed, Rawls has been castigated for taking this view by thinkers with the kind of cosmopolitan democratic inclinations we observed earlier (Habermas, 1997; T. McCarthy, 1997).

5. The conclusion drawn here should not be taken to indicate that exclusionary practices are completely avoidable. Rather, the commitment to a deepened democracy entails limits as well. Connolly (1995: 194–195) finds such limits in "general civilization values" (see also Gray, 1998: 32–33) and the openness to change necessitated by democracy. Mouffe, too, suggests that difference must be constrained by distinctly and strong democratic commitments (1992: 11–13). James Fishkin (1991: 35) argues that the ongoing practice of democracy requires a "nontyranny constraint." The extent of such limits or constraints turns in part on the sense of optimism one can maintain in the face of the risks of openness to difference. See, for instance, Connolly's (1998: 100–101) conclusion to his exchange with Frederick Dolan (1998) and J. Donald Moon (1998) and Partha Chatterjee's response to Nandy's analysis of secularism (1995, especially n. 34, p. 35).

6. What is required by dialogical or deliberative equality is a difficult issue, as suggested by Iris Young earlier. I have explored this issue more fully elsewhere (Blaney and Inayatullah, 1994).

3

State Identity and Interstate Practices: The Limits to Democratic Peace in South Asia

Himadeep Muppidi

Realist and liberal perspectives dominate the debate on the "democratic peace." Drawing on a strong correlation between the presence of democracy within states and the absence of war among democratic states, liberals argue that democracy promotes peace in international politics (Doyle, 1997; Russett, 1993, 1995). Realists dispute that argument, claiming that anarchy and the primacy of national interests leave little scope for democratic processes to affect interstate practices (Layne, 1994; Mearsheimer, 1990a, 1990b). Liberal arguments emphasize repeatedly the causal power of a state's domestic ideas and institutions in shaping interstate practices. Realists respond by refocusing the debate on the structural and material constraints in the international system. Not surprisingly, despite a growing scholarship on the democratic peace, the debate rarely moves beyond a recycling of conventional liberal-realist tenets. I believe both liberals and realists are trapped in these tedious exchanges because of a shared commitment to rationalism. I deploy an alternative, critical constructivist approach to point a way out of this rationalist straitjacket. My alternative approach is based on a different conceptualization of the relationship among *democracy, state identity,* and *interstate practices* (Muppidi, 1999a). I establish the analytical power of this framework by using it to explain the complex interstate practices of the world's biggest democracy, India.

I explore democratic India's external relations with four states that vary in terms of the presence, absence, and extent of democracy. The cases range from nondemocratic China to intermittently democratic Pakistan to democratic Sri Lanka and the United States. My empirical analysis of these cases establishes how democracy and peace are related in ways that are paradoxical and counterintuitive to the expectations of both realists and liberals.

45

DEMOCRACY AS A FORM OF STATE IDENTITY

Liberals offer two logics—a normative and an institutional one—to account for the pacific effects of democracy on interstate practices (Russett, 1993; Risse-Kappen, 1995: 24–27). On the normative logic, democratic norms foster a domestic climate of political compromise as well as an inclination toward a nonviolent resolution of disputes. These domestic norms also end up affecting the practices of democratic states in their relations with each other. On the institutional logic, the checks and balances characteristic of democratic governance slow the decisionmaking processes of democratic states. These institutional restraints also impede any easy resort to external force, rule out surprise attacks by other democracies, and thus allow greater time for the resolution of conflicts between democratic states.[1] Given the workings of these two logics, international politics ends up being conducted more peacefully between democratic states. Interactions among other states—including those between democracies and nondemocracies—do not benefit similarly and are thus expected to be far less peaceful than relations among democratic states.

Liberal scholars have responded to various anomalies in these arguments by tightening the conceptual connection between democracy and peace. Some liberals now argue that democracy produces peace only when states recognize each other as democratic. John Owen (1994), for example, notes that it is not enough for a state to have "liberal-democratic institutions" and "enlightened citizens." It must also, he emphasizes, be *recognized* and treated as if it was a "liberal democracy" by other states (Owen, 1994: 96). In other words, not only the presence of democracy is important but also its recognition by other states. Realists have contributed to this focus on state identity by arguing that whether states recognize each other as democratic or not is actually a function of the conflicts between them (Oren, 1995). That is, if states go to war with each other, they might redefine each other's identities as nondemocratic or worse. Several other important scholars and participants in this debate have also drawn direct and indirect attention to the importance of focusing on issues of state identity (Carr, 1945; Russett, 1993: 31–32; Hermann and Kegley, 1995). However limited, this shared realist-liberal appreciation of the importance of state identity allows the DP debate to be moved beyond its traditional confines and be judged, more insightfully, through the broader rationalist-constructivist debate in international relations theory (Wendt, 1992; Campbell, 1992; Weldes et al., 1999).

Democracy, State Identity, and Interstate Practices: Conceptualizing the Competing Claims

If state identity is critical for the production of a democratic peace, how do scholars conceptualize the ways in which democratic states recognize each other's identity? What processes allow states to identify with and differentiate themselves from other states? In other words, what is the conceptual relationship between democracy and state identity as it is productive of peaceful interstate practices?

Liberals. Bruce Russett (1993, 1995) is one of the most prominent liberal theorists of the democratic peace. His argument can thus be taken as indicative of some generally accepted relationships between democracy and state identity as they affect interstate practices. Russett recognizes the importance of both normative and institutional logics in the production of the democratic peace. But he also argues explicitly that the normative logic is more powerful in explaining it (1993: 119).

Based on the normative logic, Russett argues that democratic states have positive expectations of each other and lower expectations of nondemocratic states. The positive expectations of each other held by democratic states lead them to "externalize" democratic norms to their mutual relations. Such democratic norms include those that regulate "political competition," promote "compromise," and encourage the "peaceful transfer of power" (1993: 33). Moreover, given their lesser expectations about those who are not democratic, democracies are more cautious in their relations with them. Since they do not expect nondemocracies to be "restrained" by democratic norms, democracies follow the "harsher norms" of the international system toward them so as not to be exploited (1993: 33). But before states can follow the appropriate norms, shouldn't they be in a position to differentiate a democratic state from a nondemocratic one? How do they do that? For Russett, the specific question of how states are able to *identify* and *differentiate* other states does not appear to be important. He *assumes* that democracies somehow have the capacity to differentiate themselves from nondemocracies. But such an assumption would be unproblematic only if one believed the social meanings productive of relationships of identity and difference were objective and transparent to state actors.[2]

Other liberals have modified Russett's assumption about the objectivity of state identities. Owen argues that *how* states interpret other states is critical to the workings of the democratic peace. This modified focus on the specific perceptions of states allows Owen to resolve some important anomalies in the production of the democratic peace (Owen, 1994). But even as he modifies the conventional liberal perspective, Owen argues that state interpretations are also "relatively stable" understandings that fit certain objectively definable criteria (1994: 97). Owen thus seeks to balance his focus on how states interpret other states with what he presents as "objective" and conventionally accepted definitions of liberal democracy. Thus although Owen does open a small window to introduce the subjective interpretations of states, he does not, in the final analysis, break from Russett's position on the objectivity of state identities. Neither Russett nor

Owen conceptualizes the perceptions of states as predominantly subjective or as affected by relationships of power. Although both do see a role for power, this is not a power that affects how states interpret the identities of themselves or others.

Liberal theorists thus offer a distinctive conceptualization of the relations among democracy, state identity, and interstate practices. Among the liberals, one line of conceptualization sees state recognition of identities as a predominantly objective process. Another line integrates the relatively stable perceptions of states with an objective definition of liberal democracy. Both are agreed in conceptualizing state perceptions as largely objective processes. Neither conceptualization sees identity constitution as governed by relationships of power.

Realists. Realist critics of the DP have strongly contested liberals who insulate state identities from relations of power. Ido Oren, reinvigorating an older historical realist tradition, argues that the identity constitution of states is not an objective process but a changing function of conflict (Oren, 1995; Carr, 1945). Oren's argument reverses the causal logic liberals established among democracy, state identity, and interstate practices. He argues that democracies do not fight each other not because of their democratic identities but because their identities are redefined if they do fight (Oren, 1995: 178). It is power and conflict that force a change in state identities and in the conventional definitions of democracy. To that extent, state identities are subjective, interpretively malleable, and a function of power. Oren also takes care to specify the criteria that govern identity constitution and transformation. If conflict breaks out, Oren argues, states act to "maximize" the differences between themselves, which are locatable on an "objective dimension" (Oren, 1995: 153).

Structural realists, in contrast, are highly skeptical of the ability of any ideational elements—democratic meanings, state identity, or subjective perceptions—to act as the primary cause of peace or war. Given an anarchic international structure, it is the distribution of military power that produces war or peace. Democracy is of limited utility in understanding or explaining interstate practices (Mearsheimer, 1990a).

One of the more developed versions of structural realism that does have an interpretive element is Stephen Walt's balance-of-threat theory (Walt, 1988). In contrast to balance-of-power theory—which predicts that states ally in response to imbalances of power—balance-of-threat theory predicts that states ally in response to imbalances of threat. Walt identifies the main concept of balance-of-threat theory as the distribution of threats, which are based on "capabilities, proximity, offensive power, and intentions" (281). The concept of a distribution of threats subsumes the distribution of capabilities and, in thus adding an additional set of elements, is offered as a refinement of balance-of-power theory.

There are a variety of problems with this theory. But of primary relevance here is the underspecification of the main concept of the distribution of threats. Walt does not tell us exactly the nature of the relationship between the different elements that make up this distribution of threats. How is that important? The distribution of threats is an irreducibly *interpretive* category. Before we understand the distribution of threats in a region, we need to understand what counts as a threat for the actors involved in that region. Identifying certain component elements—such as capabilities, proximity, offensive power, and intentions—does not solve the problem but only begs the question to the extent that each of those elements is itself an interpretive category that could differ based on the historical meanings it is embedded in or its relationship with other elements. All of these interpretive categories require the prior reconstruction of the *intersubjective context* within which they acquire specific meanings. Without such a prior reconstruction, analysts are forced to substitute their own understandings of the distribution of threats in a particular region for those of the actors involved. Not surprisingly, much of Walt's analysis of alliances and threats is dominated by an unquestioning acceptance of the problematic of the Cold War as it appeared to the American state.[3]

Thus structural realists either ignore meanings and the ideational realm or unwittingly smuggle in their subjective conceptions of threat in understanding interstate practices. Historical realists take meanings and identities more seriously but see them as determined by conflict and power. Either way, both sets of realists downplay the role of meanings and identities in favor of power in explaining interstate practices.

Critical Constructivism and the Conceptual Limits of Rationalism

Two critical patterns are thus apparent in the conceptualizations of the relation among democracy, state identities, and interstate practices. For one set of liberals, democracy is a domestic form of powerful social meanings and political processes that, under certain conditions, affects interstate practices in ways that promote peace. Within this formulation, however, state identity is recognizably an objective process. For a second set of liberals, the identification of a state as democratic—its definition by other states—is critical and in some ways a subjective process. This subjectivity, however, is not arbitrary but has some relative stability. For both sets of liberals, democracy and state identity are *not* functions of power. For historical realists, on the other hand, power is the key to understanding the production of state identities. Whereas state power and conflict are objective features, democratic state identity is a subjective outcome of conflict. States do have objective similarities and differences, but it is the latter that are maximized when conflict breaks out. For structural realists, international structure in the form of an anarchic organization of states and the balance of power—and occasionally threats—is the key causal force. Ideas are of negligible importance when compared with material international structures. Meanings and identities are all subjective and are irrelevant or of marginal importance to understanding interstate practices.

The realist-liberal menu thus offers analysts some distinctive conceptual choices. If they adopt a liberal perspective to make sense of the democratic peace, their explanations have to prioritize the causal forces of state identity and objective meanings over and above questions of power. If they adopt a realist perspective, they must prioritize the causal efficacy of power but downplay the role of meanings and state identity. Analysts can also opt for stressing the causal importance of external material forces by adopting a structural realist position, or they can emphasize the role of institutions or norms in causing the democratic peace. What they cannot do is get out of these various binaries and conceptualize the relationship among democracy, state identity, and interstate practices as a function of social meanings, intersubjective identities, and power.

Analysts cannot do this because both liberal and realist conceptualizations of meanings, identity, and interstate practices are trapped in a rationalist framework that continually forces scholars to make mutually exclusive conceptual choices. As I pointed out earlier, identity constitution is seen as either an objective process unaffected by considerations of power or as a power-driven process in which meanings are irrelevant. But such mutually exclusive conceptualizations of identity constitution are not enough to capture the intersubjective and processual nature of the relationship among identities, social meanings, and interstate practices. The problem arises, as constructivists have pointed out, from the deeper commitment of liberal and realist arguments to a rationalist framework that sees state identity as pre-given and exogenous to interstate relations (Wendt, 1992).

Contrary to the binary choices rationalism offers, democracy is a set of social meanings and a form of power. Democracy as a set of meanings is about how people understand a distinctive way of organizing political space. Such understandings are productive of political practices such as voting and a peaceful transfer of governmental authority. They are also constitutive of material institutions such as an independent judiciary, a free press, checks and balances, and so on. The understandings of democracy, then, are productive not only of practices at the individual level (such as voting) but also of governance regimes at the structural level.

But social meanings such as democracy can also be productive of state identities. Nation-states, as "imagined communities," might take the way they organize politics seriously enough to see democracy as constitutive of who or what they are. Their social relations are then likely to be based on a differentiation between themselves and others on the basis of their democratic identity. This does not necessarily imply that such states would categorize every other democracy as a friend and everyone else as a nondemocratic adversary. They may do that, but it is not an inherent feature of having a democratic identity. It is an empirical question to be investigated, not a conceptual necessity.

But in realist and liberal analysis, the mere presence of democracy is seen as adequate to shape the identity and external practices of a state, although historically the nation-state has not been imagined through the presence or absence of democracy alone. A constructivist perspective that takes meanings seriously alerts scholars to the possibility that liberal democratic norms and institutions might be present but not be constitutive of the state's dominant identity. A state may have liberal democratic norms and institutions (fitting the objective definitions of scholars), but its identity, its understanding of itself, may be more powerfully shaped by other institutions and norms. Moreover, states that do not have liberal democratic norms and institutions cannot be defined, in terms of their identity, by that absence alone. Conceptually, what their identities are remains an open issue to be empirically investigated.

If the relationship between democracy and peace poses an interesting puzzle, then the answers must not already be contained within analysts' conceptualizations. Conceptual rigor demands that at least three minimal links must be clearly established for the democratic peace puzzle to be answered productively: (1) What does democracy mean within and for a state that possesses it, (3) is democracy, present though it may be, necessarily productive of the state's dominant or primary identity, and (3) how are the meanings that are productive of a state's dominant identity also productive of its interstate relationships?

The rationalist framework of the current debate between liberals and realists closes these questions prematurely because it fails to see the mutually constitutive relationship among social meanings, state identity, and interstate practices. Relying on an alternative set of concepts—social claims and social imaginaries—I establish a more productive way of conceptualizing and understanding the relationship among democracy, state identity, and interstate practices of war and peace.

DEMOCRACY, STATE IDENTITY, AND INTERSTATE PRACTICES

The literature on the DP treats India as a standard example of a liberal democratic state.[4] India's democratic norms and institutions have been in existence for more than fifty years. Its political governance has been characterized by regular competitive elections at central (federal) and state (regional) levels, a regular turnover of governments, a respect for political compromise as evident in peaceful changes of power, an active system of checks and balances, a vigorously free press, diverse political parties, high rates of electoral participation, and the largest electorate in the world (Lijphart, 1996). There is little dispute, then, that India possesses the features and institutions necessary to be classified as a liberal democracy. But is the possession of democracy enough to claim that the *dominant identity* of the Indian state is liberal democratic? Are democratic norms and institutions, crucial as they are for the organization of domestic politics, necessarily also productive of the Indian state's primary understanding of itself? I argue against that easy assumption.

It is conceptually incorrect to assume, on the basis of certain objective definitions of liberal democracy and their apparent presence in India, that the Indian state's dominant identity is necessarily that of a liberal democratic state. Such an assumption misses the ways in which liberal democracy was historically translated, appropriated, and transformed within the Indian political space.

Writing on this issue, Sudipta Kaviraj, one of India's most prominent political theorists, acknowledges that British "liberalism" had an important influence on Indian politics. But this influence served less to meekly clone British liberal ideas in an Indian context than to promote the power of Indian nationalism (Kaviraj, 1995). Kaviraj clearly establishes how Indian political leaders transferred liberal democratic arguments about the rationality, individuality, and autonomy of human beings to the level of the national community. Thus the idiom of domestic political discourse in India remained focused on the community and was not replaced by the standard language of British liberal democracy stressing the interest-based association of autonomous individuals. As Kaviraj (1995: 96) emphasizes, "The historical context in which the language of liberalism and democracy came to India . . . was distinct from the European context." The crucial point here, then, is not necessarily the specific details, interesting as they are, of the ways in which liberal democracy was translated in the Indian context. What is critical is the very fact of the *historical difference* in the Indian *reception* of liberalism.

This is a critical difference—a difference that shows how liberal democracy could be interpreted, articulated, and appropriated differently within a newer political landscape.[5] The minimal claim I wish to advance on the basis of this argument is that a focus on the objective presence of liberal democracy alone is not enough. It is necessary to conceptualize how the received meanings of liberal democracy were understood by the actors themselves.

This is not an argument about Indian "exceptionalism." It is primarily a caution against assuming that liberal democracy enters into historically and politically empty landscapes and clones itself unproblematically. It is a plea to take seriously the different ways in which states themselves might receive, interpret, and translate ideas of liberal democracy. If democracy is an essentially contested concept, then it is as likely to be contested within the domestic politics of the state as anywhere else.

Contestation involves questioning meanings and power. Questions of meaning involve the need to conceptualize explicitly the *interpretive relations* between liberal democratic ideas and other historically existing political meanings. Objective, textual renditions of liberalism are simply insufficient from this point of view.[6] What is required—at the least—is a careful recovery of the ways in which liberal democratic meanings are articulated historically within the political spaces productive of a state's identity. Questions of power involve the ongoing political battles liberal democracy wages to maintain its dominance over other, contesting domestic political beliefs. Liberal democratic meanings do not appear and disappear suddenly, as some of the codings of democracy for South Asian states such as Pakistan or Sri Lanka might suggest. If present, meanings of democracy are always engaged in a contest with other ideas in ways both collegial and adversarial. So what occurs in the context of Pakistan, to continue with the example, is not the periodic eruption and sudden disappearance of liberal democracy but a broader process of contestation between different social meanings, including democracy (Jalal, 1995). To understand what those contests are, one must analyze how Pakistan or India is imagined and the interpretive and social relations that are constitutive of this imagined identity (Krishna, 1994; Pasha, 1996; Khatak, 1996).

The process of contestation also suggests that liberal democratic ideas may structure some political spaces and identities but not necessarily all. Assuming that liberal democracy were dominant or hegemonic within a country, its power or hegemony could be based on concessions that seek to co-opt important oppositional forces. This opens up the possibility that a domestic space could be governed through liberal democratic institutions and yet not be productive of a state's dominant identity in a variety of ways.

Based on an exploration of such possibilities, I establish here how democratic India articulated distinctive relations of identity and difference with other, objectively similar and different states in the international system. I begin by examining India's relations with China after Indian independence.

Democratic India and Its Interstate Practices

In the 1950s China and India were significantly different countries on various apparently objective dimensions. Unlike India, China was, to use the language of the DP literature, a "nondemocracy." Unlike many of India's South Asian neighbors, it did not share a language or culture with India. As

a self-consciously communist state, China had a significantly different political system. If state actions are influenced by the objective presence or
absence of democracy in other states, Indian expectations about nondemocratic China should have been fairly negative or at least minimal in terms
of shared identities. On the objective criteria outlined in the literature on
democratic peace, China should have been seen as an "illiberal" threat to
democratic India. Notwithstanding these objective differences, Indian policymakers claimed China as an identical "brother" with whom they could
never go to war. But China and India did go to war. This unexpected turn in
the two countries' relationship allows for an exploration of how state identities might change in case of war. Does the change in state identities up-
hold, for instance, the realist prediction that war maximizes objective differences while peace produces shared identities? For these reasons, the
Sino-Indian relationship offers a good case to examine the relationships
among objective differences, socially constructed realities, and interstate
practices of war and peace.

   After analyzing Sino-Indian relations, I examine India's relations with
Pakistan, Sri Lanka, and the United States. In moving from nondemocratic
China to the democratic United States, I evaluate India's interstate practices
on a gradually increasing scale of the objective presence of standard liberal democracy. Liberal explanations assert that democratic states have positive expectations about each other and negative expectations about nondemocracies. On these grounds, one would expect that India would see
China as its greatest threat and the United States as its most secure and
peaceful friend.

Nondemocratic China and Democratic India Are Bhai-Bhai

The 1950s were the heyday of Sino-Indian relations. Indian policymakers
presented India as having had a relationship with China that extended back
many thousands of years. They argued that, differences notwithstanding,
this historical relationship helped India and China understand each other
(Nehru, 1954: 276–277). China and India were not only ancient civilizations that had long coexisted peacefully, but they had also waged a more
modern struggle against a colonizing West (Gupta, 1956: 47–60). Such representations provided the *imagined* and *meaningful* basis for a shared identity between the two states. India and China, it was claimed, were *bhai-bhai*
(brothers) (Appadorai and Rajan, 1985: 114–153).

   The effects of this shared identity on foreign policy were evident well before both countries were formally independent. It facilitated, for instance a
joint declaration by the Indian and Chinese delegates at the Congress of the
League Against Imperialism held in Brussels in 1927, condemning the use
of Indian troops in China to serve British interests. After its independence,

Indian policy toward China was also heavily influenced by these under-standings. India was quick to recognize the People's Republic of China (PRC) in 1949, only the second noncommunist country—after Burma—to do so. Indian policymakers operated through the distinctive social claim that their shared anti-imperial identity with China allowed them to under-stand that country better and to interpret its case more effectively to the Western powers (Gupta, 1956: 58). Under Prime Minister Jawaharlal Nehru, India persistently argued China's case for recognition in various in-ternational fora, including the United Nations and the conferences of Asian and African countries (Wright, 1956). It also played an active role in medi-ating the Sino-U.S. conflict over Korea. Frequent diplomatic and cultural visits took place between the two countries (Gopal, 1984). Interstate rela-tions between the two states were, not surprisingly, very warm and friendly, in the spirit of "Hindi-Chini *bhai-bhai*" (Indians and Chinese are brothers) (Appadorai and Rajan, 1985).

This shared identity of civilizational greatness and anti-imperial broth-erhood was not based on an opportunistic amnesia regarding political and ideological differences between the two countries. Democracy was seen as an important difference between the two states. Nehru, for example, was explicit about this difference in political and economic systems, pointing out that India had a "parliamentary democracy" whereas the Chinese had a "completely different" communist system that was "adapted to their condi-tions" (Nehru, 1961: 309–310). But the absence of conventional markers of democracy—such as press freedom—was not enough in Nehru's eyes to make China an authoritarian, nondemocratic, or illiberal state. China and India were both to be given the discursive space to be judged on their own terms, since each had its own "special cultural inheritance" (Nehru, 1961: 306). In Nehru's understanding the Indian or the Western system of politi-cal organization was not the general standard of measurement. China was not to be judged by its "lack" of "parliamentary democracy." What was im-portant was how the Chinese saw it (as Nehru opined, "they call it people's democracy") and Indian awareness of their mutual differences ("my point is that it is different. We know it") (Nehru, 1961: 309–310). In other words, although Indian officials acknowledged the differences in Indian and Chi-nese understandings of democracy, they did not utilize them initially to position China as a state defined by a "lack" of those democratic features India possessed.

Nehru argued explicitly that these differences did not matter when compared with the two countries' commonalities. India and China, Nehru claimed, were "great countries" that were identical in having to overcome common problems of "foreign domination" and "internal disunity." He cau-tioned Indian parliamentarians against the "superficial" arguments of "com-munism and anticommunism," noting that they were a Western "obsession" that prevented a proper understanding of international relations (Nehru, 1958: 264–265). Nehru's refusal to judge China on the basis of the democratic/nondemocratic or democratic/communist binaries was not an idiosyncratic move. It was an integral part of a broader discourse of Indian foreign policy that refused to see the world through a U.S.- or Soviet-structured Cold War imaginary (Muppidi, 1999b).

The Indian discourse on China thus articulated a link among the "greatness" of the two countries, their centuries of peaceful neighborly intercourse, and the unlikelihood of conflict between them. This articulation was productive of the dominant Indian understandings of the potential for conflict with China. Differences between China and India, although acknowledged, were presented as irrelevant because they were not seen as capable of bringing China and India into conflict. Nehru argued that whatever differences existed between India and China, they had not caused any conflict between the two states during the "millennia of history." Indian policymakers claimed repeatedly that the "thousands of years" of Sino-Indian history showed no "record" of any war between the two states. These claims appeared so "commonsensical" to Indian policymakers that in 1957 Indian defense Minister Krishna Menon declared boldly at the United Nations: "In the 4,000 or 5,000 years of our recorded relations, there has been *no aggression against our territory* by China, and we do not anticipate or apprehend anything of that kind" (cited in Appadorai and Rajan, 1985: 145; emphasis added).

Such social claims ruling out war between India and China were not rhetorical excesses trotted out for diplomatic purposes. They were deeply productive of the Indian government's foreign policy toward China.[7] The fact that these understandings were productive of Indian defense policies is evident in the fact that India did little to prepare for a war with China. As Menon remarked to his biographer, Michael Brecher, "I make no secret of the fact that we were not prepared for a war against China" (cited in Appadorai and Rajan, 1985: 145).

State identities during and after the Sino-Indian war. In 1962 the PRC invaded India. Given that the unimagined had happened, how did Indian policymakers change their social claims about China? Did they now claim that China was nondemocratic, authoritarian, or illiberal? Did they disown earlier identifications with China and emphasize those features that, as expected by the realists, differentiated China maximally from India? The Chinese invasion, not surprisingly, called into question the dominant Indian social claims about China and Sino-Indian relations. Faced with this challenge, Indian policymakers rearticulated their social claims about China in some discursively interesting ways.

Differences between India and China over their borders had already led to tensions in 1959. During that period the differences between India's parliamentary democracy and China's people's democracy—earlier dismissed as trivial—began to appear increasingly as important for understanding specific aspects of Chinese state practices. Indian policymakers argued then that this difference in political systems was making it difficult to communicate Indian intentions to the Chinese. Nehru, during a debate on China in the Indian parliament, observed that there was an "inherent difficulty" in dealing with China: the Chinese had a "one-track mind" that produced a "national trait [of] greatness." This led them to consider everyone else as naturally beneath them and as paying "tribute" to them. It also made it difficult, Nehru argued, to explain India's democratic system to the Chinese (Nehru, 1961: 362). Of course, Nehru here forgets that it was not just the Chinese who had the national trait of "greatness," and that he himself had earlier presented India and China together as "great" countries. But leaving that aside, the democratic difference Nehru had earlier dismissed as an "unnecessary question" and a "Western obsession" did acquire greater prominence with the onset of tensions in Sino-Indian relations.

Indian social claims also highlighted the democratic difference during the war. The difference was used to explain the Chinese government's ability to "condition" the Chinese people and to contrast that ability with the various constraints on the Indian government's actions (Nehru, 1964: 108). This fits well with the historical-realist expectation that democratic India's claims regarding China's democratic or nondemocratic identity would be sensitive to the peaceful or conflictual nature of Sino-Indian relations. But the democratic difference, although important, was by no means central to Indian rearticulations of Chinese identity. The democratic difference functioned, in the Indian case, primarily to account for the Chinese government's ability to mobilize its people. It was not used to explain why the Chinese had invaded India in the first place.

For Indian policymakers the dominant understanding of the Sino-Indian conflict was, interestingly, as a "betrayal" of India. A shocked Nehru observed, "We were stabbed in the back" (cited in Appadorai and Rajan, 1985: 143). This talk of betrayal, however, is puzzling from a realist perspective, because charges of betrayal make sense only within a social space where states trust each other. Such talk is not consistent with the language of an anarchic international system in which no sensible state would trust another. One can only be betrayed by those one trusts, and those could only be friends, brothers, or others with whom one has constructed a strongly shared identity. Charges of betrayal, then, are internally consistent with earlier Indian claims about China being a *bhai*. In other words, one sees continuity in India's discursive representations of Chinese identity.

Moreover, postwar China did not cease being a great country in the Indian discourse. Indian policymakers differentiated the Chinese government's actions from those of the Chinese people thus limiting to the Chinese people the greatness they had previously bestowed generously on China as a whole (Nehru, 1964: 236–237, 262). Most significantly, Indian social claims after the war redefined China not as an autocratic, communist, illiberal, or authoritarian or nondemocratic state but as an imperialist one. Moving a resolution on the Chinese aggression in the Lok Sabha, Nehru made sense of the hitherto unimaginable Chinese invasion by observing that it was a manifestation of an imperialism that had not been seen since the days of the European powers (Nehru, 1964: 230–231). China had behaved "irresponsibly," and its word could no longer be trusted (Nehru, 1964: 233–234).[8] India was merely a "victim" of this "imperialism and expansionism" (Nehru, 1964: 249–254).

Why didn't India redefine China as nondemocratic? But democracy and imperialism are not antonyms. Why didn't India, whose democratic credentials were quite strong, redefine China on the democratic dimension? India had consistently acknowledged that difference before, even if it had not hierarchized it. Moreover, the democratic difference, in a realist logic, would have maximized democratic India's difference with a patently communist China. This failure is even more significant and surprising given the international context at the time.

The Sino-Indian conflict took place at the height of the Cold War, almost overlapping the Cuban Missile Crisis. Many dominant U.S. understandings of China and India—and the corresponding scholarship during the period—were shaped by a Cold War discourse that saw the Sino-Indian conflict as a struggle between a democratic India and a communist China (C. Bowles, 1954; Schaffer, 1993). Moreover, although the Soviet Union remained neutral in the Sino-Indian conflict, India rushed to the United States for military supplies and backing (Kux, 1992). Given this, Indian policymakers could reasonably be expected to play strategically on the ideological power of the democratic difference between India and China in a highly polarized and charged Cold War context. The democratic difference thus not only represented an important objective difference between India and China but would have resonated well with India's primary ally in the crisis, the United States.

If, as the realists expect, states redefine the identities of their adversaries to maximize their differences, the democratic difference would have sufficed on both objective and instrumental grounds. But rather than redefine China as an authoritarian country, or a communist aggressor, Indian policymakers claimed the Chinese invasion was an imperialist aggression. How should Indian policymakers' failure to match realist expectations be understood?

Redefining the Chinese as imperialist and expansionist did not maximize the differences between the two states on an objective dimension. In the context of international debates at the time, imperialism was a charge the Chinese were leveling against India. The Chinese claimed the Sino-Indian conflict had resulted from Indian insistence on adhering to British-enforced imperial borders. Further, India's forcible seizure of Goa from the Portuguese had invited charges of expansionism from states such as Pakistan. Given these charges by others, Indian claims of Chinese imperialism and expansionism would not have maximized the objective differences between India and China; nor would redefining China as an imperial and expansionist state have increased India's identification with its primary helper in the crisis, the United States. To the extent that the United States had been at the receiving end of most of these charges before—especially from a stridently nonaligned India—this would not have facilitated a shared identity with a potentially new friend. By all accounts, then, Indian redefinitions of China's identity did not fulfill many objective or instrumental criteria. The Indian redefinition of China as anti-imperial and expansionist thus does not make sense in light of the expectations generated by realist and liberal conceptualizations of the relationship between state identities and interstate practices.

Social claims on China and the Indian social imaginary. A critical constructivist focus on the social imaginary—the field of social meanings and power—productive of the Indian state's identity and, derivatively, its security concerns offers a better explanation. If India and China made sense of each other through some bilaterally sustaining social claims, an interstate conflict would not constitute a break in such productions. Conflict and war, as constructivists have argued, are intersubjective phenomena that must be understood discursively (Wendt, 1992). They need to be represented linguistically and understood through social categories. If a conflict forces a change in state interpretations, those changes and the consequent redefinition must be meaningful and communicable between the actors. They cannot be totally subjective or historically arbitrary claims. On the other hand, redefinitions of the friend turned enemy cannot also be simply objective in the sense of being governed by a need to maximize some apparently objective differences. The key requirements, therefore, are intersubjectively meaningful and relayable social claims that make sense within the social imaginaries productive of Sino-Indian identities and interstate practices.

Analyzing social imaginaries is one way to recover the meanings productive of state identity, interests, and practices. It would take me too far afield to reconstruct the social imaginaries productive of Sino-Indian relations here. I will argue, however, that the worldview of Indian policymakers was constituted through a *postcolonial security imaginary* (Muppidi, 1999b). This was an imaginary within which Asia and Africa, having struggled against Western imperialism, were going to act differently in the international system. They were going to set new norms of international behavior, they would stay away from European disputes, they would work for common ideals, they would solve the problems of the vast majority of people in the non-Western world, and they would not let Western understandings of Asia or Western ideological disputes disrupt their own understandings. But most important, as new entrants on a world stage riven by European conflicts, they would resolve their mutual disputes peacefully and thus set a new standard of international politics. China, as a fellow Asian power and struggler against the West, was a critical component, an insider, within this worldview. When it invaded India in 1962 it undermined—or refused to reproduce through its actions and practices—an important element of that worldview: the peaceful resolution of disputes among Asian states. Given this context, the worst crime China could be charged with was that of betraying these ideals, this Asian worldview of the international system Indian policymakers such as Nehru so laboriously promoted.

Within this worldview an imperialist, expansionist Europe was the outsider, the Other. Asia and Africa were the Self. The identity of the Chinese government was redefined on a dimension that likened it to this Other. The redefinition made sense as an interpretive effort to relocate China outside the boundaries of the "imagined community" of anti-imperialist, non-aligned Asian states. In that sense it was meaningful and consistent with earlier Indian claims. But the redefinition was also an act of power to the extent that it was meant to isolate and distance China from its claims to any leadership, solidarity, or membership within the anti-imperial Afro-Asian community. These changes in social claims thus arose on dimensions that were not objective, arbitrary, or even merely strategic. China was redefined in Indian social claims in ways that were meaningful and powerful primarily in terms of the intersubjective discourses productive of Sino-Indian relations.

Democratic India and Democratic Pakistan:
Democracies Do Go to War

Whereas India has been democratic for more than half a century, Pakistan has had intermittent spells of democratic rule (Jalal, 1995). Pakistan's most recent period of democratic rule, lasting more than a decade, ended in October 1999 when the Pakistani military seized power and ended democratic rule in the country. But from 1988 to 1999, both India and Pakistan satisfied the objective requirements of democracies. They also saw each other as democratic. The objective and subjective requirements were thus satisfied on many counts. So what would scholars of the democratic peace tell us to expect?

Analyzing India's relations with Pakistan up to the early 1990s, Russett argues that "India and Pakistan have of course fought repeatedly and sometimes bloodily during their history as independent states." But, he cautions, "no fatalities are recorded in disputes between them during Pakistan's most democratic periods of 1962–64 and 1988–92" (1993: 20). Contrary to Russett's time-specific formulation and the expectations of liberal democratic peace theorists in general, however, India and Pakistan have fought each other—and sustained heavy fatalities—during the period when both were democracies.[9]

Democratic India's conflicts with democratic Pakistan can be analyzed through two events in the period 1988–1999. The first was a continual battle between the two states in the remote and icy terrain of the Siachen glacier in Kashmir. The second was a battle over the region of Kargil, again in Kashmir, in summer of 1999. Both conflicts were extremely expensive for the two countries in human and monetary terms. One report counts nearly 2,000 dead and 10,000 people crippled in the battle over Siachen (Bukhari, 1997). Another report estimates the cost to India of the battle in Siachen at $1 million a day (Kreisberg, 1993: 49).

On May 6, 1999, the conflict worsened when India discovered that Pakistani troops had crossed into Indian territory and occupied key posts on its side of the border in the Drass-Kargil sector of the Line of Control in Kashmir. India and Pakistan battled for nearly two months, during which both sides suffered heavy casualties. India claims the battle cost 398 Indian and 691 Pakistani lives, whereas Pakistani estimates place the number of Indians killed at 1,700 (initial estimates were 700) and the number of Pakistanis killed at 187 (Dugger, 1999). The hostilities ended in Kargil when Pakistani forces withdrew under diplomatic pressure from Washington. The Pakistani prime minister held the military responsible for acting behind his back, and the military blamed the prime minister for retreating disgracefully under external pressure. Soon thereafter General Pervez Musharraf seized power from the democratically elected but now domestically discredited prime minister, Nawaz Sharif. Thus democratic states not only go to war but it appears war can endanger democratic rule.[10]

Siachen continues to claim Indian and Pakistani lives and resources. In strategic terms the Siachen glacier is difficult to access or maintain control over for both India and Pakistan. It is in an area of Kashmir left undemarcated in the border between the two countries. Situated at an altitude of 20,000 feet, with temperatures ranging from −15 to −60 degrees Celsius, the area was considered too inhospitable to even require demarcation (Bukhari, 1997: 14). No potentially rich natural resources exist to be exploited in the region. But the peak is in Kashmir, an area of intersubjectively meaningful struggle over state identity for both India and Pakistan (Appadorai and Rajan, 1985; Mansingh, 1984; Dutt, 1984).

India's state identity—in relation to Pakistan—is that of a secular state in which people of all religions enjoy equal claims to "Indianness." Pakistan's identity is that of a Muslim state founded against the potential tyranny of India's majority Hindus. The social imaginaries structuring these two identities are thus fundamentally at odds. India, although accepting the partition of the subcontinent on the basis of territory, refuses to recognize religious claims as an adequate basis for nationhood. Pakistan's identity, in contrast, is founded on claims about the validity of religion as a basis of national identity. Kashmir was a Muslim majority state with a Hindu ruler when it acceded to India. It is critical to Indian identity as a secular state because its accession validates India's claims that a Muslim majority state is as much a part of India as a state ruled by any other linguistic, religious, or ethnic majority. To lose Kashmir on the grounds that Muslims cannot survive in India is to undermine the basis of India's secular identity. For Pakistan, Kashmir's natural place as a Muslim majority state is not in Hindu-dominated India but in Muslim Pakistan. If a Muslim majority state that borders Pakistan cannot be an integral part of the Muslim nation, then what is the basis for Pakistan's identity?

India has fought four of its five official wars with Pakistan. Pakistan and India routinely use international fora to score various diplomatic points on issues such as nonproliferation, human rights violations, and state terrorism. But Kashmir condenses and is the constitutive contradiction in the relationship between India and Pakistan. The war over Kashmir is thus a battle over state identities. The presence or absence of democracy makes little difference in this war; state identities are the primary cause (GPD, 1992).

Democratic India and Democratic Sri Lanka: Democracy Causes Conflict

In 1971 India sent troops into democratic Sri Lanka (then Ceylon) at the request of the Sri Lankan government to suppress a leftist insurgency against the ruling government (Dutt, 1984: 232). In the 1980s a Tamil rebellion in northern Sri Lanka initially received covert support and encouragement from India. In 1987 that support became overt when India's air force violated Sri Lankan airspace to drop relief packages to Tamils (Thornton, 1988: 63). Subsequently, the Indian Peace Keeping Force (IPKF) was sent to enforce a peace agreement between the Sri Lankan government and the Tamil rebels. As a result of this agreement, the Indian government waged a war against the Tamils in Sri Lanka (Thornton, 1988: 62–65). Significantly, throughout these events of conflict, cooperation, and intervention in a civil war, democratic India repeatedly asserted its commitment to maintain democratic Sri Lanka's territorial integrity. That Indian commitment was not rhetorical but was a serious social claim. Paradoxically, it also went hand in hand with active intervention in Sri Lanka's domestic affairs. Democracy and state identities were the primary reason for this paradoxical relationship. Indo–Sri Lankan relations condensed principles that articulated democracy and Indian identity in significant ways. For India, other South Asian states are significant as sovereign entities but also as states that exert political jurisdiction over cultural groups that overlap its own (see Mansingh, 1984: 265–273). Bengalis in eastern India have more in common with Bengalis from Bangladesh than with Sikhs from western India. Punjabis from western India have more in common with Punjabis in Pakistan than with Tamils from southern India. Tamils in southern India, similarly, share stronger identities with Tamils in Sri Lanka than with the Assamese in northeastern India. India thus shares borders *and* social and cultural identities with many other South Asian states such as Sri Lanka, Nepal, Bangladesh, Pakistan, and Bhutan.

Given this, for India a complex and overflowing mélange of cultural identities must be articulated together to yield the dominance of a single national Indian identity. But however powerful the social claim of Indianness, it must be constantly reproduced over and above competing linguistic, regional, religious, and other identities. Such dominance, within the social imaginary structuring India, is achieved not by erasing competing identities but by acknowledging their separateness *and* their relatedness. The Tamil is thus both Tamil *and* Indian, not just Indian. In institutionalizing the imagined identity of India, the state promotes national integration through a model that stresses unity in diversity.

Against this background, democratic politics poses a peculiar problem for India. It forces the Indian state to erase the difference between domestic and international politics within South Asia. Within that region international politics becomes intimately linked with domestic politics, and the difference between the "inside" and "outside" becomes very thin in many of India's interstate practices. A democratically organized Indian government finds it difficult to ignore a neighboring state's domestic policies, especially when they bear on issues of overlapping identity. Tamil rebels in Sri Lanka cannot be suppressed by a democratically elected, sovereign Sri Lankan government in a civil war without provoking strong reactions from the Tamil Nadu region in southern India. A democratic Indian government determined to respect democratic Sri Lanka's sovereignty would disregard this domestic reaction at its own peril. It would alienate Indian Tamils and further the claims for an independent Tamil state comprising parts of southern India and northern Sri Lanka. Even if secession were ruled out, the logic of electoral politics in a democracy would bring to power those political parties most sympathetic to the Tamil cause. Further, regional governments in southern India could lend substantive covert and overt support to the Tamil cause against the wishes of the federal government and provoke a federal-regional showdown.

India's interstate practices in South Asia, although warlike, also generally pull it back from explicitly undermining the neighboring state's territorial integrity because of the countervailing power of the Indian state's identity. The territorial integrity of its South Asian neighbors is crucial for maintaining India's own multicultural identity. Encouraging a Tamil rebellion as a way of exerting pressure on Sri Lanka is one thing, but instituting a separate state—such as Eelam—for Tamils is seen officially as strategically unwise, since it would constitute a powerful "imagined community" for Indian Tamils and thus directly threaten India's unity and integrity. Given this logic, India has also gone to war—this time with the secessionist minorities, as in the IPKF operations against the Tamil militants in northern Sri Lanka—to prevent a breakup of Sri Lanka. Democracy combines, then, with the logic of cultural and state identities to increase conflict in India's relations with other South Asian states.

India's interstate practices in South Asia are therefore governed by a peculiar need to balance overt and covert interference in the affairs of its neighbors with a concern for the maintenance of their territorial integrity and sovereignty. A vigorous Indian democracy forces the state into a warlike relationship with its neighbors on issues of overlapping identities. Sri Lanka, on the other hand, comes to a state of civil war precisely because its majoritarian democracy—based on a resurgent Sinhala nationalism—leads to a progressive alienation of its Tamil minority. The broader point is that democracy combines with territorially overlapping cultural identities to undermine peace and facilitate war. Democracy can therefore promote war, not just peace, within and between two vigorously democratic states.

Democratic India and Democratic United States: The Paradox of Insecurity

Democratic India's greatest source of insecurity is not the world's biggest nondemocracy—China—but the world's most stable liberal democracy, the United States (Muppidi, 1999b). India has fought one war with China, four with Pakistan, and none with the United States. But, ironically, interstate relations between the world's biggest democracy and its most powerful democracy have traditionally been characterized by intense insecurity.

Democracy is the objective factor present in both states. Each also perceives the other as a democracy. But the postcolonial security imaginary that is productive of Indian identity also forces it to confront the United States in various ways. This postcolonial imaginary empowers articulations that promote solidarity with Asia and Africa but a constant mimicry and mockery of the West. Pakistan and China, however conflictual the relationships, fall well within the boundaries of a shared postcoloniality for the Indian state. Notwithstanding a shared democracy, the United States has historically been articulated as different and threatening (Muppidi, 1999b). That threat has been so consistent over the past fifty years that scholars have characterized the relationship between the two states as "troubled," "strained," "fragile," "discordant," and "unstable" (Limaye, 1993; Vinod, 1991). In other words, interstate relations between two of the world's biggest democracies have been unusually insecure—although never leading to war—and anything but peaceful.

CONCLUSION

The DP hypothesis leads to an expectation that democratic India would have peaceful relations with fellow democracies in the international system and warlike relations with nondemocracies. But contrary to such expectations, democratic India's interstate practices have been more nuanced and counterintuitive to realist and liberal expectations. The Indo-U.S. relationship is extremely insecure and conflictual, putting into question the claim that democracies necessarily have peaceful relationships. Democracy has also made little difference in the India-Pakistan relationship. Both sides have gone to war when they have been democratic, and war has undermined democracy in Pakistan. Moreover, democracy itself can engender conflict and war, as in the case of India and Sri Lanka.

But these arguments do not necessarily constitute a defense of the realist position that all that matters is power and that state identities are but a function of power. India's relations with China show both the empowering and the constraining power of democratic meanings and identities. Even though India and China have differed significantly on a variety of objective criteria, democratic India has constructed a meaningful relationship of identity with nondemocratic China, consciously downplaying the democratic difference. These understandings of identity have been critically constitutive of India's military practices. The fact that India and China went to war does not demolish the power of social meanings and imagined identities. Contrary to a realist explanation, India did not redefine China on grounds easily explainable by realist accounts of the relationship between state identity and conflict. Imagined social identities thus both empowered and constrained democratic India's relations with nondemocratic China. If India and China could see each other as *bhai-bhai,* there is no a priori reason to rule out the power of social meanings such as democracy to create shared identities in other cases. Democracy and interstate practices are therefore causally related but in ways that are more nuanced than expected by rationalist theories. A critical constructivist framework better captures the causal relationships that bind democracy to both war *and* peace.

NOTES

1. Although DP theorists differ over which of the two logics is more important, some have acknowledged that the two logics are not easily separable and are mutually reinforcing; see Russett (1993: 119); Owen (1994); Chan (1997).

2. In fairness to Russett, he is open to the conceptual possibility that otherwise transparent processes of identification and differentiation could go astray. Russett explains the "imperialist wars" of democracies on non-European peoples as one such case. But his explanation of these wars sees them as arising out of a "misperception" based on "ethnocentrism" and "pseudo-Darwinian racism" (Russett, 1993: 34–35). In other words, although states could occasionally "misperceive" other states, their understandings of the identities of those states are otherwise fairly objective and not determined by considerations of power.

3. For example, even a minimally adequate understanding of the distribution of threats in South Asia requires a recognition of the social and historical reality of that region as understood by the actors there. Walt's analysis, however, assumes, among a variety of highly problematic assumptions, that the South Asian context was dominated by the prevalence of a religious conflict between "Hindus and Muslims" (Walt, 1988: 297). But India's conflict with Pakistan is not a premodern or traditional enmity between two religions but a very modern struggle between different visions of nationhood (Appadorai and Rajan, 1985; Mansingh, 1984; Dutt, 1984).

4. Most exclude the period 1975–1977, when India was under a state of emergency.

5. For a related interpretation see Chatterjee (1986, 1993). On India's different encounters with Western liberalism, see Kaviraj (1992); Chatterjee (1986, 1993); Nandy (1983, 1994).

6. Some scholars have drawn attention to the psychological aspects of leaders' or states' perceptions. Much of this work, however, takes the identity of the state or "in-group/out-group" as already given and does not investigate its production or transformation through specific constructions of identity and difference. I do not analyze this scholarship here, since it self-consciously focuses only on the political psychology of leaders. But see Hermann and Kegley (1995).

7. This did not mean these were the only views on China prevalent among Indian policymakers. Dissident views, drawn from a more traditional British imperial view, treated the Chinese with greater suspicion. But these alternative understandings were not constitutive of the dominant Indian practices toward China. On these alternative views, see Gupta (1956: 50–54).

8. It is interesting and highly relevant, though, that even in the year in which it was invaded by China, India supported China's UN representation. This speaks at one level for the strength of the shared identity Indian policymakers articulated with China. But developing this theme would take me too far afield of my main argument here.

9. Russett's theorization predates the Kargil conflict but not the conflict over Siachen; see Bukhari (1997); Thornton (1988: 60).

10. I thank Kathryn Sikkink for this point.

4

Democracy and Ethnic War

Michael Mann

The twentieth century's death toll from ethnic wars was above 60 million. Those assembling the statistics suggest that the twentieth century may have been worse than its predecessors and that violent "ethnopolitics" surged in its later decades (Rummel, 1994; Bell-Fialkoff, 1996: 21; Gurr, 1993). Although such horrors are not new to human history, few earlier historical regimes seem to have intended to wipe out or expel entire civilian populations. Ancient rulers generally wanted people to rule over. Some scholars disagree. K. Jonasshon (1998: chapter 17; cf. Freeman, 1995) instances a number of notorious historical incidents to suggest that murderous cleansing is equally ancient and modern. I concede ground to Jonasson in three realms. First, mass migrating settlers expropriating the land of natives have sometimes engaged in mass slaughter to get rid of them. Some Hun, Mongol, and Viking incursions seem to have taken this form. I discuss better documented modern cases of murderous settlers later. Second, imperial conquerors repeatedly used "exemplary repression," killing or deporting entire troublesome elites or defiant cities or local populations. Putting a city to the sword could involve thousands of deaths. But this was an exemplary signal to other cities to surrender, not the beginning of something more systematic. Assyrian bas reliefs, for example, depict a linked triptych—killing those who resist, selectively enslaving others, and accepting the submission of the rest. Third, ruthless warfare has ubiquitously killed many civilians. Depriving the enemy of food and supplies may involve laying waste to territory, burning crops and homes, killing animals. The outcome—not the object of the exercise but callously regarded as an acceptable cost—is mass civilian deaths, mostly through starvation and disease. Since all the main historical cases remain poorly documented, these issues will remain contentious.

Yet there does seem something distinctively modern about more systematic cleansing.

The overall reason is not hard to find. As Ernest Gellner (1983) and I (1986) have noted, historically most large states were essentially the private possession of upper-class elites whose cultures were quite different from the cultures of the masses. Nations did not exist, class divisions did. These were asymmetric class structures: the upper classes were capable of extensive social organization, the lower classes were not (Anthony Giddens's term is "class-divided societies"). Ethnic groups existed, but rarely did they rule or legitimate rule. Imperial regimes often perpetrated exemplary repression to maintain their rule, but they did not try to wipe out their subjects. Some empires did have a "core people" with shared ethnic or religious characteristics privileged by imperial institutions. Thus the Ottoman Empire privileged Muslims politically over Christians. Yet if Christians accepted political subordination, they enjoyed considerable rights (those commensurate with their class positions). In the Ottoman *millet* system Christian minorities possessed collective political, judicial, and cultural autonomies to an extent not found in more "modern" states of the twentieth century. All historic empires were systems of indirect rule. Rulers ruled localities through semiautonomous worthies. If localities were dominated by distinctive ethnic or religious groups, then they had to be ruled by worthies drawn from that group, supervised by governors representing the imperial authority. Thus mass cleansing of one "people" by or in the name of another was unlikely. This is more of a hazard in societies where "whole peoples" share the same collective identities and political claims.

I have written elsewhere of why in modern times rule by "We, the People" (the phrase in the Preamble to the U.S. Constitution) contained a dark side (Mann, 1999). If "the whole people" is to rule, its collective identity—and differentiation from other peoples—becomes potentially relevant to politics. A. Wimmer (1997) has presented a slightly more materialist version of this argument in relation to postcolonial states. He argues that the politicization of ethnicity is an essential part of modern state building. Only when people and state are mutually related within the sphere of a legitimate political order does the question arise as to which "people" is the legitimate owner of the state, alone entitled to its "public goods." But the dark side lay dormant for a time, for two reasons. First, eligibility for inclusion in "the people" was limited in ethnic ways liberals never talked about. Second, liberal democratic conceptions of "rule by the people" first emerged in European contexts where ethnic, religious, and other differences were subordinate to class differences. This bred a plural conception of the people. I deal with the second point first.

Although ethnicity clearly mattered in eighteenth-century countries like Britain or France, the franchise was based predominantly on property and rank. As the first liberal regimes crystallized, they focused on property (held by males). In Britain the extension of the franchise went from the 15-pound freeholder to all freeholders. Thus class continued to dominate the question of broadening the franchise. Liberal political theory has never quite perceived the significance of this. It has always misperceived the essential basis of a liberal regime by focusing overwhelmingly on the notion of individual rights and freedoms. Freedom is conceived of as of the individual from the state. Law guarantees those freedoms. Yet early liberal states did more than this. From the earliest days their practices entrenched the institutionalization of class conflict. They accepted that politics concerned the legitimate conflict of "interests," which they defined in quasi-class terms—collective groups like merchants, manufacturers, artisans, and so on (all with property, education, and thus a stake in the nation) should join gentlemen in the exercise of political rights. Their collective conflicts of interest would constitute the essential party politics of the state, and it was essentially for them that rights of assembly, petition, and others were protected constitutionally. And as the franchise was extended, so were the collective rights of other classes. It should not be forgotten that the early reform movements did not concern merely an abstract method of government but also economic redistribution. Their impetus came from the demand for fairer (and, of course, lower) taxes across the classes. If we insist on calling the ensuing political regime "liberal democracy," we should recognize that from the beginning it also contained "social" democratic aspects. Modern democracy was designed to reduce exploitation. That was its raison d'être.

This became the dominant pattern across northwestern Europe. There were exceptions. Switzerland and later Belgium had far more salient ethnic/regional differences, and these were institutionalized—alongside and often usefully crosscut by class—into the emerging political parties. Ethnic relations were also institutionalized into the structure of the state itself, although they constituted confederal and consociational power-sharing arrangements. But northwestern liberal democracy was also reinforced by the Westphalian geopolitical system between states. Its notions of the balance of power and protection for small states meant a general absence of imperialism or "exploitation" between states and regions of the northwest. In recognizing the right of the prince to determine the religion of his country, Westphalia also damped down religious conflicts. Ireland was the regional exception, oppressed by religion-centered British imperialism. Yet in general, in the region ethnicity was generally subordinate to class. Ethnic differences could be assuaged by assimilation of minorities into the relevant class status within the dominant group ("peasants into French peasants"; E. Weber, 1976).

But the problem elsewhere was that in more backward systems of indirect rule, classes were less evenly diffused across territories, and imperialism had only half swallowed up formerly distinct political units. Exploitation could be seen as being by one region/ethnicity/state. Rule by "we, the people" came to be seen in part in class terms but increasingly in ethnic and imperial terms, first in the Austro-Hungarian, then the Ottoman, and finally the Russian Empire. And with it came the doctrine of organic nationalism, the notion that since "we, the people" share a distinctive culture, character, and soul marking us off from other peoples, we should have "our own" state, free of imperial oppression. Poland for the Poles, Croatia for the Croats. O. Yiftachel (1999), writing of Israel, appropriately terms it an "ethnocratic" state—a state essentially belonging to one ethnicity. The organic ideal was initially conceived in democratic terms. Yet democracy became limited in two ways: it tended toward an ethnocratic "majoritarian democracy," tyrannizing minorities, since minorities did not possess the character the state was to express; and it tended further toward one-party rule, since if the people were singular it could be represented by one movement, perhaps even by one leader. Organic democracy, unlike liberal democracy, contained authoritarian strains, since it did not have a conception of diverse class or ethnic interest groups existing within the nation—unlike Britain and Switzerland.

The neglect of collective identities and conflicts—whether of class or ethnicity or imperialism—restricts the capacity of liberal theory to deal with the reality of ethnic wars. I outline this neglect in three main contexts: first, in supposedly "liberal" colonies, second in European countries pervaded by organic conceptions of the nation and of democracy, and third (very briefly) in the more multiethnic contexts that dominate most of the rest of the world today.

LIBERAL VIEWS OF ETHNIC WARS

The liberal view is that not democracies but authoritarian states launch mass killing. There are three relevant theories. First, a "civil society" school of social theory has argued that the best guarantee of both democracy and peace is the strength of nonstate secondary institutions within a country. The emphasis is not on class but on institutions encouraging individual citizen action and civility. These form a civil society, which is seen as essentially virtuous. Where this is weak, states will perpetrate atrocities. I will not discuss this view here, but it is incorrect. Across most cases of murderous cleansing the perpetrating communities (e.g., Nazis or Krajina Serb nationalists) have had very strong secondary institutions. Indeed, such radical nationalists have often succeeded precisely because of the greater density and mobilizing power of their civil society networks when compared with their political rivals (for the Nazis the data are very good; see Hagtvet, 1980; Koshar, 1986).

Second, a "democratic peace" (DP) school of political science has declared that democracies are essentially pacific, rarely fighting wars and, if they do, almost never against each other (e.g., Doyle, 1983). The database conventionally brought forward to support this position bears unmistakable signs of massaging, in terms of the size of either the war or the electorate. Thus large wars between states whose institutions were among the most democratic in the world at that time are excluded from the democratic camp. This seems a bit unfair for Britain, fighting the United States in 1812, or Germany, fighting the entente in World War I. Small wars of aggression fought by U.S. troops against elected governments (as in the Dominican Republic in 1954) are not counted; nor is U.S. destabilization of elected regimes in Chile or Nicaragua. The United States militarily intervened and destabilized many Third World regimes during the twentieth century (Chapter 6, this volume). Of course, the indirect enemy, the USSR, was not democratic. But the late-nineteenth-century imperial predecessors, Britain and the French Republic, were both democracies, and they also fought indirect wars through intermediaries where they could not establish direct colonies—as, for example, in the Middle East. Even starker were the practices of European colonial regimes during the first half of the twentieth century. Almost all were democratic back home, and they allowed the "white" settlers to establish democratic institutions in the colonies. But they ruthlessly repressed political parties emerging from below, including those formed according to impeccably democratic procedures, if those parties seriously challenged their domination of the colony. True, the colonial dissidents did not run their own democracy—because that was precisely what the "democratic" colonizers were preventing. The notion that the role of these imperial liberal democracies was pacific would be laughable if it were not so dangerously ideological. But these cases are not counted because those excluded are not actually seen as eligible to be considered free individuals. Collective ethnic labels defined who was and who was not an individual in the liberal sense.

Third, those studying genocide have mostly argued that it is a decidedly "statist" phenomenon. The main founder of genocide studies, Leo Kuper (1981), argued that the modern state's monopoly of power over a territory that was in reality culturally plural and economically stratified created both the political desire and the power to commit genocide against out groups. Helen Fein said flatly, "The victims of twentieth century premeditated genocide . . . were murdered in order to fulfill the state's design for a new order" (1984: 5; cf. Smith, 1987, and I. Horowitz, 1982). Human rights organizations consistently blame states and political elites rather than more "popular" groups of perpetrators for murderous cleansing. Indeed they are blamed in *all* the many cases of ethnic cleansing figuring in a Human Rights Watch book (1995). There are also several Slobodon Milosevic–centered accounts of recent Yugoslav atrocities stressing his authoritarian rule (e.g., Gagnon, 1997). These are top-down, elitist, and cohesive images of states. States appear as collective actors with premeditated goals.

This view can also color methodology. Barbara Harff and Ted Robert Gurr's very useful data set of modern cases of genocide and politicide has become widely used. It only includes cases where "one or more identifiable groups were the target of deliberate attempts by 'a ruling group' to 'bring about its physical destruction in whole or part'" (1988: 363). The inclusion of the term "ruling group" means that only state-led killing could be considered genocide or politicide. Thus their data set does not include, for example, the communal Hindu-Muslim violence in India in 1947, which killed over half a million people but was not state led. And in cases that are included, it seems to assume that the state rulers were the principal agents of the killings. This is rather problematic in cases where states were factionalized and where "popular" paramilitaries or other local or communal organizations, partly outside the control of the state, played a large role.

R. J. Rummel (1994: 12–27) takes these arguments furthest, claiming that the more authoritarian a state, the more likely it is to commit massive killings. Of course, in the fullest sense of the term, regimes that murder or deprive citizens' rights of large numbers of inhabitants cannot possibly be considered democracies, but that would be a tautology. Rummel is really arguing that perpetrating regimes were not in place by virtue of free elections. The examples of Hitler, Stalin, and Mao immediately spring to mind, and their killings tend to dominate Rummel's statistics. I would not dispute the scale of death resulting from these regimes or that it resulted from their authoritarian powers. Hitler's regime also intended those deaths, for this was genocide. Yet Stalin and Mao differed. Over 90 percent of the deaths inflicted under their regimes were not intentional but the ghastly by-product of bizarre policies of wholesale social transformation carried out by authoritarian means (the Khmer Rouge is the leftist regime under which most of the deaths seem to have been intended). True, Stalin seemed not to care that his anti-kulak and anti-Turkic policies of deportation and repression involved massive deaths, but that was not the initial intention. We shall now see that this blend of genocide/ethnocide has also occurred under democratic regimes.

COLONIAL ETHNIC WARS AND DEMOCRACY

Rummel's statistics are made half plausible only by leaving out the majority of cases of mass murder in the early modern and modern periods. They were committed against native peoples who were usually democratically organized by seventeenth to early-twentieth-century European settlers also living under mainly constitutional governments. This involved the most brutal ethnic exploitation and repeated imperial wars. The colonies lacked both of the preconditions of liberal peace back in the mother country. In parts of the Americas and in Australia, where the settlers took virtually all the fertile land and aborigines were not effective slave laborers, the settlers desired to remove them by whatever means worked. Thus forced deportations escalated well beyond bonded labor or slavery to ethnocide and genocide. This was not rare but the norm, and it continued over several centuries—resulting in the most nearly complete elimination of populations ever recorded. In the Americas most regional estimates of population losses in colonized areas hover around the 95 percent level; they must have amounted to above 80 percent for the entire continent. Since recent estimates of the total pre-Columbian population of the continent have been around 100 million, both the proportion and the absolute number of dead exceed even the most notorious twentieth-century parallels (Stannard, 1992: 74–87, 118, 146, 266–268).

Consider the present-day territories of the world's major democracy, the United States.[1] Most scholars now estimate the total pre-Columbian Indian population at somewhere between 6 and 12 million. By the time of the 1900 U.S. Census there were just 237,000 Indians, a loss of more than 95 percent over 400 years. This happened with the best records in California, where we have a better baseline figure. On their arrival in 1769, the Spanish missions estimated the native population at 310,000. By 1848, when the Gold Rush began, that number had halved. Thereafter it fell even faster as European settlement expanded. By 1860, only 31,000 California Indians remained—an 80 percent loss over only 12 years. Remember that the Nazi regime also lasted 12 years and killed 75 percent of European Jews! This was truly the Golden State Holocaust. Finally, however, things began to ease. By 1880 there were still over 20,000 California Indians, and then their numbers stabilized, growing slightly during the twentieth century.

Assimilation played little role in this monstrous cleansing. Indians were considered incapable of acquiring civilization, and settlers despised "half-breeds" or "renegades." Liberalism was based on the simple exclusion of most collective groups living in the country from the status of the free individual. Things began to change only in the twentieth century when Indian children began to be forcibly removed to Christian boarding schools, a policy known as "kill the Indian, spare the man."

Most deaths resulted not from deliberate murder but from disease. California estimates typically indicate that disease killed around 60 percent of Indians, and another 30 percent died from malnutrition and starvation. These deaths were not entirely accidental. Diseases spread most rapidly where the native population was herded close together and was malnourished—in the Spanish Missions in California and on reservations located on marginal lands. Indians fleeing these corrals were hunted down and murdered. The caloric and vitamin intakes of Indians in the missions are known to have been grossly insufficient for people forced to do heavy agricultural labor, and Mission Indians' bones are smaller than those of free California Indians (Stannard, 1992: 138–139). The settlers were not ignorant of disease mechanisms, yet they rarely took steps against epidemics to which they themselves were immune. They welcomed or were indifferent to deaths resulting directly from their own actions. The remaining native losses (about 10 percent overall in California, more after 1850) were caused by deliberate killing. The whole amounts to a massive policy of social transformation involving mixed genocide/ethnocide, comparable to that practiced by Stalin and Mao.

But there were two great differences. This genocide/ethnocide occurred under not an authoritarian but a democratic state, and the main perpetrator was not the state but the people. Politically, all European settler groups enjoyed de facto local self-rule (whatever the colonial government formally declared), since the state lacked the resources to closely supervise them. During this period these communities of settlers were distinctly democratic, yet their ethnic cleansing was usually worse than that committed by the less democratic imperial authorities. The Spanish, Portuguese, and British Crowns; viceroys and governors; and the Catholic and some Protestant churches tended to be milder toward the natives than the settlers were. In California the killings escalated as soon as rule passed from the Spanish Crown and the Missions to American settler statehood. Despite the dubious record of British North American colonial administrations, most Indians supported them and not the settler revolutionaries in the American War of Independence. Deliberate genocidal bursts were probably also more common among those ruled by the more democratic British and Dutch than among settlers ruled by the Spanish or Portuguese. In both cases we find that the greater the local democracy among the perpetrators, the more frequent the bursts of genocide.

Four U.S. presidents revered as great democrats were also great ethnic cleansers. George Washington instructed his generals to attack the Iroquois and "lay waste all the settlements . . . that the country may not be merely overrun but destroyed" and not to "listen to any overture of peace before the total ruin of their settlements is effected." He likened Indians to wolves, "both being beasts of prey, tho' they differ in shape." And he declared that the Indians must be forced west of the Mississippi and that any remaining must be broken by force. Thomas Jefferson repeatedly said Indians should be "exterminated" or "extirpated from the earth." Andrew Jackson extended the settler franchise but was elected mainly because of his renown as an Indian fighter. He boasted, "I have on all occasions preserved the scalps of my killed," and he urged his soldiers to also kill women and children—otherwise it would be like pursuing "a wolf in the hamocks without knowing first where her den and whelps were." Once president, Jackson systematically broke Indian treaties and supervised forcible deportations, killings, and mutilations of the Cherokees and Choctaws. Theodore Roosevelt declared that extermination of the Indians "was as ultimately beneficial as it was inevitable": "I don't go so far as to think that the only good Indians are dead Indians, but I believe nine out of ten are, and I shouldn't like to inquire too closely into the case of the tenth" (quotes from Stannard, 1992: 119–122, 245–246).

The 1850 California Constitution enshrined full white male suffrage but also stated that Indians were to be segregated on reservations (with the worst land in the state). Any Indians who strayed could be forcibly picked up and placed in slavery for perpetuity. The constitution also authorized the raising of murderous settler militias. In the Denver press of 1863, ten of the twenty-seven stories about Indians advocated "extermination." Obviously, not all settlers favored such atrocities. But there can be no doubting the electoral popularity of the "removal" of Indians. There was no protest movement comparable to the abolitionists (of slavery).

We also see the imprint of populism on the military means used, which were not particularly "statist." True, regular armies assembled by the colonial state could kill more Indians than any other local force. Governments also often approved and financed the killing. The federal army played a horrific role, with forced deportations becoming death marches. Yet the army tended to be called in at the urging of local settlers, when local militias could not cope with the Indian resistance that major cleansing drives provoked. Settler militias also provided the main genocidal thrust. "My intention is to kill all Indians I come across," said Colonel Chivington, a former Methodist minister and militia leader in Colorado. He exhorted his men to "kill and scalp all, little and big"—including children, since "nits make lice." These were normally part-time volunteer forces recruited from among the settlers and receiving a wage (sometimes a scalp bounty). In California the state legislature raised $1.1 million to pay them in acts of 1850 and 1851, with Governor Burnett declaring that "a war of extermination will continue to be waged between the two races until the Indian becomes extinct." The vigilante posses, part-time militias, and ranger forces described themselves as "a free people in arms"—volunteers bringing to murder their everyday settler skills as herders and hunters, their knowledge of the terrain, and their familiarity with handguns. Militia leaders appealed for "experienced woodsmen" in Eastern militias and "Indian fighters" in Western ones. The Second Amendment to the U.S. Constitution ("the right to a duly constituted militia") is only now coming under attack. Yet its original main purpose was far from sacred: it was to kill Indians.

This was also ethnic war *between* democracies, since in North America (as in some parts of Central and South America and in all of Australia) native political institutions were also usually democratic—indeed, more so than those of the settlers. Political participation was more "direct" than representative, but the rights of most ordinary males (sometimes also females) of the Indian nations were far greater than those of the citizens of representative democracies. They could freely leave the nation; they could refuse to fight for it. I should add that these were not pacific Indian democracies, since they fought many wars against each other. The democratic peace school has excluded groups like the Indian nations from their calculations on the grounds that they lacked permanent, differentiated states of the "modern" type. Although this is convenient for purposes of data massage, it is illegitimate even by their own definitions. For Indian nations did develop permanent constitutional states through the mid–nineteenth century— for example, the Cherokee in 1827; the Choctaw, Chickasaw, and Creeks in the period 1856–1867. The major cause of this development was U.S. government pressure for "responsible" government with which it could negotiate (Champagne, 1992). Predictably, the negotiations turned into enforced deportation.

It is a terrible story, one that—unlike slavery—most Americans have forgotten. Unlike the descendants of slaves, the descendants of the murdered Native Americans are few and politically marginalized. This genocide was a total "success," since it was forgotten. Hitler and Himmler both referred to U.S. genocide as part of their inspiration. Some of the world's greatest liberal democracies repeatedly committed mixed ethnocide/genocide against other democracies. If we counted the cases where "the people" of the United States, Canada, and Australia committed mass murder on the individual Indian and aboriginal nations and communities, we could probably tip Rummel's statistical scales over to conclude that democratic regimes were more likely to commit genocide than authoritarian ones. But I have no wish to reverse the statistical artifact, only to observe that in many such regimes entire groups of humans were being excluded from the collectivity of the people.

Was this a *necessary* connection between the two sides of liberal democracy, between genuine democracy and genocide? Not in one sense. The emergence of liberal democratic regimes in the northwest European core did not depend on genocide in the colonial periphery. Representative government was caused indigenously from within Europe. We are dealing with two separate phenomena—one in the motherlands, the other in the colonies. Yet there was another connection. Since the imperial authorities, especially those of Spain and Portugal, were not committed to rule "by the people," they were less likely to develop theories emphasizing the ethnic commonality of all settlers. These were still class-divided states. In contrast, settlers wished to legitimate rule by the "people" yet sought to limit membership of the people to Europeans. Thus they were likely to develop the theory of "the people" as ethnic (and eventually racial). This was not an accidental but a logical connection.

The process continued in North America, parts of South America, and Australia until there were virtually no more natives to exterminate. The colonists could then forget their origins and delude themselves with their unique, pacific virtues. Cleansing remained strongest where white settler populations were still expanding, as in Australia, and in settler groups involved in the "scramble for Africa," which was now involving latecomers to colonialism such as Germany and Italy. The last case of authoritarian colonial genocide was in Ethiopia, ruled by fascist Italy. But the last more democratic case was in a German colony, South West Africa, now called Namibia, which is well documented. Again, the colonial state and the missionary churches were relative moderates compared with many settlers, who wanted to go beyond the mix of severe discrimination, harsh labor exploitation, and conversion and simply get rid of the natives. Their language was more likely to dehumanize the natives by labeling them "baboons." Some demanded "a clean sweep, hang them, shoot them to the last man, give no quarter" (Bridgman and Worley, 1997: 8). These settlers provoked the Herrero native rising of 1908 in order to secure that goal. The governor and Berlin were pressured into authorizing the imperial army to force the Herrero into a waterless desert. Only 15,000 of 80,000 Herrero remained alive by 1915, a loss of 80 percent in only a decade—virtually identical to California in the 1850s. As usual in the colonies, it was a church organization (the Rhineland Missionary Society) that pressured a vacillating imperial government to eventually stop the slaughter (Drechsler, 1980; Poewe, 1985).

Today, this type of murderous cleansing still continues in the backlands of Latin America and Asia in the form of attempts to seize the land and thus eliminate small indigenous peoples living in marginal forests, swamps, and mountains. Some of the perpetrating regimes are authoritarian, some are democratic. It now makes no difference, since the indigenous peoples are few in number and rarely vote. This is what "rule by the people" has brought across much of the world in modern times. In colonial situations, what was ostensibly liberal democracy and in practice was delimited by ethnic and imperial exploitation was responsible for ethnic wars, usually against even more democratic regimes. This is the reverse of liberal theory.

ORGANIC DEMOCRACY AND ETHNIC WARS IN EUROPE: FROM THE BALKANS TO THE BALKANS

I will not chronicle here the rise of organic democracy in Europe (see Mann, 1999, 2000). I will only instance its most murderous incidents, at the beginning and the end of the twentieth century, in the Balkans. In its last

years the Ottoman Empire was attacked by liberal movements in the mid-
to late-nineteenth century that initially demanded more universal democratic rights. Some Greeks, Serbs, Bulgarians, Albanians, Armenians,
Turks, Kurds, and Arabs began to demand that millets and other forms of
local government should be democratized and be subject to a parliament,
not to imperial despotism. Resistance by the imperial authorities led European dissidents to demand their own "national" states. As conflict intensified, Greece, Serbia, Bulgaria, and Albania broke away from the empire.
Their democratic aspirations became organic; they excluded Muslims and
Turks and ultimately murdered and deported millions of them. The Young
Turks, aspiring to create a Turkish democracy, retaliated against the remaining Christian minorities of the empire—and in 1915 their deportations
of Armenians escalated into genocide. These had all begun as liberal reform
movements espousing democratic ideals. The pressure of local struggles
and the availability of nation-state ideals then turned them toward organic
nationalism and the perpetration of atrocities aimed at achieving an ethnocratic state.

The great powers had learned near the end of this dreadful process that
these collective tensions required constitutions containing not only individual rights but also entrenchments of collective communal rights. Yet they
sought to impose those rights only on the Turks, and they showed excep-
tionally bad timing. Just as their international inspectors were traveling
across Turkey toward their tasks, World War I (the final destroyer of the Ottoman Empire) sent them scurrying home again (J. McCarthy [1995] details
the Christian escalations, Vahakn Dadrian [1995] the Turkish ones). In the
post-1918 peace treaties the victorious powers established nation-states
with a 70 percent ethnic majority everywhere in Central and Eastern Europe and its periphery (except for Yugoslavia and Czechoslovakia). The
constitutions protected the rights of all individuals, and some added limited
local autonomies for minorities. But they entrenched neither confederal nor
consociational rights for minorities in the state. Post–World War II settlements furthered the process, sometimes moving borders, sometimes peoples, in the pursuit of monoethnic states.

The Soviet Union and Yugoslavia became the main exceptions to the
rule of the monoethnic state across greater Europe. With the terrible exception of Stalin's murderous deportations, their regimes consciously damped
down ethnic tensions with authoritarian versions of confederal/consocia-
tional means. Major ethnicities were given "their own" subordinate-level
republics, and republican and statewide central committees were carefully
ethnically balanced. It seemed to work, but unfortunately the people wanted
democracy. When both regimes collapsed, ethnic tensions rose again in
contexts where rule by "we, the people" could take plausible ethnic col-
oration. Although these contexts are too complex and diverse to summarize

here, they do not reveal a simple positive correlation between ethnic war and authoritarian regime. Some of the most murderous clashes (e.g., in the Armenian/Azerbaijani conflict and in the Russian devastations of Chechnya) were initiated by regimes that were in power because they had won fairly free elections. They had been supported by the majority people, which subsequently supported ethnic combat in the name of its own collective defense. Conversely, at least two semiauthoritarian regimes, in Turkmenistan and Uzbekistan, have continued Soviet-era policies of ethnic tension suppression (see various chapters in Dawisha and Parrott, 1997).

The Yugoslav collapse has happened amid the full glare of international publicity and so is easily the best-documented case of the process of descent into ethnic war (see Woodward [1997] and Udovicki and Ridgeway [1997] for good synthetic accounts). It can be divided into three phases. The first phase involved the collapse of the Yugoslav Federation and the emergence of putative nation-states with organicist tendencies. This occurred primarily through democratic electoral processes during 1990 and early 1991. Civil society played a substantial role. The densest networks of voluntary associations were possessed by communist and nationalist parties. They could most easily mobilize these to secure a high vote. But communism was substantially discredited. Most people wanted democracy, not authoritarianism. This left the nationalist parties as the best organized and thus triumphant.

Nationalist parties won parliamentary majorities in substantially free elections in Slovenia and Croatia. When these new regimes could not get the Serbian regime to agree to an asymmetric federation (giving each republic distinctive autonomies), they broke away—soon carrying the more cautious Macedonia with them, where nationalists had also won an electoral majority. Bosnia was the only predominantly multiethnic republic. But 90 percent of its electorate had voted for the three rival nationalist parties, not for multiethnic parties—again in a substantially free election. Serbia was a little different, since Milosevic and his SPS (the Socialist Party of Serbia, a nationalist but also the former communist party) was the only movement that could add some authoritarian manipulation into the elections. Nonetheless, half the Serb opposition was more nationalist than Milosevic, and all the main parties supported his bargaining position—strengthening the federation to ensure Serb predominance and rejecting asymmetric federalism. Moreover, all the Serb parties favored the same default position: if negotiations failed, then unite and protect Serbs through territorial expansion of Serbia—that is, establish a greater Serbia.

Some kind of collision inevitably followed from these predominantly democratic processes. Slovenia broke away with little bloodshed (as did Macedonia). Croatia's breakaway started an ethnic war. I have not the space to attempt a proper explanation of this, but a major clue is found in the constitution of the new independent and democratic state of Croatia. It proclaimed that "the Republic of Croatia is comprised as the national state of the Croatian people and all minorities who are citizens of Croatia, including Serbs, Muslims, Slovaks, Czechs, Jews [etc.] . . . for whom equality with those citizens of Croatian nationality is guaranteed."

The first words contain a typical organicist formula (the Croatian state is for the Croats, not for other peoples). But it then qualifies this with a typical liberal guarantee of the individual rights of non-Croats. Yet for the many Serbs and Bosnians living in Croatia this represented a *reduction* of their political rights. They had been defined as an "equal nation" within federal Yugoslavia, and various federal and consociational institutions had entrenched their national rights collectively wherever they lived. Now they were promised the lesser status of a minority such as Czechs or Jews, who in federal Yugoslavia had enjoyed only individual civil rights under the law. Individual rights were insufficient, collective confederal or consociational rights were necessary, so particularly argued Serbs. Croat nationalists argued identically when they were in the minority. The Bosnian Croat leader Mate Boban told British journalist Ed Vulliamy that he could not accept the constitution of Bosnia-Herzegovina, since "although it defended individual rights, it did not defend the rights of the . . . Narod" (evidence in International Criminal Tribunal for Yugoslavia, Blaskic trial, April 24, 1998).

Unfortunately, the major powers had formally liberal constitutions, so they believed a guarantee of individual rights was sufficient protection for minorities. That was probably not correct. Serbs argued that areas with local Serb or other ethnic majorities should have political autonomies (federalism) or that ethnic minorities should have their representatives entrenched within the central state (consociationalism). But the great powers were wedded to a liberal version of the nation-state ideal and simply failed to understand arguments couched in terms of collective rather than individual rights. Thus they applied no outside pressure on Croatia—nor had they on Slovenia. That was a mistake, although the main responsibility for what followed lay with indigenous groups, not foreign powers.

Murderous ethnic cleansing did not follow from this alone (it did not do so in Slovenia or Macedonia). The second phase of descent into violence involved struggles within the minority Serb and Croatian communities in Croatia and Bosnia, pitting moderate and radical nationalists against each other. The radicals proved to have two advantages. One remained electoral. Referenda were held to ask each ethnic group whether it wanted its own state. This proved an ethnic loyalty test, and so the radicals won overwhelming majorities, which considerably legitimated their rule. But the radicals were also better organized for violence, and their supposedly "popular" paramilitaries suppressed the moderates at the same time they began provocations against the ethnic out-group. Thus phase two contained a mixture of relatively democratic and relatively authoritarian politics.

The third phase began when Milosevic took his disastrous gamble on force and Croatian president Franjo Tudjman responded with "no surrender." Using the power of the Serb-dominated federal army flanked by "popular" paramilitary and security police units, covertly organized within his own state apparatus, he launched a full-scale ethnic war. This was met with determined armed resistance and then murderous retaliation by some Croats, Bosniaks, and Albanians. During the wars, the authoritarian yet legitimate power of all these regimes increased (as happens in most wars). Tudjman and Milosevic partly manipulated later elections, and in 1997 Milosevic may have stayed in power only by using force. Yet both men retained their electoral majorities (Milosevic in alliance with extreme nationalist parties) because each electorate (with some help from regime manipulation of the media) believed that atrocities were being perpetrated by the ethnic enemy, not by its own side. The result was almost total ethnic cleansing. All the states and statelets of the former Yugoslavia (if we decompose the ostensibly confederal Bosnia-Herzegovina into its real political entities) are now over 70 percent monoethnic. Those areas that were fought over are more than 90 percent monoethnic. They are ethnocratic states. Perhaps a few minorities will return, although in Kosovo cleansing (of Serbs) will likely continue for some time.

The Yugoslav case is more complex than the colonial cases. No ethnic group in Europe has possessed the enduring ethnic solidarity and ferocity of the colonial settlers. In consequence, the descent into ethnic war has been more contingent and less consensual or "democratic." The Yugoslav descent did start democratically. Aspirations toward democracy turned toward organic democracy and then toward the ethnocratic state—in part because multiethnic ideals were tainted by authoritarian communism. Yet this only lurched toward and into full-scale ethnic war amid a very mixed process of electorally partly legitimated authoritarianism in the name of the people. This is a much more double-edged process than that described in liberal theories.

ETHNIC WARS ACROSS THE GLOBE

Indeed, the Yugoslav pattern may be fairly general across the globe. Modern ethnic conflict usually seems to be initiated by broadly popular and democratic processes inside ethnic groups in tension. Indeed, authoritarian regimes fearing popular forces often seek to restrain this. But out of the conflict much greater authoritarian political and military powers emerge if the situation escalates to mass murder. The majority of the German electorate voted for revisionist radical nationalist parties; but Hitler's seizure of power and the top-down radicalization of the Nazi movement led to mass murder, which neither ordinary Germans nor ordinary Nazis had envisaged (Broszat, 1981). A late process of top-down radicalization among many perpetrating groups is perceptible just before outbreaks of actual genocide (from Young Turks to Hutu advocates of majoritarian democracy). Moderates among each aggressor ethnic group are then violently suppressed, and the outgroup is murderously cleansed.

Yet very few cases of ethnic tension escalate anywhere near this level. The best studies of "ordinary" ethnic rioting are of the Indian subcontinent. Paul Brass (1997) and Stanley Tambiah (1996) have shown that intercommunal murderous violence between Hindus and Muslims or Sikhs and between Sri Lankans and Tamils has risen in periods of vigorous competitive electoral politics and declined in periods of authoritarian national government wielding martial law (another nail in the democratic peace coffin). They also argue that the key in riots themselves is whether local and regional police authorities intervene with ruthless force.

Donald Horowitz's (1985: part 4) extensive survey of the recent history of southern countries shows that almost all of them are riven by the politicization of ethnic more than class identities. Class parties were common before and immediately after independence but then mostly decayed or were transformed into ethnic parties. Almost all democratic parties explicitly or implicitly represent one ethnicity or a coalition of ethnicities. These cases show a persistent (although not quite universal) tendency to unravel into ethnic rioting and suppressions. In the worst cases, however, they regress to repressive military dictatorships exhibiting a "natural history of ethnic attrition." They first violently repress their main ethnic rival, then suppress in turn almost all the factions that had made up their own original ethnic coalition until their power rests only on an army and police force recruited from their own local kin and neighbourhood base plus foreign or marginal mercenaries. Horowitz instances as the worst cases Sierra Leone after 1968, Uganda between 1966 and 1979, Syria since 1963, and Saddam Hussein's Iraq. None of these regimes has legitimated itself in ethnic terms, but all launched what were in effect "ethnic wars" on their own citizens.

Of course, this is not the typical outcome. What is distinct about most of the South is the multiethnicity within states. Tanzania lies at one extreme, supposedly with 120 distinct ethnicities. Yet many states have five or more distinct macroethnicities. In most countries tensions have grown involving some political and communal violence between ethnic groups. At the extreme this could result in local, regional, or even national disintegration, accompanied by massive repression. Yet large-scale ethnic wars have been rare because it is very difficult to achieve stable government without cross-ethnic coalitions of parties and military elites. Fifty ethnic groups, none dominant, may cause instability. Five loosely aggregated macroethnicities may generate considerable violence, even occasional civil war, but rarely intentional mass ethnic cleansing. No ethnicity is strong enough to accomplish this on its own on more than a local scale. Even if one does, it is not likely to make explicit appeals to ethnic solidarity or organic nationalism since it has to find allies from other groups. These contrary tendencies seem to produce far more regime fluctuations, oscillating from democratic to authoritarian regimes, perhaps with somewhat mixed and unstable regimes predominating.

CONCLUSION

My account of the modern rise of ethnic wars has differed greatly from liberal theory. Overall, mine has been more of a bottom-up than a top-down account, for ethnic wars are part of the dark side of democracy. The entry of "the sovereign people" created the potentiality for an upsurge in ethnic killing as the masses demanded democracy. This was initially masked by the fact that class overwhelmed ethnicity within most of the first liberal regimes in Europe, whereas imperialism was restrained by the Westphalian system of geopolitics. Yet it was starkly revealed when ostensibly liberal regimes were exported into colonial situations where the greater the democracy among the settlers, the more likely was ethnic war—launched predominantly against native democracies. The dark side was also revealed in most of the rest of Europe where class exploitation was subordinated to ethnic and imperial exploitation. In the South, ethnicity and imperialism have also predominated over class, although the most common situation is multiple ethnicities contesting the politics of a single state. These lend themselves less to ethnic cleansing than initially to confederal/consociational power-sharing arrangements, often stretched to the breaking point and prone to repression and/or disintegration.

Elsewhere (Mann, 2000) I argue that the greatest danger of murderous ethnic cleansing is where we find two cross-border ethnic groups plausibly claiming rival political sovereignties over the same cross-border area and where nationalism is fueled by imperialism. One nationalist group plausibly claims to be a "proletarian nation," the other exhibits embittered "imperial revisionism." The proletariat claims "justice" against "exploitation"; the threatened imperial nation claims its hereditary political property rights, honor, sometimes its very survival, are threatened. Moral outrage grows to justify what others see as aggression as self-defense or retaliation.

I have argued that in cases such as these, processes of organic democracy may lead to the brink of ethnic cleansing and war. Yet it is conjoined democratic and authoritarian forces that lead over the edge, with the latter increasingly predominating as conflict becomes truly murderous. Outside of colonial situations we glimpsed much more double-edged political processes than those posited by liberal theory.

These widespread modern tendencies are not easy to reverse, and liberal theories do not help much. They breed hypocrisy about the past failures of our own societies, and they misspecify the nature of our past successes.

Political and geopolitical peace has not come from an unmediated relationship between free individuals—or between individuals freely associated together in a civil society—and a state. When liberal regimes worked well, they also institutionalized class relations. They did not transcend them, of course, for class conflict still endures. Successful liberal regimes continue to generate political parties and social movements with something of a class base. A few countries like Switzerland also managed to institutionalize ethnic conflict. Since most subsequent societies have entwined class and ethnicity or subordinated class to ethnic or imperial divisions, they require forms of collective institutionalization that are very different from those of Britain or the United States but that come closer to those of Switzerland, supplemented by some form of international security system that can have effects similar to those of the Westphalian system—which today would probably require far more direct international intervention.

Thanks to writers like Arend Lijphart (1977), we know roughly what these forms look like. They are either confederal and consociational, or they offer electoral incentives to parties that manage to attract votes from more than one ethnic community. But we also know how difficult they are to institutionalize securely (see several chapters in Montville [1997] and D. Horowitz [2000]). Across the South they persistently break down into communal violence and state repression. For example, Uganda was widely lauded as an example of consociational stability in the late 1980s. In 2000 it was widely condemned as a repressive "no-party" regime.

But the secular trend of the entire modern period I have identified in this chapter suggests that today much of the ethnically divided world may have three main choices:

1. African-style more or less permanent instability, leading to erratic outbursts of violence but rarely to all-out ethnic war
2. European-cum-colonial-style ethnic wars and cleansing producing nation-states to the 70 percent level of monoethnicity, which seems to allow the majority to relax and the minority to put up with second-class citizenship; as the German chief quoted by Tacitus said of the Romans, "they make a desert and call it peace"
3. Constitutional and international security guarantees of confederal/consociational/electoral incentive regimes that do not formally resemble the constitutions and international autonomies of most of the "liberal" and "advanced" countries but that resemble, if in a different ethnic form, the real domestic and geopolitical histories of the institutionalization of collective conflicts

But merely by recognizing these choices, we are a little nearer to a solution.

NOTE

1. In what follows I have relied heavily for California on Almaguer (1994: 107–130) and for elsewhere on Churchill (1997: 129–288), Champagne (1992), and Stannard (1992).

5

Military Professionalism and the Democratic Peace: How German Is It?

Timothy R.W. Kubik

> By always asking what German history was not, rather than what it was, one also runs the risk of posing questions to which the answer is always "No."
> —David Blackbourn and Geoff Eley (1984: 10)

Historians and political scientists of the twentieth century relied on an understanding of the course of German political and social development that posits an "alternative course" *(Sonderweg)* when compared with the rise of Western liberal democracies such as Britain, France, and the United States (Meinecke, 1950; Gerschenkron, 1962; Moore, 1966; Dahrendorf, 1967; Wehler, 1985). In the 1980s, however, historians of Germany began a debate that challenged this sense of "German exceptionalism" by arguing that although Germany's historical development was unique, it was not so wholly divergent as to suffice as an explanation for Germany's illiberalism, authoritarianism, and militaristic aggression in the first half of the century.

Far from an irrelevant debate in an unrelated discipline, the work of Blackbourn and Eley (1984) is directly relevant to both the content and the form of contemporary studies on democracy and the use of force. In terms of content, the image of militarism in German history plays a peculiar historical role that Ido Oren (1995) has addressed as much for its absence as for its explicit inclusion. Yet there is also a formal problem. The "fact" that democracies do not make war on each other may be the closest thing to an empirical law the science of international relations has discovered, or so Jack Levy (1988) and all subsequent Levy citations assure us. Yet in asserting this negative fact *(democracies relate to armed force such that wars do not occur*, or *dRf=~w)*, scholars of the "democratic peace" (DP) also run "the risk of posing questions to which the answer is always, 'No.'"

The majority of this chapter furthers Oren's explorations of the historical image of German militarism in the literature on the democratic peace in the context of this formal problem. Few social scientists would allow that revisions of historical accounts are in themselves conclusive evidence for the proof or falsification of a theory. That said, there is increasing awareness that historically distinct interpretations of the past are a problem for all research agendas when these affect their formal assumptions—a problem that cannot be resolved through statistical manipulations alone (Lustick, 1996). With enough change in the world of the historian, the evidence earlier generations of social scientists offered for their general laws eventually comes to have a historical air about it. As a result, rather than continue to serve as a basis for the accumulation of knowledge, the histories that produced such data slip back under the purview of historians—chiefly those interested in the subtleties of historiography or the philosophy of history (Ross, 1991; Schmidt, 1997).

This cycle is perhaps more true, or at least more manifestly obvious, of German history than of the history of any other nation. The quarrels among historians of Germany offer political and social theorists an opportunity for more careful consideration of the formal relationships we are inclined to establish between democracy and the use of force, precisely because there are so many interpretations. Indeed, these various interpretations of a single question of German history provide a comparative sampling that will help to illuminate the forgotten side of the reciprocal relationship between democracy and the use of force. A close reading of competing histories may help us to arrive at a positive fact about that relationship; that is, it may help us to understand what democracies *do* with their militaries, not only what they *do not*.

WRITING HISTORY AND THE IDENTIFICATION OF CAUSAL RELATIONSHIPS

According to social scientific definitions of democracy in international relations literature, the German Empire of 1871–1914 is held to fall short of the qualifying conditions that separate democracy and autocracy (Doyle, 1996; Gurr, 1990; Russett, 1993). Although this position is not without support among leading historians of Germany (Craig, 1978; J. Sheehan, 1978; Berghan, 1982b; Wehler, 1985), Oren (1995) has made a convincing case for the subjectivity of these perceptions within international relations theory in general and among advocates of the democratic peace in particular.

I accept that this debate will, as Oren notes (1995: 156, n. 26), remain subject (and hence subjective) to professional historical reconsiderations such as those among historians of Germany in the 1980s as well as the changing nature of German relations with the rest of the world (Oren, 1995: 184). Yet if the assessment of imperial Germany's *political* institutions remains open to debate, in much of the social scientific literature today there is a twofold silence regarding Germany's military institutions, as well as the role those institutions play in liberal and republican theory.

Oren (1995: 156) remarks: "It is the 1917 image of Germany, greatly magnified by the experience of 1933–1945, that pervades current American social science." Although there is little or no mention of the central role German military institutions played in framing this image in the scholarly literature addressing this problem after World War II, the central figure appears not in the person of an autocrat such as Wilhelm II or Adolf Hitler but is rather the German military as a whole and the Great General Staff in particular. Symbolized by the immediately recognizable images of the *Pickelhaube* and *Stahlhelm* that adorned so many books on German history after World War II, the unique institutional structures and spirit of Prussian or German militarism were more often treated as the independent variable that explained the tendency to autocracy and illiberalism in Germany rather than the other way around (Vagts, 1959; Demeter, 1965; Craig, 1955; Huntington, 1957; Janowitz, 1960; Büsch, 1962).

From Oren's perspective (1995), we can understand why this would be true with regard to Germany after the war. Yet this militaristic image continued to play an important role in much larger debates regarding war and society despite changes in the popular image of Germany after the "economic miracle" (Berghan, 1982a; Giddens, 1985a; Wehler, 1985; Geyer, 1986; Mann, 1988, 1996). Scholarly debate was not over democracy and autocracy but—perhaps surprisingly—about institutions and norms. As Volker Berghan (1982a: 4) notes, "Germany's militarism came to be seen by many as a paradigm. . . . even when people wrote on other cases of militarism, the German example was, in one way or another, often at the back of their minds." It is odd, therefore, that the image of German militarism receives little consideration in the contemporary social scientific literature on the prospects for democratic peace.

I will argue that where Germany is concerned, we are not dealing with a cumulative narrative but rather with a formal theoretical transition with profound consequences for the identification of dependent and independent variables. Even if one grants the statist perspective critiqued elsewhere in this volume, *at least* two historiographies are at work here (ultimately I will suggest six), and each implies a different causal relation between regime type and the use of force. These other histories must be silenced to allow the literature of the democratic peace its voice, such that from the perspective of earlier work on this question a gaping hole exists in the literature sur-rounding the prospects for democratic peace—a hole through which an en-tire army might be driven.

I will argue that it is precisely the army in its modern, professional form that stands in this hole, ready to execute the will of the juridical sov-ereign state in a manner much more consistent with classical realist theory in international relations than with liberal or democratic political theory and that the connection made to republican theory, such as found in Kant, is therefore ultimately untenable. Theorists of the liberal or democratic peace have silenced the military and its use by treating it as a variable entirely de-pendent on domestic political structures and norms of the state, "politically sterile and neutral," to quote Samuel Huntington (1957: 84).

An equally important "fact" of the democratic peace is that the con-stant omission and undertheorization of the military as an independent vari-able rest on an earlier generation's historically conditioned desire to remove war from democratic theory and practice altogether. The success of this si-lencing not only preserves the basic image of the "bad" state as militaristic, it also allows theorists of the democratic peace to ignore the role of the mil-itary in society and therefore to literally define democracy as the absence of war, while at the same time these democracies yet retain their militaries. Put another way, it allows a series of questions about the relationship be-tween democracy and the use of force to which the answer is always, and perhaps all too reassuringly, "No."

MILITARY PROFESSIONALISM IN GERMAN HISTORIES

Debates over German exceptionalism (Blackbourn and Eley, 1984: 2, n. 3) allow us to examine specifically the assumptions imported by scholars of international relations regarding the German military and the way in which those assumptions mislead with regard to two crucial variables. The first of these assumptions has to do with the general impact of mass society on the internal dynamics of states and on the military in particular. The second pertains to the presumed relation between mass societies and total war.

Mass Societies and Democratization

German historians writing in the 1960s and 1970s, such as those surround-ing Hans-Ulrich Wehler (1985) and the so-called Bielefeld school, actually supported the general pattern of development advanced by theorists of the democratic peace. The rise of a mass society in the industrializing areas of the Ruhr and Berlin did in fact lead to internal pressures for an expanded franchise, and this expansion also produced demonstrable changes in the structure of the Prussian and, later, German governments. It has long been argued, however (Dahrendorf, 1967; J. Sheehan, 1978; Wehler, 1985), that because these reforms stopped short of producing a full-fledged bourgeois parliamentary democracy, German liberalism remained confined to an "illiberal society" (Sheehan, 1978). Drawing on these histories, the German Empire can indeed be dismissed from the list of states under consideration as "democratic."

Oren (1995) is correct to criticize this argument on the grounds of its ahistorical imposition on the German past. As Eley (1996), Dorothy Ross (1991), and Brian Schmidt (1997) note, during the nineteenth century many in the United States and Britain held the German constitutional model to be superior to that of their own country, particularly with regard to the freedoms citizens gained from the implementation of bureaucratic rationality and administrative efficiency in the Weberian sense. Although Zeev Maoz (1997) can offer counterexamples to these positive views, all such counterexamples prove is that the issue remains debatable, even among historians. Thus there is a need for scholars of international relations to consider other histories, and here Blackbourn's (in Blackbourn and Eley, 1984) comparative contribution seems much more likely to persuade than the prolonged exchange of received opinions.

At the core of Blackbourn's essay, and his subsequent research as well (Blackbourn and Evans, 1991), is the notion of a "silent bourgeois revolution" that, although it clearly lacked the dramatic upheavals of more typical revolutions, nonetheless resulted in "changes at many levels: in the law, in the advance of mechanical civilization, in patterns of sociability and the formation of a 'public'" (Blackbourn and Eley, 1984: 176). Crucial to this argument is a historical analysis of political and administrative reform at the *local* level of urban magistracies and rural governments rather than through parliamentary coalitions (Blackbourn and Eley, 1984: 276–285). By arguing that reforms at this level were able to satisfy the demands of the German bourgeoisie, Blackbourn posits a refutation of the general notion that democracy in its liberal, parliamentary form is necessary in order to satisfy the demands of the people. As Tarak Barkawi, Mark Laffey, and Mark Rupert argue elsewhere in this volume, democracy need not necessarily be tied to representative elites in a centralized political structure but may take other forms depending on cultural context. Admittedly another controversial proposition, this theoretical shift allows Blackbourn and Eley (1984: 292) the conclusion that "Germany was much more the intensified version of the norm than the exception."

In terms of the literature on the democratic peace, this interpretation affords a possible definition of the democratic response to mass society that has little to do with those variables codified in the standard empirical literature. Blackbourn and Eley's history not only challenges the notion that the democratic peace is a distinct and novel development in international relations theory, as Oren (1995) suggests. It also requires of these theorists a much broader empirical database before the notion of a "democratic" German Empire can be dismissed out of hand. More interesting for my purposes, however, is the impact Blackbourn and Eley's thesis has on the image of the German military as an institution within that questionable democracy.

The Response to Mass Society and Total War

In analyzing the relationship between mass societies and total war, historians of Germany agree that liberal normative pressures for reductions in armaments were ultimately ineffective in Germany at the parliamentary level. Indeed, after the passage of the first Army Bill in 1860, there were public pressures for increases in military expenditures to support and promote German expansion into the international arena. From the perspective of systems-oriented international relations theories, we might explain this phenomenon by means of a "security dilemma" (Herz, 1950) that resulted as neighboring states pursued (or were expected to pursue) similar increases. Hence the rise of Germany's "army of millions" would be understood as a rational government response to changes in the international system, a structural realist analysis that clearly treats the military as a variable entirely dependent upon the sovereign's ability to read the international system.

Liberal theorists who would challenge this interpretation by drawing upon analyses of particular states, however, are equally guilty of assuming that military forces will always function as an extension of the rational will of a sovereign yet democratic power, desirous of peace yet confronted by war beyond the confines of their "civil" society. Even where exceptions to this rule are found among liberal theorists (Friedberg, 1992), there is still a sense that liberal institutions outside of the government promote military restraint as part of a rational calculus over which the military has little or no influence. Yet Berghan (1982a: 29–37), Wehler (1985: 157–181), and Blackbourn and Eley (1984: 118–126, 263–264) all agree that it was the existence of a relationship between the military and German civil society that led to public calls for increases in armaments.

The nature of this relationship is explored in the following section. What is important to note at this point is that a point of agreement actually exists between realist and neoliberal analyses with regard to the appropriate response to the dynamics of an anarchic international system: the state must control the military. This agreement is the direct result of the fact that both groups hold a common image of the German military as a "state within a state" (Craig, 1955), despite what they think of the state that encompassed it. On a theoretical level, Michael Mann (1988: 18) is surely correct to discount the corollary that the state's organization is derived from its military organization (Hintze, 1975)—itself a legacy of the historiography of an earlier, more militant age—yet that does not absolve international relations theorists from taking into consideration the state's internal responses to the problems of military organization in a mass society.

Scholars of international relations resorting to the image of German militarism must also acknowledge that the democratic pressure for the franchise yielded an internal politics (Wehler, 1985) that produced what might be called an internal "security dilemma" over sovereignty and the control of military forces. This acknowledgment would directly challenge structural realist and liberal statist assumptions that the military is merely an executive arm of the state, for although these tensions may have been felt most sharply in Germany, they were in fact faced by all European states that experienced the rise of mass societies—a point contemporary historical sociology has clearly established (Giddens, 1985a; Mann, 1988).

Edward Mansfield and Jack Snyder (1995) have proposed a general theory regarding democratization and war that tracks such transitions and serves as a partial critique of social scientific literature on the prospects for a democratic peace in that it suggests that the mere presence of democratic institutions is insufficient if they are not adequately developed and stable. According to their argument, "In this transitional phase of democratisation, countries become more aggressive and war-prone, and they do fight wars with democratic states" (1995: 5).

This is an interesting corollary to the literature on the democratic peace, but it is in no way the structural realist critique of the literature it purports to be because it nonetheless assumes the validity of the core liberal argument. Mansfield and Snyder (1995: 19) simply push back the liberal argument that it is "elites" (now threatened internally) who "use nationalist appeals to compete for mass allies with each other and with new elites" and that this competition often leads to internally defensive wars. This is akin to what Mann (1999) terms the "dark side of democracy." Yet as the focus of Mansfield and Synder's critique is the creation of an external rather than an internal enemy, their analysis actually aids proponents of the DP by explaining away many of the problem cases that result from close or questionable coding decisions. What Mansfield and Snyder obscure that Wehler, Mann, and Giddens do not is that these transitions involve social and professional choices with regard to the role that the military plays in a society we might otherwise be prepared to categorize as "democratic"—choices the military is able to influence. Denying these states the status of democracy is equivalent to denying that there is a place for debate on the role of military forces in any democracy so defined, which may indeed be part of the ideology of democracy Mark Rupert critiques, in Chapter 8. Regardless, it is formally equivalent to asking questions to which the answer is always, "No."

With this notion of an internal security dilemma, however, we can re-open the central questions surrounding Huntington's (1957) appropriation of Harold Lasswell's (1941) theme of the "management of violence." To the extent that the management of violence can be addressed in terms of democracy or autocracy, Huntington establishes that civilian control of the military in democracies has usually been understood as relying upon an institutional solution. In reviewing those arguments from Anglo-Saxon political theory that have traditionally pitted liberal society against the military (1957: 143–162), however, Huntington returns to the idea (and ideal) of military professionalism, which he identifies earlier in the work as the direct result of democratic norms more than democratic structures.

Along with the modernizing forces of mass society and the nation-state (1957: 32–33), Huntington frames his subsequent analysis of military professionalism with the initial proposition that proponents of democracy "attempted to shape military institutions in its pattern also. They substituted the representative ideal for the aristocratic ideal" (1957: 33–34). Such an ideal, normative image of military professionalism is crucial for Huntington's notion of "objective civilian control." As his introductory remarks conclude, professionalism contributes to the "existence of a single recognized source of legitimate authority over military forces" because "a professional officer is imbued with the ideal of service to the nation" (1957: 35). Here the statist bias becomes manifest. Institutional checks on the use of force traditionally associated with democracy remain a source of conflicting and dividing loyalties. Professionalism, defined by Huntington as "service to the nation," becomes the only acceptable democratic response to the internal security dilemma regarding the management of violence.

Ironically, this interpretation of professionalism as an anti-ideological embodiment of universal rationality has a much greater tradition in German history and social theory than it does in the political or social theoretical traditions of the United States. Terms such as Georg Hegel's *Beamtenstand* (1952) or Max Weber's *Weltrationalität* (1947) required translation into English during the twentieth century precisely because they were not a part of Anglo-Saxon political and social discourse but rather were an integral part of the cultural context Karl Marx (1978) termed "the German Ideology." Yet at the same time Huntington was promoting the virtues of such professionalism in the United States as a solution to civil-military relations, scholars of German history were placing some of the blame for Germany's illiberal autocracy on many of the same virtues (H. Rosenberg, 1958; Demeter, 1965; Habermas, 1968).

If the ideological notion of professionalism Huntington invokes may actually be to blame for German militarism rather than the best check against it, there is a clear need for a broader theoretical and comparative perspective on this question—not least because it presents a serious challenge to the advocates of the democratic peace who, in their silence on the military, appear to share Huntington's conclusions that democracy and military professionalism go hand in hand. Many of the contributors to this volume are engaged in such work. Yet to continue with the (re)writing of German military history as a vehicle for exploring this question despite political, generational, and methodological differences, German historians such as Detlef Bald and colleagues (1985), Wehler (1985), Eley (1996), and Michael Geyer (1986, 1990) all share a common position regarding the effect the rise of technical professionalism had on the old Prusso-German military. In their own way, each author suggests that it was not the Crown itself, as an archaic, feudal institution, that retained control of the decision to use force but in fact a group of "military professionals" who established control on the basis of expertise in the management of violence, and then used this new expertise to buttress conservative principles that had otherwise lost their hold on society. Reading back through these stories in German history will provide a different view of Kant's theoretical work prior to these events and thus ultimately change our understanding of Kant's wish for perpetual peace.

Wehler's discussion of the army in Wilhelmine Germany insists that "the sovereign's right of command survived as an essential element of late absolutist rule" (1985: 146–150). The "one sided emphasis on technical military thinking" (1985: 153) comes to play an equally important role in explaining Germany's decision to use force in 1914, however, for Wehler supports the view found in Chancellor Theodor von Bethmann-Hollweg's memoirs that as "laymen," Germany's political leadership "could not presume to pass judgement on military options, let alone military necessities." Thus, Wehler concludes, "the First World War did not result from many years of deliberate planning, but simply from the ruling elites' incapacity to cope with growing problems in a world which was rapidly heading in the direction of democratic forms of government" (1985: 200). In Wehler's account, it was therefore not the centralized power of authoritarian government that plunged Germany into war but the manifest deficiencies of that power when confronted by (or offered) a military option. Theoretically then, the structure of Wehler's historiography is much more in keeping with the model advanced by Mansfield and Snyder (1995).

Blackbourn and Eley (1984) have been critical of the overall role exceptionalism plays in Wehler's work without wanting to overturn all of his conclusions. Thus, like Wehler, their general framework is much more of a challenge than a support to Huntington's overall thesis. Although Huntington develops much of his image of military professionalism on the Prussian model like Gordon Craig (1955), he describes the "tragedy of professional militarism" (Huntington, 1957: 99–124) as the direct result of the military's untimely surrender of that professionalism to politics and to mass politics in particular. Such surrender, however, plays into the exceptionalist thesis Blackbourn and Eley sought to diffuse and according to which an eruption of the masses was the logical outcome of Germany's failed bourgeois revolutions. Like so many of the apologists for the German military after World War II (Ritter, 1972; Demeter, 1965), Huntington's image of military professionalism looks back to the quasi-aristocratic General Staff officer as an idealized check against the forces of mass society (1957: 464–466). Yet if Blackbourn and Eley (1984: 80) are correct that few genuinely frustrated bourgeoisie were waiting to explode in Germany, there is little need for this idealized check.

Nor, however, do Blackbourn and Eley then proceed to blame the "German Catastrophe" (Meinecke, 1950) on the "backwardness" of the Junkers and their military institutions. Instead, in another point of agreement with Wehler (1985) and Berghan (1982a), the frantic pace of modernization in Germany provides the best explanation (Blackbourn and Eley, 1984: 292). Whereas Wehler (1985) views the German military as an institution clinging to its position in the midst of a domestic struggle for power, Blackbourn and Eley's (1984) overall historical narrative allows that the military may have experienced modernization as well. It was not just a backward institution in a modernizing society but rather one that modernized at a pace that was threatening to many inside and outside the barracks halls.

This allowance has been well substantiated in the detailed work of the Social Scientific Institute for the Study of the Bundeswehr (Bald, 1977; Bald, Bald-Gerlach, and Ambros, 1985), and Arden Bucholz (1991) has documented an important period of transitional modernization along "managerial" lines during the early twentieth century. My own analysis of the "scientific" historiographical practices adopted by the Great General Staff in the second half of the nineteenth century also supports these conclusions (Kubik, 1997b: chapter 5). Yet the work of Michael Geyer (1986, 1990) has done the most to promote the notion of a highly modernized German military in the imperial period.

Like Himadeep Muppidi in Chapter 3 of this volume, Geyer's general point in reexamining the Prusso-German military is that "traditions never simply exist and continuities do not just roll along. They have to be maintained by continuous renewal in a changing national and internal environment" (1986: 529). Thus we cannot treat the German military simply as a monolithic site of tradition or reform. In his attempt to analyze the German officer corps as a profession, Geyer (1990: 188) suggests that "it was decidedly not aristocratic privilege, but the military's ability to control and mobilize resources autonomously, that enabled the Prussian military to withstand popular rebellion and constitutional challenge. The newly gained (reformist) autonomy, in other words, was the prerequisite for the (restorative) struggle to sustain anti-constitutionalism."

Rather than place the roots of German militarism in the age-old traditions of a "backward" Prussian militarism, Geyer instead locates militarism in what the Prussian government and many of its subsequent historians referred to as the "revolution from above," which occurred between 1806 and 1819 and again during the late 1850s and early 1860s (Bald, 1977). Particularly with regard to the military in the earlier period of reform, this "revolution" was designed to make Prussia a modern and highly developed state—a response to the decisive defeat of the old Prussian regime at Jena and Auerstadt in 1806–1807.

It is also wrong to assume that the modernization implemented simply tapped into the nationalistic militarism of the masses on behalf of the nation-state. Rather, Geyer (1986) offers an account of the Prusso-German military that emphasizes the resistance to mass participation in the military on the part of the older Junker families during the late 1800s while denying that this resistance led to a reactionary "feudalization" or "militarisation" of the bourgeoisie for elite purposes (1990).

What, then, was the nature of Wilhelmine militarism, and what, if any, social compromise did it sanction? Instead of describing the Liberals' agreement to the Army reforms of the 1860s as a failure of the German bourgeois, Geyer (1990: 189) sees:

> The mutual agreement of core groups within the military and the bourgeoisie on the autonomy of experts and . . . the embrace of professionalism as the principle for the social organization of violence. Within the military context, it hinged on the rise of the general staff and its "scientific strategy." Within bourgeois society, it depended on the acknowledgment of a mutually beneficial division of labour between the social organization of production and the social organization of violence.

Geyer's analysis fits Huntington's professional ideal quite nicely. As he later notes, "Both the social organization of violence and its articulation in terms of expertise were profoundly bourgeois" (Geyer, 1990: 191). Indeed, to anticipate my conclusions, this does seem to be what liberal democracies do with their militaries: they isolate them and tolerate them so long as they fulfill their assigned function in the division of labor and do so in a professional manner.

Yet the problem here for theorists of the democratic peace—and opponents of militarism in general—is that Geyer developed this case to explain why the unified respect for the division of labor and professional expertise actually undermined both military autonomy and civilian control. The bourgeois compromise that separates the military from society in such a way as to treat it as a concealed rather than a celebrated extension of the sovereign state produces an endless need for negotiating the terms of this compromise regarding the management of violence. To effect this concealment, these negotiations themselves must ultimately be concealed from the public. Huntington's ideological model works, but only when one assumes that the compromise between "democracy" and "professionalism" can endure. Yet if anything, the structural dynamics of the compromise work against this. Where the military professionalism of nineteenth-century Germany existed to "contain violence, to make it purposive, and to turn it into an asset of the state along classical realist lines" (Geyer, 1990: 197), following World War I the consensus of twentieth-century Germany was to place the military in the service of the people (*Volk*) (Geyer, 1990: 198). As the notion of professionalism changed, so too did the notion of whom to serve. Thus the institutional questions Huntington sought to eschew return once more.

Perhaps most concerning, this change in the concept of professionalism was the direct result of the German military's self-cultivated military "science," namely, the demand for increasing resources to respond to the phenomenon of total war produced by that "science" (Kubik, 1997a, 1997b, chapter 5). Geyer's (1986: 533) earlier summary of this compromise is worth quoting in full: "[The military's] enemy was not civilian society, but society's demand to participate in the process of determining strategy, which became a key problem with the concurrent rise of mass participation in national politics and mass armies."

On this account, we might say that whereas civilians ultimately acquiesced to the demands of their military experts, those demands were made all the same in accordance with notions of a division of labor that fostered a desired form of "objective civilian control." Based on these very notions of a professional division of labor within a democratic society, the autonomy of each side risked being destroyed by the discursive authority of the other, compelling a constant process of (re)negotiation. In 1914 this process of compromise was exposed, and therefore both sides faced a crisis sufficient to propel the armed forces and the society that respected their professionalism into war. Although the compromise was different, the same can be said of 1939, where the people—broadly understood as is appropriate for the context—propelled the armed forces. Such transitions would suggest that "military professionalism" is a decisively historical rather than structurally enduring phenomenon, and this in turn undercuts liberal normative claims to its lasting influence.

Although most scholars have come to recognize imperial Germany as a society in rapid transition from its preindustrial agrarian past to something resembling a modern industrial society, there is still a strong temptation to retain the image of the military as something irrevocably tied to the preindustrial past in a way that made it reactionary or allowed it to be swept away by the forces of modernization it sought to resist. Yet much as David Blaney (Chapter 2 in this volume) argues regarding the democratic peace, those who succumb to this temptation unwittingly reify the theoretical division between state and society their analyses are often meant to question. If the military is a part of society and if society is in transition, then it stands to reason that we might look for evidence of that transition in the military as well.

KANT'S REPUBLICANISM AS A
CHALLENGE TO MILITARY PROFESSIONALISM
IN DEMOCRATIC SOCIETIES

We are now in a position to consider liberal arguments on behalf of the democratic peace at their source, the philosophical program set out by Immanuel Kant. Although Nicholas Onuf and Thomas Johnson (1995) argue that Kant's republicanism may have been unfairly appropriated by liberal democratic theorists who fail to understand the historical context of his views on commerce, cosmopolitanism, and the state, I think it is more instructive to probe this appropriation on the question of the military. As we shall see, Kant (1983) and Michael Doyle (1996) are essentially at odds on the crucial issue of the relationship between the military and society and whether the latter can adequately check the former.

According to Kant's program, several "definitive articles" must be realized together: republican constitutions, the sovereign rights of free nations in federation, and cosmopolitan rights of individuals traveling in those free nations (Kant, 1983: 348–360). Yet from the perspective of the German histories examined in the previous section, the crucial causal nexus of Kant's argument may be the "preliminary article" where he argues that the expansion of the franchise will lead to a general reduction in warfare because the citizenry is directly obligated to military service in exchange for the franchise.

Historically speaking, the role of a militia in a republican constitution is certainly more important as a context for Kant's analysis at that time than the physiocratic notion that war would be judged too expensive by a free society. Three years prior to the publication of "Perpetual Peace," on September 20, 1792, French Carmagnoles repulsed the standing armies of the First Coalition—including Kant's Prussians—in defense of their newly proclaimed republic at Valmy. The poet Goethe, who was present at the battle, concluded that "from this place and from this day forth commences a new era in the world's history" (quoted in Creasy, 1995 [1852]: 340). In the context of an event of such concrete political importance as Valmy, it is hardly surprising that Kant might identify this form of military organization as a crucial preliminary to his own view of a cosmopolitan world order.

Talk of a citizen militia no doubt appears utopian in the age of total war and military professionalism and is perhaps thus often overlooked by systemic realists who, like the Great General Staff, have a vested interest in the idea that all wars are now necessarily total. On the other hand, second-image analysts drawing on select experiences of the twentieth century likewise fear universal service and the idea of the "people in arms" as a form of mass militarism that leads to war. It is nonetheless the case that a citizen militia is a central tenet of Kant's republican program. Standing armies *(miles perpetuus)* as extensions of the Crown must give way to the self-armed citizen *(civis armatus)* serving as the manifestation of the popular will. Indeed, only in this way can one assure that the cost of war—literal or figurative— will be borne by the citizens rather than by an overweening sovereign.

This is not merely an attachment to an archaic ideal but a theoretical necessity. Later, in his definition of republican government (1983: 351), we find Kant's identification of the causal relationship between republican military organization and perpetual peace that makes this preliminary necessary:

> The republican constitution also provides this desirable result, namely, perpetual peace, and the reason for this is as follows: If (as must inevitably be the case, given this form of constitution) the consent of the citizenry is required in order to determine whether or not there will be war, it is natural that they consider all its calamities before committing themselves to so risky a game. (Among these are doing the fighting themselves, paying the costs of war from their own resources, having to repair at great sacrifice the war's devastation, and, finally, the ultimate evil that would make peace itself better, never being able—because of new and constant wars—to expunge the burden of debt.) By contrast, under a non-republican constitution, where subjects are not citizens, the easiest thing in the world to do is to declare war.

Doyle (1996) cites precisely this passage in advancing his arguments for the democratic peace, and yet he bases much of his overall case on other points of Kant's program. Nowhere in Doyle's text does he mention the military organization required by a "republican constitution," which Kant sets forth very clearly in his preliminaries (1983: 345, art. 3). I will follow Doyle's lead in quoting from this preliminary article at length.

> Standing armies (i) shall be gradually abolished. For they constantly threaten other nations with war by giving the appearance that they are prepared for it, which goads nations into competing with one another in the number of men under arms, and this practice knows no bounds. And since the costs of maintaining peace will in this way finally become greater than those of a short war, standing armies are the cause of wars of aggression that are intended to end burdensome expenditures. . . . The voluntary, periodic military training of citizens so that they can secure their homeland against external aggression is an entirely different matter.

When this preliminary is taken into account, the weight of structural constraints against war in nations with republican constitutions becomes undeniable. In a very literal sense, the citizenry will bear the cost of war because the citizenry will be called upon to serve in it. This is entirely different from the claims made by contemporary advocates of Kant who merely acknowledge that in a democracy the citizenry is potentially liable to bear the physical or commercial costs of war and will take this into account before lending political support. In a modern nation-state developed according to Huntington's model, a standing professional army composed of a small percentage of the population will do the fighting. Democratic institutions may still have some role in limiting the use of force, but from a genuinely republican perspective such an army makes the liberal link between democracy and peace seem vacuous. The structural necessity of congressional approval for war pales by comparison to that which would be had from larger citizen participation in military service, especially since even in our day the constitutionality of this necessity is a matter of debate.

In this light, Mann's sense of a "spectator-sport" militarism (1986: 183–187) is perhaps more relevant to our own time. In 1914 patriotic Germans joyously celebrated the military's decision to engage a small minority of their country's population (864,000 out of a population of 67 million in 1913, or slightly more than 1 percent of the population—1.29 percent to be exact) in a calculated risk (Wehler, 1985: 148). The expert planning and rhetoric of the Great General Staff assured both the political leaders and the public at large that the calculations had been adequately worked out. They had not. In 1991, 76 percent of U.S. citizens supported U.S. involvement in the Gulf War (Morin, 1991), yet under two-tenths of a percent (roughly 550,000 out of 260 million) served. The fact that the calculations of the Joint Chiefs were better has little if anything to say about their relationship to democracy.

From the perspective of Kant's republican plan for perpetual peace, no significant institutional check exists in U.S. democracy to prevent the use of our standing army. Instead, the spectator-sport variety of militarism Mann (1988: 185) describes—in which there is "no real or potential sacrifice, except by professional troops"—goes a long way toward encouraging the use of force in much the same way the more notorious sport of kings once did in the ancien régime. It is simply not the case that a significant number of citizens bear the burden of the decision to use force in war in a modern, liberal democratic society. That decision is made by military professional managers who are rarely—if ever—elected and are subject only to public opinion, a constraint the military is increasingly adept at influencing, if not controlling. The soldiers who serve under these "managers of violence" are no less pawns than those of the ancien régime. We, like our aristocratic predecessors, can afford to use war as a continuation of policy and even to be entertained by it once in a while.

Yet it is not my point to argue only that the issue of the military in modern society is a crucial, independent variable in Kant's schema that has not been realized. Nor would I necessarily recommend that we revise the empirical studies to learn whether nations with militia forces are more pacific than those with standing armies. Instead, I would keep our focus on the host of narrative and theoretical concerns surrounding the role of the military in society and the ways in which the progressive peace has been predicated upon the essential absence of the military in liberal democratic society without full consideration of the absence this role plays. If the realm of liberal security regimes is in fact predicated upon the standing armies of modern states, Kant's vision is not only far from realized, but the democratic peace is in itself nothing particular in the history of political and international theory, even though these militaries may be, for all intents and purposes, invisible. The democratic peace is simply the renegotiation of classical realism in disguise.

SUMMARY ANALYSIS

Traditionally, analysts of social/military relations have adopted Alfred Vagts's (1959) distinction between a more traditional, heroic "militarism" and a "managerial" or "liberal" militarism such as is found in states where civilian control of the military is secure. If, however, German military history is taken to illustrate the adaptation of heroic militarism to managerial practices, then the acceptance of this adaptation by the bourgeoisie as an alternative to direct military service, and the global diffusion of this alternative through states erected on the professional model, make global forces of modernization much more problematic for those who would see the developing conditions for a perpetual peace.

Given the reductive tendencies inherent in blaming the incidence of war on either the reactionary legacies of the past or the demagogic forces of the future, there seems a need for a more discriminate typology. Consideration of the case of German militarism shows at least four separate histories at work, and therefore there is a need to analyze them systematically.

To enumerate the first two of these four, the liberal institutionalist argument (Doyle, 1996) draws from the history of constitutional thought in the Anglo-Saxon world, whereas the liberal normative argument (Owen, 1994) looks to a separate, individualistic aspect of that same tradition. These arguments assume a historical relationship between the military and society in which the need for the military is a hangover from a past that society is moving to undo through the establishment of democratic political institutions and/or norms. As a result of this zero-sum relationship, the problem of the military in society is something the state, in its progress toward theoretical perfection, will take care of itself over time.

At slight remove from these two arguments is the transitional liberal institutionalist argument (Mansfield and Snyder, 1995; Wehler, 1985), which basically accepts the liberal institutionalist model while noting that the transition to democratic institutions is often difficult. Although more discreet, this argument lends more support to the first two positions than it challenges them.

Finally, among liberal theories there is what I will call normative military professionalism (Huntington, 1957; but Janowitz, 1960, is also appropriate). Although its proponents imagined it as realistically distinct from the more common liberal/idealist constitutional and normative arguments, this view nonetheless derives its notions of objective civilian control from a liberal belief that separation of the military from society in pursuit of its independently determined professional needs contributes to democratization and thus reciprocally toward peace. Thus I would categorize the argument as normative liberal overall.

Two strongly contrasting historical patterns make the opposite arguments. The first of these, drawn more as an afterthought or justification for the horrors of the twentieth century, can best be understood under the heading "mass militarism." Whether in the form of the German apologists (Ritter, 1972; Demeter, 1965) or more recent historical sociological accounts such as those of Mann (1996) or Giddens (1985a), global forces of modernization in the form of mass society and industrial warfare are held to produce a new source of energy in support of a militarism that actually challenges the interests of the state and therefore poses a serious challenge to the assumptions of liberal ideology, if not to liberal elites.

Although arguments in this vein present an important alternative, I hope to have shown through my analysis of German militarism that although the masses are often blamed for their nationalistic and militaristic zeal, war remained something initiated by elites—broadly understood (Mann, 1988: 158). Thus in a way, this militarism is structurally indistinct from that which the liberal tradition attacks. The socioeconomic background of the actors may have changed, but the problem remains the same. Thus the solution might as well remain the same: progress away from states governed by elites will eventually lead to peace. Clearly, this is what Kant had in mind writing in 1795.

But elites are constituted by modern societies for concrete reasons, most of which have as much to do with perceived progress as with reaction (M. Weber, 1947). Thus the problem of mass militarism is perhaps best understood by the proponents of what might be called bureaucratic professional militarism. Similar to Mann's "deterrence-science militarism" (1988: 178–180), an isolated, professional military bureaucracy will eventually yield a challenge to civilian authority of a form authority cannot resist because it lacks the material and discursive resources to do so. This is true even where military forces are constituted on the democratic principle of a rational division of labor. Here we find a link to earlier republican concerns about the role of military professionals such as those found in Niccolò Machiavelli (1965), Alexander Hamilton and colleagues (1961), and, as I have argued, Kant (1983). We also find concerns similar to those expressed by Lasswell (1941) that, although they were directed against Germany and not meant to apply to its democratic rivals, might nonetheless still shed some light here.

We should not rule out the sociopolitical possibility of a militaristic compromise between armies and liberal commercial societies that is something more than an elite manipulation of interests within the state. Such a compromise may, as Muppidi suggests, depend as much on historical and cultural particulars as on democratic norms and institutions. Unfortunately, the historical nature of this possibility is ignored in contemporary literature on the democratic peace. The reasons for this oversight have been elaborated in detail, but they can be further organized systematically into three general categories, shown in Table 5.1.

Both the liberal institutionalist and transitional liberal arguments subscribe to what Giddens (1985a) refers to as a "container state" model for civil-military relations. Accordingly, militarism is something that can be regulated by state institutions and on its own poses no threat to the state as long as these institutions are properly structured. The present volume expressly criticizes this approach, but two other arguments remain to be summarized: the "sociology of the state" and the "sociology of the military."

The normative liberal and mass militarist arguments are of some interest to theorists of the democratic peace because they argue for eventual changes in the structure of the state that might affect the state's ability to control the use of force. As Blaney and Shaw explore in more detail in Chapters 2 and 9 of this volume, the driving force of these analyses remains the values attributed to the state as a coherent unit of analysis, even though society now has a causal role. Sociologies of the military, however, yield two further conflicting possibilities.

Normative military professionalism remains marginally attractive in the democratic peace literature for two reasons. Norms such as "service to the state" are at the foundation of the paradigm shift that justified the existence of military professionals to a liberal society. Huntington's notion of "objective civilian control" allowed the politicians to wash their hands of waging war and leave it to the generals to follow orders. Theorists of the democratic peace are thus willing to consider these norms as evidence because the norms do not challenge the fundamental assumptions of political control offered in the container state models, even if the agency of such control resides with the military rather than with the state itself.

Table 5.1 Categories for Relating Democratization to the Incidence of War

Civil-Military Framework	Relationship of Democracy to Force	
	Peace	War
"Container state"	Liberal institutionalism	Transitional liberal
Sociology of the state	Normative liberalism	Mass militarism
Sociology of the military	Normative professionalism	Bureacratic professionalism

Bureaucratic military professionalism, on the other hand, is a direct threat to the democratic peace literature because it takes a long, historical view rather than a short-term, static view of the existence of democratic institutions. Seen from this perspective, the military may subscribe to democratic norms during times of stable democratic rule, but long-term prospects for corruption arise when liberal societies choose to ignore their military needs and instead defer to those who have an unreliable professional interest in making war.

CONCLUSION: THE PROSPECTS FOR PEACE?

Realizing the political agency of the military is tantamount to admitting that however great the distaste for war in a free society, simple promotion of that free society will not lead to utopian peace unless the military remains an issue for public debate and social choice in a genuinely democratic culture. My primary aim has not been to disprove or critique the current social scientific literature on its own grounds but to encourage those writing in this historiographical and theoretical tradition to consider the appropriated nature of these grounds and whether it is appropriate to continue to stand on them in our contemporary debates.

What do democracies do with their militaries? If the comparison to Germany's bureaucratic military professionalism is understood as part of that nation's transition to democracy, the answer to this question is a professional compartmentalization that removes force from view by means of a socially acceptable division of labor. This removal may occur through heroic idealization, as it did in the Wilhelmine period in Germany, or through political camouflage of the sort Tarak Barkawi describes in Chapter 6 of this volume. Regardless, this compromise makes the authority of the military all the more powerful when it is needed, whether that need is felt by elites or by masses with no direct links to the military. The "fact" that democracies are less likely to use force instrumentally does not mean that force plays no role in them but that it plays a different role, one usually seen only when the military is frustrated in achieving its self-understood mission (Feaver, 1996).

Global social forces of modernization and democratization may promote freedom of speech and exchange in previously authoritarian states, and such may lead to "normative" constraints on the decision to wage war. Yet these tendencies alone provide no structural promise of Kant's perpetual peace because the military retains the ability to influence and even change those norms. Modern militaries possess the political, intellectual, discursive, and material resources to redefine the normative concerns of political institutions to such a point that politicians are disinclined—or even unwilling—to exercise their restraining function, and this presents a theoretical challenge to social scientific literature on the pacific tendencies of liberal democracy.

Taking this challenge seriously, today the hopes Kant expressed for a perpetual peace rest solely in historically variable normative constraints, and that which is historically variable provides no permanent or "lawlike" guarantee. Social scientific research on this issue may have yielded an interesting statistical anomaly (Farber and Gowa, 1995), but it cannot speak of an institutional or organizational framework to be promoted as a viable foreign policy in the name of a lasting peace. Worse yet, if one accepts the arguments of military professionals uncritically as the inevitable result of the rise of mass society and total war, these twin forces of global social change may be directly antagonistic to Kant's vision. Peace, on Kant's model, will become perpetual only when the *miles perpetuus* is confined to the dustbin of history. For now, however, liberal democratic theorists, and perhaps thus also liberal democratic societies, appear to prefer to keep this ancient relic out of sight and out of mind, if not necessarily out of practice.

NOTE

I am grateful for Ido Oren's comments, as well as those of others at the Social Science Research Council (SSRC) workshop, "Democracy, the Use of Force, and Global Social Change," at which the chapter was first presented. Thanks also to Nick Onuf for his comments and to Tarak Barkawi, Mark Laffey, and the SSRC for the funding necessary to bring these thoughts to light. My title is inspired by Walther Abish (1980).

6

War Inside the Free World: The Democratic Peace and the Cold War in the Third World

Tarak Barkawi

From its resurgence in the 1980s, discussion of the "democratic peace" (DP) has acknowledged some of the problems posed by the militarized covert operations carried out by the United States against elected governments in the Third World during the Cold War.[1] Rather less trouble has been taken over the more widespread use of U.S. military and police power, often operating through clients and proxies, to suppress or eliminate popular forces identified as communist throughout the dominions of the free world. Neither of these forms of organized violence meets the threshold of interstate war as defined in the Correlates of War (CoW) databases used to establish the proposition that democratic states do not wage interstate war on one another. I do not seek to argue otherwise. Rather, I take up a logically prior question generally ignored by both critics and proponents of the DP: Are the conceptions of "state" and "interstate war" used in the CoW databases and the DP proposition appropriate for analysis of use of force between core and peripheral powers? If not, it is unwarranted to assume that the zone of peace extends to core-periphery relations, regardless of whether or not this or that covert operation or use of force by the United States in the Third World is a formal exception to the DP. The significance of the DP as a statistical finding would be considerably reduced, largely applicable only to a Western context where many other variables may account for the lack of war.

For proponents of the DP proposition, U.S. militarized covert operations do not amount to interstate war. In many cases, these operations clearly meet the classical, Clausewitzian definition of war: the use of force to achieve political purposes. But CoW structures its definitions of wars and states in terms of sovereign borders, creating a distinction between intra- and interstate wars. As a consequence, *juridical* considerations become dominant, such as the relation of military operations to interstate borders or whether "official" national armed forces are used in battle. Karl von Clausewitz's realist as well as his historical sensibilities would be roused, for war is not waged with legalities. From a historical point of view, no necessary correspondence exists between sovereignty and the social and political processes productive of war. Wars should be analyzed with concepts appropriate to the historical context in which they are fought. As will be seen later, proponents of the DP utilize the juridical features of CoW's conceptual apparatus to *remove from analysis* the ways in which the United States waged war in the Third World. In so doing, they largely avoid grappling with the questions such war waging raises for democracy, both at home and abroad.

I first contrast CoW's conception of "interstate war" with a Clausewitzian approach sensitive to the historical context of use of force in the periphery during the Cold War. Second, I provide a critical analysis of the discussion of militarized covert operations in the democratic peace literature. Given the fact that U.S. policymakers were trying to subvert various international and domestic legal conventions regarding the use of force, it is relatively easy for proponents of the DP to demonstrate that such operations do not reach a threshold of interstate war ultimately based on those very same conventions. I then turn to two aspects of U.S. use of force in the Third World obscured by CoW's conceptual apparatus: that the crucial geopolitical distinction is not between sovereign states but a world of two blocs, and that an inherent component of U.S. strategy was the utilization of foreign military manpower. In conclusion, I offer a preliminary analysis of the international relations of democracy and war between core and periphery during the Cold War.

CoW AND THE COLD WAR IN THE THIRD WORLD

CoW's conception of interstate war is defined in terms of a system of sovereign states, categorizing war in relation to recognized sovereign borders. A core distinction is made between intra- and interstate wars.[2] The operational definition of "state" is therefore fundamental. CoW uses population criteria, membership in the League of Nations or the UN, and formal diplomatic recognition by great powers to determine whether an entity is a state and hence a member of the states system. An interstate war is an armed clash between the armies of two or more sovereign states that results in at least 1,000 battle deaths. Intrastate or civil wars occur primarily within the territory of a sovereign state. For such wars to be classified as "internationalized," the national, regular armed forces of a foreign state must be present, regardless of any degree of foreign material aid or clandestine involvement (Small and Singer, 1982).

As a statistical artifact, then, the democratic peace is produced by empirical indicators based upon internationally recognized, territorial sovereignty (Russett, 1993: 13–14). Those indicators assume what should be empirically investigated: that historically wars have fixed and regular relations with sovereign statehood. In fact, with respect to the projection of coercive power, the nature and meaning of sovereignty change over time and place. As the history of European imperialism and its aftermath attests, a key feature of relations between core states and peripheral powers is the making and remaking of sovereign boundaries. Far from being an "objective" indicator of sovereignty, the right to withhold or grant international recognition to the government of a peripheral state is a *tool* of imperial control and great power politics.[3] As Stephen Krasner (1999) has pointed out, sovereignty is little more than "organized hypocrisy." When it suited U.S. interests, sovereignty could be emphasized as, for example, in representing the North Korean invasion of the South as a case of international aggression, or it could be downplayed. When justifying the U.S. invasion of the North, the U.S. ambassador to the UN referred to the 38th parallel as an "imaginary line" (quoted in Cumings, 1991: 769).

But sovereignty and the various lines superpower diplomacy drew on the map had little to do with the social forces productive of war in the Third World. The two great conflagrations of the Cold War, in Korea and Indochina, were rooted in the social upheaval of occupation in World War II and popular struggle against the reimposition of colonial and neocolonial rule.[4] In both conflicts, relations with sovereign borders were multiple and contingent. Indeed, although both are classified as "interstate war" by CoW, they could equally be understood as internationalized civil wars, as Koreans invaded South Korea and Vietnamese invaded South Vietnam, with all sides receiving external support. The contingent place of sovereign borders in these conflicts raises the question of whether CoW's conception of interstate war is meaningful in the context of the Cold War in the Third World. In sharp contrast to the European states system, interstate war in CoW's terms has *never* been a predominant form of war *between* core states and peripheral powers. Claims made on the basis of this conception of war involving the United States and the Third World, whether regarding its presence or its absence, should be treated with caution.

In contrast to CoW, Clausewitzian analysis of war is sensitive to historical change on the social and strategic terrain upon which political authorities and their military forces operate. *On War,* in part, analyzed the advent of national peoples in modern warfare. A twentieth-century Clausewitz, Raymond Aron noted, would address nuclear weapons and guerrilla insurgency (Aron, 1968: 67). These were the phenomena that structured superpower competition in the periphery. The threat of nuclear war meant that superpower forces neutralized one another by their mutual presence. Wherever their regular armies faced each other directly, as on the central front in Europe, "there [was] no alternative to peace," President Eisenhower remarked (quoted in Aron, 1968: 2). This enforced nuclear peace meant the local forces of clients and proxies became vital instruments for conducting superpower competition, especially if actual fighting was involved. The risk of escalation increased exponentially if U.S. and Soviet forces were simultaneously involved. The periphery therefore took on central importance as a site of armed conflict. There the superpowers pursued their political purposes through resort to armed force. Moreover, the demarcation lines between the blocs were in many cases unclear, especially in Asia, creating space for strategic maneuver.

As a result of these historical transformations, "war" understood as open violent conflict between legally recognized powers declined in significance after 1945.[5] One reason for this was the development of structures of international law designed to halt international war and overt aggression. A liberal state like the United States, seeking the legitimacy of international opinion, was consequently limited in the overt deployment of its national forces for aggressive purposes. But far more important was the discipline that the threat of mutual nuclear suicide enforced on the superpowers' use of their regular, national forces. In particular, only the forces of one superpower could become directly engaged in any one locality. If the forces of the other side were present, they had to have some international juridical status other than that of legal combatants. In this way, as discussed later, the juridical status of superpower forces (e.g., advisers) provided diplomatic cover for force projection. These legal fictions did not mean war was dead as an instrument of policy. Superpower competition did involve large-scale organized violence within and between the territories of nominally sovereign and variously dependent secondary states. In Korea and Indochina the United States inflicted casualties equivalent to those the great powers suffered in World War II (Cumings, 1991: 769–770; Duiker, 1995: 270). But equally characteristic of the Cold War in the Third World was a form of permanent military action conducted between internal security forces and their armed and unarmed opponents. As Aron suggested, nuclear weapons force the creation of new distinctions in the modalities of war in order to limit its violence (1968: viii). Even before considering any domestic democratic constraints the United States faced in overt use of national forces, there is every reason to suspect that after 1945, strategists, to paraphrase Clausewitz, would seek "the continuation of war by other means."[6]

Is CoW's conceptual apparatus appropriate to these new modalities of war? A key assumption by CoW is that military forces necessarily belong to the sovereign state under whose flag they serve. The political entities and military forces that wage war, however, do not necessarily correspond with the categories of juridical sovereignty. During the Cold War new forms of an old practice, the use of foreign military forces, were developed. The Europeans had raised large armies and police forces from colonized populations for purposes of imperial control and great power competition. These colonial armies were, juridically speaking, part of the sovereign armed forces of European imperial powers. After decolonization, the superpowers turned to building up the local forces of nominally sovereign client states—raising, advising, and supporting a number of forms of police, military, and intelligence organizations. They also raised a variety of ad hoc, often multinational paramilitary forces. Forces of these types were generally at the "sharp end" of the Cold War. CoW's focus on the national armed forces of sovereign states is thus particularly ill suited to analysis of the role of core powers in peripheral warfare during this period. If a superpower's regular, national forces are not present as combatants, CoW does not consider that state to be at war. Proxy wars can be classified as civil wars, even though their course, nature, and outcome are shaped by external involvement (cf. Deutsch, 1964).

As with states and war, CoW's conception of imperialism is structured by the juridical status of colonies. For CoW, "imperial" and "colonial" wars ended with the passing of the formal European empires (see Small and Singer, 1982: 52; Wayman, Singer, and Sarkees, 1996: 6). Once the new states in the Third World were internationally recognized, they could be party to intra- or interstate wars and wars against nonstate actors but not to imperial war. As can be seen, CoW's typology is not neutral or objective with respect to contending theoretic approaches to the study of world politics. Specific assumptions about war and international relations are built into the data, whereas other possibilities, such as neocolonialism and neocolonial war, are excluded. In this sense, the tests of the democratic peace proposition against CoW's data are always already biased. In particular, CoW's typology does not allow for the possibility of informal empire in a sovereign states system and the use of clients, proxies, and foreign forces to rule and wage war in that empire. But it was precisely in terms like these that many analysts of the Cold War conceived of the respective spheres of influence of the superpowers (Aron, 1974; Kolko, 1988; LaFeber, 1984; Wendt and Friedheim, 1996)

Assumptions about relations between military forces and sovereign statehood made by CoW do not reflect the real relations between political authority and coercive power in informal empire. This is a fundamental issue: war involves the use of force by political entities. Indicators and typologies of war must analytically capture the nature of relations between such entities and their military power. Behind CoW's sovereign statehood lies Max Weber's definition of the state, which draws a close relationship among the state, coercive power, and rule over a territorially demarcated area. In international relations there exists a *juridical* demarcation of the globe in terms of sovereign states. Yet in informal empire relations of *ruling*, the maintenance of an "order [that] is continuously safeguarded within a given *territorial* area by the threat and application of physical force" can diverge markedly from the *sovereign territorial* demarcation of the globe (Weber, 1978: 54). Although Weber assumed for modern states that state, rule, and sovereign territory coexist in the same space, there is the obvious possibility that legal, administrative, and coercive dimensions of rule are not coextensive in space. This possibility entails critical scrutiny of conceptions of state, rule, and war that rely on juridical assumptions. For example, the United States was able to switch regimes in Guatemala; it possessed the ultimate say on how and by whom Guatemala—and many other Third World states—was to be ruled. Many secondary powers, such as those in Eastern Europe, "shared" their coercive monopolies over sovereign space with a superpower patron (see Wendt and Friedheim, 1996: 246). Even former great powers like Germany and Japan were shorn of their political-military autonomy and integrated into transnational military alliances. Within the superpower blocs there were of course many degrees of dependency and autonomy with respect to various issues. Rule in any context is always a matter of degree. Nonetheless, relations between great powers in a sovereign state system can be distinguished from those between core states and peripheral powers in the context of informal empire.

   Relations of informal empire and global struggle with the Communist bloc were the context of U.S. use of force in the Third World rather than that of a sovereign state system. Proponents of the DP, however, use the juridical dimensions of CoW's category of interstate war, as well as other arguments, to establish that U.S. militarized covert operations against elected regimes in the Third World were not in fact wars between democracies.

THE DEMOCRATIC PEACE, COVERT OPERATIONS, AND THE COLD WAR

The DP literature assesses covert operations from the perspective of its own categories, generally emphasizing two points. First, such operations were not interstate war by CoW rules, and second, they reflect limited imperfections in U.S. democracy. This way of framing what is at stake in covert operations obscures the historical and international context in which they were conducted. U.S. policymakers were pursuing political objectives through use of military means in a manner appropriate to the strategic situation that confronted them as they understood it. As will be seen, resort to covert means was driven not by domestic democratic constraints on overt use of U.S. military forces but by strategic calculation.

Potential exceptions to the DP considered in the literature include the operations in Iran (1953), Guatemala (1954), Indonesia (1957–1958), Brazil (1960s), Chile (1973), and Nicaragua after the elections in 1984. Laos, which had an elected government and conducted competitive elections with universal franchise during the early period of U.S. covert involvement, is overlooked.[7] It is relatively easy to establish that paramilitary operations like those in Guatemala or Indonesia were not interstate war by reference to aspects of CoW's definition, principally the requirement for overt use of national armed forces and that for 1,000 battle deaths.[8] Some ad hoc points are made in the literature, such as the role of liberal interventionism and anticommunism in inspiring U.S. action or the fact that, with the exception of Chile, the targets of these operations were not "fully democratic" (Russett, 1993: 121). But CoW's definition of interstate war primarily rescues the DP from invalidation in its own terms in these cases.

In arguing that the Central Intelligence Agency (CIA) operation in Guatemala was not a war, proponents of the DP refer only to the efforts to unseat the democratically elected Jacobo Arbenz in 1954 rather than to the decades of guerrilla insurgency that followed (e.g. Weart, 1998: 220–221). In that operation the CIA raised a small mercenary force, composed of Guatemalan exiles and Latin and North American mercenaries, of about battalion strength. It was trained in Nicaragua and invaded Guatemala primarily from Honduras, fighting several minor actions with the Guatemalan army.[9] The CIA supplemented its invasion force with a small air force of approximately a dozen ground attack aircraft of World War II vintage piloted by employees of the CIA's proprietary airline, Civil Air Transport (CAT), which later became Air America. These aircraft flew strike missions against shipping, troop trains, and Guatemalan army units. Ultimately, the Guatemalan officer corps—sympathetic to the oligarchy, which objected to Arbenz's land reform policies—refused to crush the invasion, and Arbenz resigned. Colonel Castillo Armas, the leader of the invasion force, was installed as head of state and promptly received U.S. recognition as the legitimate government of Guatemala.[10]

The military weakness of the Arbenz regime was decisive, and only a few hundred were killed and wounded in the fighting and aerial raids. This is insufficient for war to have occurred on CoW's account, given its criterion of 1,000 battle deaths (Small and Singer, 1982: 50). The problem with such a criterion is that it refers to the severity or intensity of war rather than to its intrinsic nature in modern context: the use of force for political purposes. A measure of the intensity of a phenomenon cannot stand in as a definition of that phenomenon (Duvall, 1976). As a consequence of this faulty definitional strategy, in certain apparently "obvious" cases of interstate war, CoW has had to be flexible with respect to battle deaths. The Falklands War, for example, resulted in over 900 but fewer than 1,000 battle deaths but is still considered an interstate war. Spencer Weart sets his definition of war at 200 combat deaths (1998: 13). At what number of deaths does armed conflict become war? The fact that the Arbenz regime was toppled so easily is indicative of its lack of military strength, not of the nature of the policy used to oust it. The 1,000 battle deaths criterion poses an additional problem peculiar to war between core and peripheral powers. The weakness of the latter often means large-scale violence is not necessary to defeat them or that such violence is dispersed in time and space. For CoW, such "low-intensity conflicts" do not amount to war precisely because they do not involve organized violence on a large scale (Small and Singer, 1982: 56–57). Yet these conflicts are low intensity only by comparison with European warfare. Their consequences often have been decisive for local populations. The use of a paradigm of war derived from one context for analysis of another is precisely what I seek to critique.

The other facet of the CoW definition of war invoked in analysis of the Guatemalan operation is that, officially, U.S. armed forces were not involved (Weart, 1998: 220). For an intervening state to be at war, CoW requires that its national armed forces participate and suffer casualties regardless of the degree of clandestine involvement (Small and Singer, 1982: 218–219). CoW does not always insist on open use of national armed forces, seeing through the People's Republic of China's (PRC) insistence that only "volunteers" were aiding North Korea during the Korean War. Similar suspicions, however, do not apply to U.S. militarized covert operations. The 1954 conflict in Guatemala is classified as a civil war with the explanation that "there was no formal American participation in this war, although the CIA armed, trained, and financed the winning rebel force" (Small and Singer, 1982: 324). The use of the term "formal" is crucial here, as without the "informal" CIA operation there would have been no civil war. Similarly, Bruce Russett argues the Guatemalan operation was not an interstate war because it was not "openly fought by military units of the United States" operating in an "organized fashion" (1993: 123). Naturally, in a *covert* operation a state does not openly or formally use its official military forces; that would be inconsistent with the very idea of such operations. Rather, CIA paramilitary operatives hired, trained, supplied, and advised foreign mercenaries. Where necessary, personnel from the U.S. armed forces were seconded to the CIA. CAT employees were often former U.S. Air Force (USAF) officers or were recruited from Southeast Asia; nationalist Chinese pilots flew many of the missions in Guatemala and, later, in Indonesia. The use of foreign personnel, especially in combat roles, was necessary to avoid the risk of domestic and international publicity if U.S. personnel were to fall into enemy hands. But the use of foreigners does not change the fact that they were part of *U.S.* operations. By taking seriously U.S. efforts to conceal its role, proponents of the DP are in effect accepting at face value the "plausible deniability" of covert operations in social scientific analysis, even though everyone is aware that the CIA wholly armed and financed the invasion of Guatemala!

In making a firm connection between interstate war and the use of national armed forces, CoW's categories fail to evince a sufficiently realistic suspicion of the various coercive instruments of statecraft. CoW's emphasis on the sovereign legalities of conflicts provides generous cover to states seeking to cloak their policies of war—cover advocates of the DP are only too happy to make use of. There are further ways in which the DP literature obscures the historical and strategic background of militarized covert operations. The operations are placed in the context of imperfections in U.S. democracy that, it is argued, allowed them to occur. For Weart, the roots of the Guatemala operation are to be found in nationalism and "prejudice," which can lead officials to perceive "Communists or dark-skinned people" as an "out-group" not deserving of the tolerance and respect democrats and democracies usually reserve for one another (Weart, 1998: 208, 229). As "leftists" can also be treated in this manner (1998: 227), one wonders what kind of democracy Weart is talking about. Russett claims the resort to covert operations was actually evidence of the effectiveness of U.S. democracy in "limiting intervention" and forestalling "open military action," although it was not effective enough to prevent them entirely (1993: 123–124), implying that U.S. officials would have preferred to invade Guatemala overtly. More convincingly, Michael Doyle places such operations in the context of the interventionary moment in U.S. liberalism (Doyle, 1996: 35–44). These arguments, however, underestimate the prominent place of covert operations in containment strategy.

From 1947 the United States developed an apparatus for the conduct of a variety of covert operations in which it could "plausibly deny" its involvement, at least in the short term (Blum, 1995; McClintock, 1992; Prados, 1996). These operations became a significant and regular feature of U.S. strategy in the Cold War. They were one instrument in the global struggle against communism. The Eisenhower administration saw covert action as a way of making containment affordable (Gaddis, 1982: 157–158). More important, covert action was a means of responding to the perception that communist successes were the result of conspiratorial methods. As George Kennan put it in a 1947 letter endorsing a proposal to supplement the covert action mission of the new civilian intelligence agencies with a Department of Defense (DOD)–run "guerrilla warfare corps": "I think we have to face the fact that Russian successes have been gained in many areas by irregular and underground methods. I do not think the American people would ever approve of policies which rely fundamentally on similar methods for their effectiveness. I do feel, however, that there are cases where it might be essential to fight fire with fire" (quoted in McClintock, 1992: 28).

Although Kennan notes a potential public legitimation problem, the nature of the perceived Soviet threat was the reason for fighting fire with fire. Covert action, then, not only provided a means to avoid domestic and other international constraints on the overt use of national forces but was seen as a way of meeting the peculiar nature of the communist threat. It was not primarily a second choice of policymakers who would have preferred overt intervention but were domestically constrained in the use of national forces. Quite aside from domestic or international political repercussions, the United States lacked sufficient national forces for large-scale deployments in every case of communist aggression.

H. W. Brands points to a threatening aspect for U.S. officials of the peaceful and electoral accession to power of social democratic and communist leaders in the Third World: it implied a public rejection of American values and the U.S. model (1993: 56–57). In this sense, such instances were more damaging to U.S. interests and prestige than obvious cases of Soviet aggression. To respond to such situations with overt U.S. aggression would be self-defeating. Democracy in the Third World, if voters made the wrong choices, was a threat to U.S. interests. Viewed from the perspective of the threat faced and the purposes of U.S. policy, covert operations were an appropriate means. Indeed, in a case like Guatemala, overt U.S. intervention, aside from its other costs, might well have generated more resistance. Hence within the framework of containment, covert operations were good strategy, at least in the short term.[11]

Containment strategy has additional significant implications for analysis of democracy and war. Some proponents of the DP argue that democratic norms of respect and tolerance between self-governing peoples prevent recourse to war between democratic states (see Maoz and Russett, 1993). If covert operations are placed in their containment context, however, it becomes clear that the nature of a perceived communist threat was fundamental to U.S. policy rather than any democratic process by which communists, or those regarded as such, might come to power. Fearing the electoral victory of Salvador Allende's Popular Unity movement in the 1970 elections, Henry Kissinger remarked, "I don't see why we need to stand by and watch a country go communist due to the irresponsibility of its own people" (quoted in Prados, 1996: 317). During the covert operation in Indonesia, initiated in part in response to the electoral success of the Indonesian Communist Party (PKI), John Foster Dulles cabled his ambassador, "They [the Indonesians] cannot turn over their country to communism without something being done about it by the free world" (quoted in Kahin and Kahin, 1995: 168). Clearer statements of the relative importance in U.S. foreign policy of anticommunism over democratic norms of tolerance and respect can hardly be imagined.

Attention to the Cold War in the periphery brings to light a strange feature of the discussion of covert operations in the DP literature. It is odd, in analyses of relations of democracy and war, that only a few relatively minor operations are considered, given that a regular and prominent feature of U.S. policy was to back authoritarian client states and equip them with a coercive apparatus designed primarily to defend them against internal unarmed and armed popular challenges. Once popular forces in the Third World resorted to mass political mobilization and especially armed insurgency, small operations to "switch regimes" no longer sufficed; the United States had to turn to a strategy of "foreign internal defense"—training, advising, and supporting the security forces of its clients. U.S. policy sought to violently suppress popular forces in favor of narrowly based elites dependent on foreign backing. Precisely as questions of democracy and war come to the fore, the literature on the DP is silent because such wars rarely amounted to interstate war, much less wars between democratic states.

The reason for this silence is to be found in the distinction between interstate and intrastate wars. Like CoW, the DP assumes that war in any context can be typed according to its relations with sovereign borders (Weart, 1998: 27). Only covert operations even approximate interstate war, and U.S. military assistance to authoritarian regimes generally occurred in the context of intrastate war and hence is not considered pertinent to the DP. This distinction between intrastate and interstate war, however, was not relevant to the ways in which U.S. strategists constructed the communist threat or sought to respond to it.

CONTAINMENT, FOREIGN FORCES, AND THE "DEFENSE" OF THE FREE WORLD

The crucial geopolitical distinction in containment strategy was not sovereign statehood but a world of two spheres. By conceptualizing sovereignty in largely juridical terms, CoW overlooks the ways in which U.S. strategists understood the relationship between sovereign boundaries and the communist threat. It was on the basis of this understanding that the United States deployed its military resources. Sovereign borders and the international juridical status of combatants were something policy had to adapt to or work around. Only by attending to the strategic context of containment can the extensive provisions the United States made for what it called "overseas internal defense" be understood, a term that itself suggests manifold relations between the inside and outside of sovereign borders.

During the Cold War, U.S. strategic thinking conceived U.S. interests in global terms, seeking to secure a space called the free world. Insurgencies in the Third World struck at "the weak point in *our* defenses," according to Secretary Caspar Weinberger (quoted in McClintock, 1992: 334; emphasis added). "Containment" represented a project of international hegemony, the maintenance of which often required resort to force *within* the perimeter of the free world as defense against external attack (Cumings, 1993: 549). Inside that perimeter the United States worked to establish a set of political economic relations conducive to the flourishing of the U.S. economy, associated transnational capital, and the continued dominance of U.S. power. Containment was at once an ideological representation of these purposes, in that it obscured the economic imperatives behind U.S. policy, and the framework upon which U.S. officials based their strategy. Threats to the free world were understood by policymakers to arise from *external* sources, even if they manifested themselves *internally*. Communists, and others inimical to U.S. interests who were effectively elided with communists, were seen as *foreign* to the free world, regardless of their social origins or juridical status—for example, their nationality. Hence in the many insurgencies in which U.S. national and client forces were involved, most U.S. military and civilian officials perceived their opponents as *external aggressors* and conducted operations accordingly.

Allen Dulles, who headed the CIA in the Eisenhower administration, described the covert operations in Iran and Guatemala in these terms:

> In Iran, a Mossadegh, and in Guatemala, an Arbenz had come to power through the usual processes of government and not by any Communist coup as in Czechoslovakia. Neither man at the time disclosed the intention of creating a Communist state. When this purpose became clear, support from outside was given to loyal anti-Communist elements in the respective countries—in the one case to the Shah's supporters; in the other, to a group of Guatemalan patriots. In each case the danger was successfully met. (Dulles, 1965: 207–208)

The presupposition that the Communist threat was always a form of externally inspired aggression, even when it took internal forms, is crucial to Dulles's curious logic. The elected and highly popular Arbenz government, seeking more just distribution of land, is perceived as an even more underhanded method of installing a communist government than the Soviet-backed coup in Czechoslovakia, which overthrew an elected government. U.S. intervention through a mercenary force was required to respond to the external threat represented by Arbenz. Mercenaries, as with the contras in the 1980s, are seen as the true "patriots" by virtue of their use in an anti-communist campaign. As communism is foreign to the free world, communists by definition cannot be patriots, since their ultimate allegiance was perceived to be to the Kremlin.[12] An assistant secretary of state in the Truman administration, calling for action to oust Arbenz, argued, "No one is

more opposed than I to interfere in the internal affairs of other nations. But
. . . we may be compelled to intervene. . . . I should like to underscore that
because Communism is so blatantly an international and not an internal affair, its suppression, even by force, in an American country, by one or more
of the other republics, would not constitute an intervention in the internal
affairs of the former" (quoted in McClintock, 1992: 138). It would not be
intervention because the threat is external; intervention and involvement in
internal war is, in U.S. strategic thinking, a response to external attack.

Prior to the Guatemala operation, Secretary Dulles pushed for an Organization of American States resolution condemning communism in the
hemisphere. Although he was forced to accept an amendment specifying
"dangers originating outside the hemisphere" (LaFeber, 1984: 121), Dulles
interpreted the resolution as "an extension of the Monroe Doctrine to include the concept of outlawing foreign ideologies in the American Republics" (quoted in Kolko, 1988: 104). But communism was not foreign to
the free world. Communist and social democratic parties were popular in
the Third World after 1945, as they sought more equitable social, economic,
and political conditions in the wake of decolonization. Their popularity and
ability to mobilize anticolonial and nationalist sentiment can only be understood in terms of the local social relations and political dynamics out of
which they arose. By understanding such movements as externally inspired,
the United States placed itself in opposition to the social forces of which
they were a part.

Conceiving of popular challenges by anticolonial, nationalist, and revolutionary movements as externally inspired attacks enabled coercive responses. To see such movements as products of their own social contexts,
as many of the more perceptive but less influential counterinsurgency
thinkers did, would mean that various social welfare and political reform
policies would have to be pursued in order to "defeat" them—policies at
odds with the political-economic purposes behind U.S. policy. So such
movements were usually seen as closely coordinated efforts by the USSR
to bring countries into the "communist orbit" (Cable, 1986; Kolko, 1988;
LaFeber, 1984). In 1957, after reviewing events in Korea, the Philippines,
Vietnam, Laos, Cambodia, Burma, Iran, Trieste, and Guatemala, Eisenhower claimed they were all instances "of Soviet pressure designed to ac-
celerate Communist conquest of every country where the Soviet government could make its influence felt" (quoted in Gaddis, 1982: 140). As
Gabriel Kolko (1988) notes, the consequence of this expansive vision of the
communist threat was to place U.S. foreign policy in opposition to change
in the Third World and to cast it as the backer of status quo regimes in an
era of great social upheaval.

The popularity of their struggles enabled insurgent movements to mobilize significant military troops, supplemented to a greater or lesser extent

by the support of communist-bloc countries. The United States developed the notion of "overseas internal defense" to defend client states from this threat—raising, training, and advising their armies and other security forces. Some insurgent forces recruited and operated within the borders of a single sovereign state, whereas others made use of sanctuaries in neighboring countries. The client armies they faced in battle were armed and equipped by the United States. Hence regardless of how they are categorized by CoW, wars of containment were constituted through domestic *and* international processes, a conclusion impossible to arrive at from an initial assumption that "interstate" and "intrastate" refer to different types of war. The social context of war between core and periphery during the Cold War was one of the mutual constitution of the domestic and the international.

This mutual constitution is evident in one of the primary instruments of U.S. containment strategy: foreign-recruited forces. A consistent concern of U.S. policymakers during the Cold War was to develop means of utilizing "local" or "indigenous" manpower to counter communist aggression in the Third World. As Eisenhower put it, "The United States could not maintain old-fashioned forces all around the world," so it sought "to develop within the various areas and regions of the free world indigenous forces for the maintenance of order, the safeguarding of frontiers, and the provision of the bulk of the ground capability" (quoted in Gaddis, 1982: 153). The "maintenance of order" refers to the internal security mission of such forces. As part of its strategy of flexible response, the Kennedy administration sought to meet the threat posed by wars of liberation. "What Chairman [Nikita] Khrushchev describes as wars of liberation and popular uprisings," Secretary Robert McNamara said, "I prefer to describe as subversion and covert aggression" (quoted in McClintock, 1992: 174). The administration developed a high-level coordinating committee called the Special Group (Counterinsurgency), which in 1962 approved an "Overseas Internal Defense Policy" (see McClintock, 1992: 161–178). The policy sought to limit the role of the United States to support of the indigenous effort with training, advice, and matériel. U.S. Special Forces were designed to mobilize, advise, and lead foreign guerrillas. In Indochina, they would raise and operate with tens of thousands of Hmong and Montagnards. An extensive apparatus was developed to train Third World militaries, as well as police and intelligence forces, in counterinsurgency skills (McClintock, 1992). Training in the United States of Third World officers occurred on a large scale as well. Between 1955 and 1981, nearly 400,000 passed through various programs (Neuman, 1986: 28–29).

The Nixon Doctrine was specifically concerned with limiting the role of U.S. national forces in "other types of aggression," stating that the United States would provide military and economic assistance but would "look to the nation directly threatened to assume the primary responsibility of providing the manpower for its defense."[13] The Reagan administration continued these policies. According to Secretary Weinberger, programs such as supporting the El Salvadoran Army and training other Third World militaries were designed "to reduce the probability that United States armed forces could be committed in foreign battles" (quoted in McClintock, 1992: 351). Ronald Reagan also sought to develop a mirror image of the perceived Soviet strategy of internal aggression through "pro-insurgency." Support was given to Angolan and Afghan insurgents, and a light infantry raiding force was raised to conduct operations in Nicaragua. As can be seen, foreign forces were a fundamental and integral part of U.S. strategy throughout the Cold War.

The systematic relations between the United States and its foreign forces are obscured in the CoW data by the presumption that armies necessarily "belong" to sovereign states, a very misleading proposition in relations between core and periphery. For CoW, a power using foreign forces qualifies for involvement neither in internationalized civil war nor in interstate war. This is a major oversight because a key feature of any analysis of war is the organization of force. The United States constituted significant military power from foreign populations. In its heyday, the Army of the Republic of Vietnam (ARVN) was one of the four or five most powerful armies in the world. It was used for U.S. force projection throughout Indochina, providing the bulk of the forces for the invasions of Cambodia and Laos as well as for the war against the Vietnamese communists. The United States developed the ARVN's military power for its own purposes and saw it as part of the armed force at the disposal of policy (e.g., Richard Nixon's policy of "Vietnamization"). Juridically derived measures of the sovereign state and its coercive apparatus used by CoW diverge from forms of the international organization of violence in the post-1945 period. The juridical nationality of military manpower and the counting of national military deaths have no necessary relation to the powers waging war.

The issue is not whether CoW codes specific cases correctly but that its indicators are not an adequate guide to the real relations between political authority and military force. In juridical terms, for example, South Vietnamese forces were those of a sovereign state. Yet U.S. pilots flew combat missions in Republic of Vietnam [South Vietnamese] Air Force (RVNAF) aircraft (supplied by the United States) in the early 1960s.[14] Sufficient numbers of Vietnamese pilots had yet to be trained. In order to maintain the fiction that U.S. Military Assistance Command, Vietnam (MACV) personnel were not engaged in combat at that time but were merely advisers, a Vietnamese national flew with the U.S. pilot even though he played no role in flying or fighting with the aircraft. This was done to ensure that if the plane were shot down a Vietnamese body would be present, so MACV could claim the U.S. body was simply that of an adviser "conducting training in a combat environment." In what sense is the nationality of the pilot a crucial issue? It is crucial in terms of *representing* the U.S. advisory effort as one of support for an allied sovereign country under attack. Carrying a Vietnamese "dummy" pilot was a form of diplomatic cover for U.S. projection of force in the context of its early involvement in Vietnam. As the United States was constrained in the overt use of its national forces, under cover of "advise and support" it used its national military professionals to "stiffen" the South Vietnamese formations it was in the process of constituting. Later, RVNAF aircraft would be flown by Vietnamese pilots, but the essential relationship of dependence on the United States for training, aircraft, and logistical support remained unchanged. Throughout its involvement, the U.S. inability to exercise direct control over RVN forces was the price paid for waging war with client forces. But "colonialism by ventriloquy," as it was sometimes called, is still a form of colonialism.[15]

The parody containment strategy made of the juridical status of combatants was frequently evident. The CIA, for example, sought "stateless" foreign personnel to staff its paramilitary forces. Free Poles, who had flown for the Royal Air Force in World War II and remained in Britain after the communist takeover of Poland, were recruited to fly missions supporting anticommunist forces in Albania. Later, they were part of the aerial "foreign legion" the CIA provided to the Permesta forces it backed in Indonesia in 1957–1958. When two Poles were killed flying CIA-directed strike missions against the Indonesian army, a CIA officer remarked that it did not matter "because none of them had been Americans" (quoted in Conboy and Morrison, 1999: 90). Later in the operation, a USAF pilot seconded to the CIA was shot down by the Indonesians. Suspecting he would face harsh treatment if captured with no identification, the pilot carried—against orders—his U.S. military identification and other official paperwork. His capture played a significant part in convincing the United States to scale back and ultimately abandon its support of the Permesta rebellion (Conboy and Morrison, 1999; Kahin and Kahin, 1995). Both the Guatemalan and Indonesian operations involved relatively minor commitments of U.S. military power. Even so, in both, small air forces provided by the CIA played decisive roles. In Indonesia the CIA was backing a weak military rebellion against an elected central government. But as two historians writing for the U.S. Naval Institute's Special Warfare series commented, "The Permesta struggle had become largely synonymous with the rebel bombing campaign," and that campaign was almost wholly a CIA-run affair (Conboy and Morrison, 1999: 122).

"Plausibly deniable" army and air forces were not necessarily limited to such a small scale. In Laos the United States fought, as William Colby put it, a twenty-year "nonattributable war" (quoted in Castle, 1993: 94). The 1954 Geneva Accords prevented both the United States and the USSR from deploying military personnel in Laos, even as advisers. As a consequence, U.S. military ability to advise and support was channeled through the civilian aid programs of the U.S. Embassy in Vientiane in order, in Henry Kissinger's words, to "avoid a formal avowal of American participation for diplomatic reasons" (quoted in Castle, 1993: 57). To prevent communists from coming to power electorally, the CIA initially tried to influence and finally rigged elections, producing Soviet-style results of over 99 percent of the vote for some of its favored candidates (Castle, 1993: 19; Stevenson, 1973: chapters 1–3). CIA intervention polarized Laotian politics. Leftist and nationalist forces turned to the Pathet Lao and its North Vietnamese supporters whereas the United States backed a right-wing military government, in support of which it ultimately developed large ground and air forces from a variety of U.S., Laotian, and "third-country" personnel. Nearly 30,000 Hmong, known as L'Armee Clandestine, were mobilized with the support of U.S. Special Forces, suffering some 10,000 killed over the course of the war (Castle, 1993: 122; Fall, 1969). Once again the CIA directly controlled strike aircraft, flown by conveniently discharged USAF pilots in planes with Royal Laotian Air Force markings. The U.S. ambassador in Vientiane, known as the "field marshal," adopted the role of general officer in command, coordinating significant USAF assets based in Thailand.

The war in Laos provides an image of the conduct of the Cold War in the periphery: U.S. and Soviet aircrew observing one another as they flew supply missions for their respective clients (Castle, 1993: 24–25). In July 1971 Under Secretary of State U. Alexis Johnson stated before the Senate Armed Services Committee that "the only U.S. forces involved in Laos are in the air. We have no combat forces stationed there." He went on to explain that as "under the Geneva Agreements we were prohibited from having American military personnel in Laos . . . [the] CIA is really the only other instrumentality we have" (quoted in Lens, 1987: 104). This "instrumentality" was the only way the U.S. executive could conduct operations, given the international and domestic constraints it faced. It made widespread use of U.S. as well as foreign military troops, just not in open fashion, making Johnson's statement legally correct. Analytic indicators of relations between political authority and military forces must address such instrumentalities. CoW dates U.S. involvement in Laos from 1964, approximately nine years after significant U.S. paramilitary activity began in the country, because that was when significant USAF assets began operating and the use of U.S. advisers became more widespread. The U.S. Congress was outfoxed for some time longer. In constitutional terms, the war in Laos was fought with, in Sidney Lens's apt phrase, "untraceable troops" (1987: 105).

The involvement of the United States in internal war, whether with foreign or national forces, was the predominant form of reciprocal organized violence between it and the Third World during the Cold War. Distinctions

between the foreign and national and the clandestine and "official" elements of U.S. military power were significant in terms of containment
diplomacy and U.S. and international law but not in terms of determining
whether the United States was waging war. The various forms of cover used
for U.S. and third-country personnel are indicative of the way in which the
legal status of superpower forces was in itself an aspect of their military
competition in the periphery. Yet international legalities must not obscure
the military operational realities. An executive authority used force in pursuit of its aims. In Laos, the U.S. war involved the subversion of elections
and the use of foreign forces. And it involved the subversion of the war
powers of the U.S. Congress, a consequence for democracy not recognized
in the debate over the democratic peace in which the United States is simply coded as "democratic."

THE INTERNATIONAL RELATIONS
OF DEMOCRACY AND WAR

Historical sociology and state-society approaches to international relations
focus on the mutual constitution of domestic and international processes.[16]
It need hardly be remarked that the internal processes of peripheral states are
uniquely susceptible to and shaped by the influence of international factors
of all kinds, including foreign involvement in their internal wars. As Naeem
Inayatullah comments, "How can the inside of any Third World state be seen
as disconnected from the outside of the world system?" (1996: 71).

Much less appreciated are the ways in which involvement in peripheral
wars shape the nature of core powers. The mutual constitution of the internal
and external can be observed in the case of U.S. unconventional warfare in
the Third World during the Cold War. The United States developed an extensive organizational and military apparatus for the conduct of "foreign internal
defense." Aspects of this apparatus have been discussed in the preceding
pages. They range from the covert operations functions of the intelligence
agencies to the development of an internal warfare capability for U.S. national armed forces. They also include the provisions made for the constitution of foreign military, police, and intelligence forces. Overall, these developments led to a dramatic increase in the war-making powers of the
executive branch of the U.S. government; that is, they had obvious consequences for U.S. democracy. Foreign forces raise direct questions about the
democratic control of war-making powers. They provide executive authority
with an end run around democratic constraints on war-making by sparing the
citizenry the costs of military service and evading legislative war powers.

The constitutional apparatus for the regulation of war powers is designed to control the use of national forces. Foreign forces are considered

by the legislature only in terms of the budget for foreign military assistance, not in their war-making capacity as instruments of U.S. policy. Foreign forces constituted through the CIA were largely exempt even from this form of congressional oversight. They provided the executive with troops largely outside the control of the legislature, especially prior to the increased congressional activism that developed from the latter stages of U.S. involvement in Vietnam. Issues such as these relate directly to consideration of relations between democracy and war but are not part of the DP debates as currently constituted. They fall under the broader rubric of the "international relations of democracy and war."

Covert operations were a means of carrying out foreign policy without normal democratic constraints. Crucially, these operations were generally only "covert" or "secret" from the perspective of the American public. Citizens and elites in the target country were often well aware of U.S. involvement. U.S. domestic secrecy enabled policymakers to evade many of the causal mechanisms suggested as explanations for the democratic peace. "Black budgets" and ineffective or nonexistent congressional oversight enabled the executive to evade the legislature. Oversight was further hampered by the fact that many operations, as well as the state terror of client security forces, were carried out by foreign nationals, not U.S. government officials subject to U.S. law. Secrecy also prevented electoral incentives from deterring the executive. Not only was the operation of the "free press" hampered by secrecy, but reporters and editors were often tacitly complicit—out of "patriotic" motives and shared ideology—or actively complicit by spreading disinformation, as was the case with the Guatemala operation (Kahin and Kahin, 1995: 158; Schlesinger and Kinzer, 1982; N. Sheehan, 1988: 315). The fear of failures becoming public, especially after the Bay of Pigs, was incentive for further secrecy. Although covert operations were developed in response to a perceived external threat as one weapon among many in the Cold War arsenal, they simultaneously enabled the executive to conduct foreign policies that might not have met with public approval. Public discussion of foreign policy was hampered by lack of knowledge of just what policies were being pursued.

Additionally, the intelligence and covert operations apparatuses developed in response to a foreign threat were employed domestically, directly undermining the civil and political rights of U.S. citizens. With the announced intent of uncovering foreign influence on domestic political dissent, the CIA instituted a number of programs to collect intelligence on dissident organizations and their activities. Beginning in 1952, an extensive mail-opening program was instituted for mail from foreign countries to Americans on a "watch list" that included the American Friends Service Committee, several congresspersons and senators, and even John Steinbeck. Files were maintained and surveillance conducted on thousands of antiwar groups and activists. Several agencies—most notably the Federal Bureau of Investigation but also including the DOD, CIA, the National Security Agency, and the Internal Revenue Service—conducted domestic surveillance, justified by fears of foreign influence, on what was constitutionally legitimate political activity. In 1968 around 1,500 U.S. Army agents were undercover in the antiwar movement. Even the civil rights movement was seen as susceptible to communist influence, and surveillance was justified in national security terms.[17] Evidently, the "foreign" threat was manifest inside the United States as well (see Campbell, 1992).

Most U.S. use of force in the Third World during the Cold War took the form of intervention in state-society conflicts in which the United States was involved on the side of narrowly based client states facing popular insurrection and the fighting was done predominantly by client state armies, paramilitaries, and police. It was in these internationalized internal conflicts that war decided questions of democracy, of whether and how the people would rule. From the perspective of U.S. containment strategy, popular forces seeking more democratic conditions of just distribution of material values and political power were perceived as externally inspired communist subversion requiring a military response. The crushing of popular revolt through military and police action is generally understood as antidemocratic. The use of interstate war as the only indicator of "war" in the DP proposition *removes from analysis* these forms of war waging and their relation to questions of democracy. Concepts of war and democracy erected on juridical distinctions between the inside and outside of sovereign states have no necessary or consistent relation to the social and political forces productive of war. In the context of relations between Third World states and the United States, these distinctions obviate the possibility of informal empire and hence of wars of informal empire.

War is a matter of the clash of armed forces in definite historical and social contexts; it is not conducted with legal distinctions or the juridical division of territory. The relations between democracy and war will be shaped by historical context, attention to which is necessary for meaningful analysis. I have not argued that U.S. use of force in the Third World invalidates or is an exception to the DP proposition but that the analytic categories of the latter are simply inapplicable. The effect of this argument is to reduce the scope of the zone of peace to a largely Western context. Coupled with more robust definitions of democracy, which hold that few or no democracies existed prior to the twentieth century, the geographic and temporal scope of the zone of peace is reduced even further. It can then be accounted for by alliances among the Western democracies against first the fascist and then the communist challenge and by the creation of new democracies in Germany and Japan through victory in total war. In historical context the statistical artifact of the "democratic peace" is much less significant than it at first appears.

NOTES

I thank Aaron Belkin, Susie Carruthers, Lisa Disch, Bud Duvall, Lynn Eden, Dan Froats, David Holloway, Mark Laffey, the members of the International Relations Colloquium, University of Minnesota, the participants in the MacArthur Consortium conference "Democratization: International and Domestic Security Dimensions," February 23–25, 1996, and the participants in the Social Science Research Council workshop on the state of the field of international peace and security, "Democracy, the Use of Force and Global Social Change," May 1–3, 1998, for comments on earlier versions of this chapter. The chapter was revised with the support of the John M. Olin Institute for Strategic Studies, Center for International Affairs, Harvard University, and the Social Science Research Council–MacArthur Foundation Program on International Peace and Security. An earlier version of this chapter was published as a MacArthur Consortium Working Paper in Peace and Cooperation, Center for International Security and Arms Control, Stanford University.

1. See Cohen, 1994; Doyle, 1996: 35–44; Forsythe, 1992; James and Mitchell, 1995; Ray, 1995: 36–37; Russett, 1993: 13, 120–124; Weart, 1998: chapter 13.

2. CoW has added a third major category of wars, "extra-systemic wars." See Wayman, Singer, and Sarkees, 1996. This category is used for wars between sovereign states and nonstate actors. It is still defined in terms of sovereignty, as "extra-systemic" refers to entities that are not members of the sovereign states system.

3. Needless to say, the recognition of sovereignty by bodies such as the League of Nations or the UN is no less political.

4. This characterization is more generally accepted in the case of Indochina. For Korea, see Cumings, 1981, 1991.

5. This is reflected in the CoW data. After 1945 there is only one instance of interstate war between first-rate powers (the border fighting between the Soviet Union and the PRC in 1969), and only 18 percent of all wars are classified as interstate.

6. Thanks to Dan Froats for this phrase.

7. Blum, 1995: chapter 21; Castle, 1993; Fall, 1969; Prados, 1996: chapter 14; Stevenson, 1973; Warner, 1996.

8. U.S. military forces were not used overtly in either operation, although U.S. military personnel participated in both covertly. Although casualties in Guatemala were far below 1,000, in Indonesia they exceeded 20,000 over the course of the CIA-backed Permesta rebellion (Kahin and Kahin, 1995: 305).

9. For this reason I suspect, as well as the fact that CIA bombing raids were flown from Honduran and Nicaraguan airfields, Kalevi Holsti (1996: 216) bizarrely classifies the Guatemalan operation as one of Honduran and Nicaraguan intervention! This is a salutary lesson in the absurdity of classifying war by reference to sovereign territory.

10. For the Guatemalan operation, see Blum, 1995; Cullather, 1999; Gleijeses, 1991; Prados, 1996; Schlesinger and Kinzer, 1982.

11. As elsewhere in the Third World, U.S. support in Guatemala of an authoritarian and military regime in the face of a social democratic challenge served to

polarize politics. The left eventually turned to armed rebellion, creating a threat to U.S. interests much more expensive to combat in the long term.

12. See Brands, 1993; Campbell, 1992; Paterson, 1988. For Charles Wolf the Soviet Union had "proxies" or "surrogates" in the Third World whereas the West had "cooperative forces." See Wolf and Webb, 1987.

13. From a clarification of the Nixon Doctrine provided by the White House, quoted in Gaddis, 1982: 298.

14. Sheehan, 1988: 64. One could see the USAF markings on the planes underneath the freshly painted South Vietnamese colors.

15. "Ventriloquy" is evident in the many instances in which the United States had client governments "officially request" U.S. military aid, advise and support, or deployments to defend them against attack. See Castle, 1993: 18, for an example from Laos.

16. See, for example, Abrams, 1982; Halliday, 1994; Mann, 1993; McNeill, 1982; Shaw, 1988; Shaw and Banks, 1991; Tilly, 1992.

17. See Brands, 1993: 110–115; Halperin et al., 1976; Lens, 1987; Theoharis, 1978; Wise and Ross, 1974.

7

Warfare, Security, and Democracy in East Asia

Bruce Cumings

A new and interesting literature has emerged since the end of the Cold War, arguing that the proliferation of democratic governments in the 1980s and 1990s—whether in formerly communist nations or in those run by right-wing authoritarian systems—holds out the hope of a long peace in our time because of the propensity of democracies not to fight each other.[1] Other chapters in this volume assess this argument, but I want to examine the origins of contemporary democratic systems in Japan, South Korea, and Taiwan and to argue that the happy outcome of democratic governance cannot be understood apart from the warfare that afflicted East Asia from 1931 to 1975 and the security divisions that have constructed the map of the region from 1945 to the present. All three countries are simultaneously democracies and semisovereign, penetrated states, nested in a U.S. hegemonic regime that was made and remade in the early postwar period and that has easily outlived the end of the Cold War and the collapse of the Soviet Union.

I also will argue that a transnational and regional security approach to understanding political development in the region can explain why Japan has a strong democracy and a weak civil society, why South Korea has a strong civil society and (finally) a strong democracy, and why Taiwan has both a weak civil society and a weak democracy. (In this chapter I speak of democracy and civil society not interchangeably but with the assumption that the two concepts are inextricably related.)

To the extent that this is true, my argument would undermine a cardinal assumption of the "democratic peace" (DP) literature—namely, that we can best understand our world by assuming a norm of sovereign nation-states, which can be categorized as democratic or authoritarian, rather than by examining transnational systems and hierarchies of power that may enhance or retard democratization. Explicitly and implicitly I also argue against a nation-specific modernization ontology that assumes a direct relationship between economic and political development. As for the concurrent presumption that the United States has been behind the spread of liberal democracy and market capitalism, I argue that attention might better be directed to a history in which democracy in Northeast Asia came to Japan only in conditions of abject defeat and foreign occupation and to South Korea and Taiwan in spite of U.S. support for decades of authoritarianism. Moreover, the democratic United States was at war in Asia from 1941 to 1975, with two of the wars (Korea and Vietnam) resulting from native attempts at national independence and decolonization. Meanwhile, market capitalism has had little to do with East Asian development, as the International Monetary Fund made clear with its attempt to reform the South Korean political economy in 1997–1998. I frame my argument at the beginning and end of this chapter with a non-Asian country that is central to all of my analysis, namely, the United States. I briefly examine contemporary U.S. debates about democracy and civil society, and in the conclusion I will argue that the United States itself is by no means free of the link between warfare and democracy.

The question of whether democracies fight each other, as analysts of the problem frequently note, depends on two key terms: What is war, and what is democracy? Bruce Russett limits his purview to interstate wars in which more than 1,000 people die. Spencer Weart defines war more specifically as "violence organized by political units against one another across their boundaries," in which organized combat produces at least 200 deaths (1998: 12–13). For both authors, therefore, the two major wars of the postwar era, in Korea and Vietnam, do not by definition figure into their calculus. Russett's book has no index entries for either war (although the reader might infer from their exclusion that Korea and Vietnam belong to either the category of civil war or wars of national liberation—both of which he excludes from his analysis) (1993: 12–15). Weart, on the other hand, appears to rule out Korea and Vietnam because neither the North nor the South was a democracy, while appearing to assume that in both cases the northern communists were the basic cause of the wars (1998: 197–198, 205).

As for the question What is democracy? Russett deploys the typical U.S. political scientist's answer by assuming that Robert Dahl's procedural definition of democracy, or polyarchy, is definitive; as we will see later there is no reason to take that definition as a given. Weart's discussion of democracy is more nuanced and extensive than Russett's; although he focuses on the domestic structure of political republics (paying no attention to structures of the international realm), ultimately he departs from that focus to argue that only an established democratic *political culture* can guarantee that two states having such a culture will not fight each other. His definition thus involves both the procedural formalities of republican democracy and rooted beliefs (in tolerance, compromise, fair play) that make for a democratic civil society (Weart, 1998: 9–21 and passim; on political culture see chapter 5). Both authors firmly believe their books prove the case that democracies never fight each other (or, in Russett's words, "almost never" do so [1993: 3–4]; Weart's adverb is "scarcely ever" [1998: 36]). If so, peace in our time would seem to be guaranteed because the advanced industrial countries are all democracies, according to both authors; elsewhere it will depend on creating democratic republics and political cultures where none may have existed before—a much more daunting proposition.

Weart has an open-minded and commonsensical approach to his subject, and perhaps for that reason he almost gives away the "democratic peace" game by saying that ultimately, no matter how we might classify political regimes, "the real question is how leaders of the time characterized their rivals." Given, for example, Thomas Jefferson's view during the War of 1812 that Britain was not a democracy but an aristocracy—and a rotten and corrupt one to boot—"cannot leaders always find an excuse for war in the flaws of a foreign regime?" His answer—that such distortions have only surfaced historically "when a regime was already in an ambiguous border zone"— merely begs the question, in my view (Weart, 1998: 133, 137). In Korea and Vietnam both sides characterized themselves as democracies; neither Russett nor Weart would accept this categorization, but U.S. policymakers certainly argued for the democratic character of both southern sides, whereas many supporters of the northern sides believed the republics supported by the United States were autocracies—and rotten and corrupt ones to boot.

A more challenging case is postwar Japan. Weart clearly classifies Japan as a democratic republic with a democratic political culture, and so would I. But as trade conflict with Japan grew in the 1980s, as we will see later, some influential Americans began to argue that Japan was not really a democracy and had an authoritarian political culture falling into a new category defined by "Asian values." Furthermore, Japan deployed a predatory form of neomercantilism that made for an alternative type of capitalism and a rival to the United States. Interestingly enough, Weart's analysis also takes him into this thorny and difficult terrain of national character, cultural difference, and binary categorizations of self and other that are questionable, to say the least.[2] It would appear that democracy is less a defined system than a perception in the eye of the beholder, which can change as conflict between two countries grows. We can better understand this paradox when we examine contemporary U.S. debate about civil society and democracy.

CIVIL SOCIETY AND DEMOCRACY IN WEST AND EAST

For much of the 1990s the U.S. political spectrum from right to left was suffused with deeply conflicted concerns about U.S. democracy and civil society. Most commentators pointed to a host of common symptoms: citizen apathy and disinterest in voting, the pathologies and dangers of the public space (in cities), high rates of crime amid a more general breakdown of morality, the disintegration of nuclear families, cynicism about the political system, the debasement of public debate (particularly on television, the primary medium for delivering that debate), and an absence of political and national leadership. If these concerns were understandably deepened by the failed impeachment of President Bill Clinton, they nonetheless long predated that episode and continued after it was settled.

Harvard political scientist Robert Putnam has been lauded across the U.S. political spectrum, from the left-leaning *Nation* to the conservative *Economist,* for his books *Making Democracy Work* (1993) and *Bowling Alone* (2000).[3] The first book is a study of civil society in general and within the specific confines of Italy, but it begins with a discussion of the widespread despair in the United States about public institutions and democratic possibilities, continues with the exemplary civic virtue of northern Italy and the lack of it in southern Italy, and ends on a pessimistic note: "Where norms and networks of civic engagement are lacking, the outlook for collective action appears bleak. The fate of the Mezzogiorno is an object lesson for the Third World today and the former Communist lands of Eurasia tomorrow, moving uncertainly toward self-government" (Putnam, 1993: 183).[4] Putnam thinks Robert Dahl and Seymour Martin Lipset were right in stressing the contribution of modernization to democracy: "Nothing is more obvious even to the casual observer than the fact that effective democracy is closely associated with socioeconomic modernity, both across time and space" (Putnam, 1993: 11). He also rehabilitates Gabriel Almond and Sidney Verba's *Civic Culture* (1963), calling it "a modern classic" in the vein of Alexis de Tocqueville's *Democracy in America* (Putnam, 1993: 11).[5]

Putnam's own theory draws heavily on the Weberian/Parsonian pattern variables that Almond and Verba used nearly forty years ago, renaming them "norms of civic engagement," "social structures of cooperation," and the like. The quality of a democratic citizenry depends on its "civic virtue," according to Putnam, and like Weart he argues that the presence of this virtue gives us the best explanation for well-functioning civil societies and democracies—resting on civic engagement, political equality, the attenuation of individual striving in the interests of community, "solidarity, trust, and tolerance," and a network of civic or secondary associations: indeed, a key indicator of "civic sociability" is the "vibrancy of associational life" (Putnam, 1993: 86–91).

Simultaneously, however, contemporary writers of great influence argued that civil society is inherently a Western concept and practice and that it is absent in the remaining communist countries, the thing most in need of creation in postcommunist countries, and the thing mostly absent in East

Asia—whether in authoritarian Singapore, democratic Japan, or the newly industrialized countries of South Korea and Taiwan. In this discourse, which became common in the United States, the ills and pathologies of U.S. civil society curiously disappear, to be replaced surreptitiously by an idealized construction drawn from John Locke and Tocqueville. In the democratic peace literature we also find a similar Kantian discourse that privileges the West but not "the rest."

Samuel Huntington made such views famous, if not notorious, in his book *The Clash of Civilizations* (1996), which sought to fashion a new paradigm for post–Cold War global politics; according to Huntington, the Putnam/Almond and Verba model of modernization yielding parliamentary democracy fits with Atlanticist civilization but not with any of his five other global civilizations. But perhaps Karel van Wolferen's *Enigma of Japanese Power* (1989) is the best recent example of the argument that East Asia industrialized without civil society and without an Enlightenment. This book would merit no more than a footnote were it not so influential in U.S. circles: at one point in late 1993 van Wolferen performed the feat of having articles published simultaneously in *New Left Review, Foreign Affairs,* and the *National Interest,* thereby blanketing the spectrum of intellectual opinion from left to right.

For van Wolferen "the West" connotes a site of "independent, universal truths or immutable religious beliefs, transcending the worldly reality of social dictates and the decrees of power-holders"; Japan, however, is a place where people adjust their beliefs to situations in "a political culture that does not recognize the possibility of transcendental truths." Japan for van Wolferen is an enigma, led by a mysterious, opaque "System" that "single-mindedly pursu[es] some obscure aim of its own." The System "systematically suppresses individualism," he writes; nor do the Japanese accept Western logic or metaphysics, going all the way back to "the Greeks." The "crucial factor" that proves these generalizations is "the near absence [in Japan] of any idea that there can be truths, rules, principles or morals that always apply, no matter what the circumstances" (van Wolferen, 1989: 1–10, 23–24). Koreans might think the same thing of Japan, but van Wolferen does not like any of the East Asian political systems: "The Japanese, Korean and Taiwanese experiences show that a third category of political economy can exist, beside the Western and communist types." These states represent "a largely uncharted economic and social-political category" (1989: 5–8, 23–24).

To anticipate arguments I develop later: the greatest power of our time, the United States, was at war in East Asia from 1941 to 1975. It fought two of the bloodiest wars in the twentieth century in Korea (1950–1953) and Vietnam (1961–1975), stalemating with one enemy and losing to another because of the extraordinary sacrifices of huge numbers of people—mostly peasants—in Korea, China, and Vietnam. Through all this, Japan, Korea, and China also ought to have become liberal, van Wolferen and many others imply—namely, to have developed stable democracy and an open civil society. Of course, many analysts now argue that some did: South Korea and Taiwan are celebrated as victories for democracy, coming (predictably) toward the end of a process of "modernization" in which a middle class emerged triumphant. But the path to this end was hardly smooth; instead it was filled with decades of torment and turmoil: Sturm und Drang and then—and only then—democracy.

Like van Wolferen, the recent civil society literature identifies civil society and pluralist democracy with the West: these things originated in Western Europe and migrated to North America and the British Commonwealth and hardly anywhere else. Non-Western societies are simply not suitable settings for civil society and republican democracy, Putnam suggests. *The Civic Culture* reported these Western conceits straightforwardly in 1963, a time of higher U.S. self-confidence and less self-awareness; only in the United States and Britain did the authors find "a pattern of political attitudes and an underlying set of social attitudes that is supportive of a stable democratic process." In the other nations they studied (West Germany, Italy, and Mexico), "these patterns are less evident" (Almond and Verba, 1963: x).[6]

Jürgen Habermas is the world's preeminent theorist of civil society, or what he calls the public sphere *(Öffentlichkeit)*. His life work has combined a deep knowledge of the continental tradition and its heights (especially for him in the work of Kant, Hegel, Marx, Nietzsche, and Weber), with an unusual interest in positivist and systemic Anglo-Saxon social science. From the latter he draws upon the Parsonian concern with norms, roles, and systems of both that influenced Almond, Verba, and Putnam (e.g., Habermas, 1984).[7] Habermas's work is on a much more sophisticated plane, and yet he also privileges the West as the site of the origin of his "public sphere" and its contemporary problematic, as well as its ultimate redemption. Surely he ought to know better, yet he concluded one of his books on "modernity" with this statement: "Who else but Europe could draw from its own traditions the insight, the energy, the courage of vision—everything that would be necessary to strip from the . . . premises of a blind compulsion to system maintenance and system expansion their power to shape our mentality" (Habermas, 1987: 367). This is not an unusual emphasis for Habermas, even if it is unusually blunt; his entire work is imbued with "the claim that the modern West—for all its problems—best embodies" the values of rationality and democracy (White, 1995: 9). Thus he shares the same prejudices of his cherished predecessor Max Weber (Habermas is most of all a Weberian) but not Weber's passionate and intelligent comparativist project—and in a time when Weber would certainly recognize his own provincialism, were he still talking about "only in the West." But perhaps we had better sample the original Weber, since we do not know what he would say now: "Only the occident knows the state in the modern sense, with a professional adminis-tration, specialized officialdom, and law based on the concept of citizen-ship. . . . Only the occident knows rational law. . . . Furthermore, only the occident possesses science. . . . Finally, western civilization is further dis-tinguished from every other by the presence of men with a rational ethic for the conduct of life" (M. Weber, 1981: 312–314).[8]

A person we can call "the early Habermas" had a different view. In his 1961 book *The Structural Transformation of the Public Sphere,* Habermas (1989) showed how the liberal (or bourgeois) public sphere, a limited but vital civil society in the eighteenth century, turned into a bureaucratized, alienated public space still marching under the banner of the French *philosophes'* ideals of civic virtue.[9] The primary cause of this transforma-tion was the arrival of masses of laborers in Europe's cities; thereafter we had a bourgeois public sphere and a *"plebeian* public sphere" that repre-sents the entrance of the masses onto the political stage (Habermas, 1989: xvii–xviii). Habermas thought the Chartist movement was the specific cause of this change—that is, the moment when organized labor first burst upon the industrial scene. Habermas summarized his account of the de-composition of the liberal public sphere as follows:

> Marx shared the perspective of the propertyless and uneducated masses who . . . would employ the platform of the public sphere, institutionalized in the constitutional state, not to destroy it but to make it into what, ac-cording to liberal pretense, it had always claimed to be. In reality, how-ever, the occupation of the public sphere by the unpropertied masses led to an interlocking of state and society which removed from the public sphere its former basis without supplying a new one. (1989: 177)

Thereafter a general fear of people in the mass yielded a procedural politics that gives us "tolerance" but not the substance of participatory democracy. Is this a better explanation of the democratic malaise the Putnams of the world point to or not? In my view, Habermas delivered in 1961 an unan-swerable critique of actually existing liberalism. But implicitly this discus-sion raises a question prior to all this: What is democracy?

WHAT IS DEMOCRACY?

For Adam Przeworski democracy exists if another party can win an elec-tion.[10] Joseph Schumpeter also preferred this form of politics, yielding a circulation of party elites. The premier U.S. democratic theorist, Robert Dahl, would not disagree; although he places more emphasis on political equality as a key prerequisite for democracy than Przeworski or Schumpeter, their basic schemes of pluralist democracy are rather similar. As C. B. Macpherson put it, "The Schumpeter-Dahl axis . . . treats democracy as a mechanism, the essential function of which is to maintain an equilibrium [between] two or more élite groups for the power to govern society" (1973: 78). In our terms, this is mere procedural democracy, less interested in developing the civic virtues of participation than in restraining civil society. Dahl's account, like Putnam's, is also marked by the implicit idea that democracy is what you get in the West but not elsewhere for the most part, and it is passively satisfied with the outcomes of procedural justice.[11] Yet Dahl is the primary theorist used by the political scientists who have produced most of the democratic peace literature.

A contrary perspective is provided in an important recent book, *Capitalist Development and Democracy* (Rueschemeyer, Stephens, and Stephens, 1992), offering a perspective supported by the East Asian evidence I will survey later. The authors begin by agreeing with Lipset's famous judgment that economic development and pluralist democracy are positively related. But they offer very different explanations for this correlation. The political outcomes of development have to do with four elements, in their view: (1) the pattern of agrarian transition, (2) the empowerment of subordinate classes through industrialization (the middle class, but especially the working class), (3) the type of state structure, and (4) transnational power relations (something all the other accounts of democratization leave out). The authors also have a sense of timing, especially the persistence over time in certain "late"-developing countries of particular agrarian social relations, industrialization patterns, roles for the state, and variant positions within the world system.

Capitalist development is associated with democracy because as a by-product of growth it transforms class structures, undermining old ones and creating new ones. The new middle classes, however, will fight to the point of their own democratic representation but not beyond; after that, they will seek to restrict working-class representation (just like Mill and Tocqueville, Putnam and Lipset, in other words—a "yes" but then again a "no"). And here we have a nice explanation for the continuing absence of labor representation in South Korea and Taiwan and the fecklessness of the two "labor" parties in Japan—the socialists and the communists. In the United States the Democratic Party functioned as a business/labor coalition from 1932 through the 1980s, but the "neodemocrats" who were in power in Washington thought they had to attend to the interests of the middle class, to the detriment of the old Democratic coalition. Perhaps this means the middle class will also seek to disestablish working-class representation.

As for the international element, Rueschemeyer, Stephens, and Stephens (1992) rightly emphasize that geopolitical and other great power interests generated direct interventions and support for repressive states. In the case of East Asia, prewar Japan's authoritarianism was in part an outcome of the breakdown of the world economy and outside economic pressure from the United States and Britain (although neither supported its repressive state). Meanwhile Japan's postwar democracy has "nested" in a U.S.-dominated security regime: U.S. policing of East Asian security left Japan alone to be "developmental"; its status as an "economic animal" shorn of military and political clout in the world was a clear and conscious result of U.S. strategy. I argue later that the authoritarian regimes that prevailed in South Korea and Taiwan until the end of the 1980s can be seen in part as the completion of a Japan-centered economic and security sphere in Northeast Asia. With all this in mind, let me now turn from West to East.

WARFARE, SECURITY, AND DEMOCRACY IN EAST ASIA

A shorthand way to grasp how war and democracy have interacted in East Asia would be this: Japan became a democracy after 1945 but only after the cataclysm of war and military occupation; South Korea, a democracy by 1998 but only after the cataclysm of revolution, war, division, and decades of military dictatorship (1961–1987) and sharp political struggle; Taiwan, a democracy by the 1990s but only after revolution, war, national division, and forty years of martial law (1947–1987). Now we can backtrack to look at the state structures and regional forces that operated in the region in the twentieth century.

I argue that state structures—whether those of authoritarian or democratic regimes—are shaped by a matrix of domestic (or internal), regional, and global experience growing out of interactions between state and society and metropole and periphery. States are both *shapers of* domestic social forces and regional influences and are *shaped by* those same forces. As metropolitan states seek to shape their environment, they react by successive openings and closures, or degrees of each, and thus create changes in state structure and state-society relations (known in the twentieth century as New Deals and New Orders). They also effect openings and closures in their regions, making them more or less penetrable by external forces, and thus they make and remake regional orders (known by names like the Good Neighbor Policy or the Greater East Asian Co-Prosperity Sphere). Regional dynamics also arise from a matrix of metropolitan power involvements, contemporary and historical, and are not simply the reflection of the character and will of the central metropolitan power. Regions will have a mix of economic and security interests; indeed, the boundaries of a region often coincide with international security lines. Different regional contexts vary in their intensity and explanatory power for domestic state structure.

Let me summarize (with drastic compression) what premodern state structures in East Asia looked like. Premodern China and Korea exemplified agrarian-bureaucratic states characterized by relatively well-developed central bureaucracies that competed with social forces (landed classes especially) for scarce resources and did not penetrate much below the county administrative level. The state, ever in search of revenues, was predatory rather than developmental. China fostered limited trade with its neighbors (the tributary system) and had limited security concerns (e.g., the Ming intervention against Hideyoshi in Korea in the 1590s). But China provided strong ideological legitimation (the Chinese world order, Confucianism) and a clear model for peripheral state structures to emulate (exemplified in the Korean and Vietnamese civil service and their statecraft).

Japan, on the contrary, had a fundamentally different structure of parcelized sovereignty, feudal domains associated with a strong military tradition, and a weak central state (although stronger than those in classical European feudalism). Before the nineteenth century ended it was the only East Asian society to resist Western imperialism effectively (all three East Asian countries in the 1860s sought a "restoration" as a means to stave off imperial conquest, but only Japan succeeded—through a state-directed revolution disguised as the Meiji Restoration). As modern Japan developed, it expanded into a region of multiple imperial rivalry, overlaid on the residues of the Chinese Middle Kingdom, or tributary system. It overcame the Chinese residue in the 1894–1895 Sino-Japanese War by detaching Korea and Taiwan from the Chinese world order, then overcame the Russian threat in 1905 and British and U.S. threats in 1931 (Manchuria) and 1941 (by becoming hegemonic in East and Southeast Asia, if only for four years).

The modern Japanese state thus emerged in two phases, each phase having much to do with "timing of insertion" into the world system, late industrial development, and warfare. The first experience was the Prusso-Japanese phase in the late nineteenth century, a state that was bureaucratic, meritocratic, developmental, and exclusionary. The second experience was Japan's New Order in the 1930s, which added a corporate character and ideology to the state while deepening its developmental character through heavy industrialization schemes that brought high growth rates to Northeast Asia. Japan's regional imperial strategy in the 1930s was architectonic, transnationally administrative (with transnational state agencies, banks, and firms), developmental (the largest heavy industrial spurt in the Northeast Asian region occurred in the mid- and late 1930s), and ideologically pan-Asian and racial. This state, however, existed within a general configuration of total mobilization for war and thus was highly exclusionary, with a vastly distended military and police component at home and in the colonies. Unlike liberal and communist states, Japan had no democratic pretensions or legitimation; rather, Japan's leaders pushed warrior ideals and denigrated Western democracy as weak and spirit sapping. But Japanese colonial authorities were state builders in Taiwan, Korea, and Manchuria—with resulting highly centralized, autonomous, penetrative state apparatuses and national policing systems. The colonial governments were coercive, administrative, and entrepreneurial security states, and they survived virtually intact in postwar South Korea and Taiwan. These postwar states were fashioned in a cauldron of imperialism, industrialization, and warfare.

On August 15, 1945, General Douglas MacArthur issued General Order Number One, announcing the division of Korea, China, and Vietnam and a unilateral occupation of Japan. This happened fundamentally because the United States feared the anti-imperial, antisystemic, revolutionary nationalists who soon took power in North Korea, China, and North Vietnam; their incipient alliance with the Soviet Union; and their addiction to the Soviet model of industrialization. The U.S. occupation demolished the Japanese military, eliminated rural landlords, and reformed the big firms (*zaibatsu* became *keiretsu*), but it left the state bureaucracy alone to govern Japan. The United States established a lateral penetration of and leverage over the Japanese state by keeping bases on its territory and establishing a defense dependency while shaping the flow of important resources like oil to Japan. The obliteration of the Japanese empire in 1945 was followed quickly in 1947 by a U.S.-sponsored restoration and reintegration of areas still available to Japan (Taiwan, South Korea, Southeast Asia). The United States also wrote the rules of regional interaction, but for the first three decades after 1945 it encouraged or tolerated protected home markets and hot-house industrial development in Japan, South Korea, and Taiwan. The American way of democracy, or what Huntington called the "Tudor polity model" of constitutional pluralism, was weakly advocated by the United States and failed to develop throughout the region.

The postwar restructuring of the Japanese state by a seven-year U.S. occupation, however, left the country with a strong democratic system and a weak civil society. The state was externally penetrated and weak in relation to society (but Japanese society remained docile by virtue of occupation-sponsored reforms, especially the incorporation of labor into "peak bargaining" with the state and big business); the state was strong in relation to the domestic economy and was legitimated by democracy at home and constitutional prohibitions on the use of military force abroad. Japan thus became for decades a single-party democracy under the Liberal Democratic Party (LDP), an anticommunist party funded at its inception in 1955 by the Central Intelligence Agency (CIA) (for reasons of security); the LDP remained in power continuously until 1993, when it suffered a brief hiccup, and remains in power today.

South Korea appeared to follow the Tudor Polity model with its 1948 constitution, written with the help of Americans in the occupation, but that was mere formal appearance. Korea's First Republic was a harsh and deeply corrupt authoritarian state, finally overthrown in a popular rebellion in 1960. A military coup in 1961, however, led by officers who had been in the Japanese military, revived the 1930s model of a total security state (symbolized by the ubiquitous Korean Central Intelligence Agency, founded in 1961) and state-led neomercantile industrial development. That authoritarian model brought rapid industrial development but collapsed in 1979–1980 with the assassination of Park Chung Hee, only to be revived by his disciple Chôn Tu-hwan in 1981; whereupon it finally died in 1993 with the accession of an elected civilian government. The presupposition of the dictators—the essential enabling element of their power—was that Washington would support them as long as the Soviet or the North Korean security threat remained palpable, an assumption that held true until the Cold War ended and was punctuated dramatically by the massacre of protesters in the southwestern city of Kwangju in 1980 (which happened on Jimmy Carter's watch).

Taiwan was influenced by both the 1930s Japanese and the 1920s–1930s Chinese nationalist experience on the mainland, yielding a single-party authoritarian system that governed under martial law from 1947 to 1987. Its security was underpinned, first, by alliance with the United States from 1950 to 1979 and since then by surreptitious and often purposely ambiguous U.S. security guarantees (given Washington's greater interest in the People's Republic of China [PRC] after 1979). In the 1990s Nationalist Party dominance gave way to a multiparty electoral system. Civil society was weak in Taiwan throughout the twentieth century, whether during the Japanese colonial period or from 1945 to 1998. The reasons have to do fundamentally with the absence of a land question and the infertile soil for Taiwanese nationalism (which was never remotely comparable to Japanese or Korean nationalism and has had to contend with mainlander "nationalism" since 1945) (Cumings, 1999).

Both Taiwan and South Korea had huge, distended militaries—way out of proportion to country size—but both represented a bulwark against communism on the mainland; both military structures represented a completion of the Japanese state in a regional sense (if South Korea and Taiwan did not have strong militaries, Japan could not have a weak one). Both states had significant autonomy from society by virtue of their capture by exiles; the main result of this was a reformist land redistribution, which was complete in both countries by the early 1950s. Both were deeply penetrated by a U.S. military and Agency for International Development regime, and both were inveterately exclusionary toward labor.

South Korea and Taiwan were "penetrated" by external power, namely, the U.S. security regime. What does that mean concretely? First it means an open spigot of money. From the beginning, U.S. aid flowed to Korea and

Taiwan in comparatively huge amounts, all of it justified by the security considerations of the Cold War. In the late 1940s the total U.S. aid level to the Republic of Korea (ROK) alone was about $220 million per annum (U. Johnson, 1984: 97)—more than Truman Doctrine aid to Greece and Turkey combined. The entire ROK national budget for FY 1951 was $120 million, with $27 million formally earmarked for defense (actually about 80 percent went for defense and internal security).[12] Analytically, therefore, U.S. money subsidized a state policy in which President Syngman Rhee and the social formation he represented used the strong colonial bureaucracy to repress their enemies and perpetuate their social position; domestic state revenues paid for coercion, and the United States paid for everything else. Much the same was true of Taiwan.

One high point for this flow of resources was 1957, when Korea drew $383 million in economic assistance from the United States as against $456 million in domestic revenue. But military aid made for an additional $400 million, not to mention another $300 million for the cost of maintaining U.S. troops in Korea. This military aid figure alone was higher than that for all of Europe and quadrupled the total military assistance to all of Latin America.[13] We often hear that Korea had an annual per capita income of $100 in 1960. Yet one analyst came up with an annual U.S. per capita assistance figure of $600 from 1945 to 1976—that is, $600 for every Korean man, woman, and child for thirty years.

Unlike Japan and Taiwan, civil war raged up and down the Korean peninsula in the early 1950s, which in odd ways helped to loosen the grip of what modernization theorists like to call "tradition." What the Japanese had begun with their massive mobilization of the Korean population in 1935–1945 and the national division had intensified in the late 1940s, the Korean War completed: Koreans of all classes were now thoroughly dislocated from their local roots. Everyone was jostled, pushed, or thrown bodily out of their social niche. The capacity of agrarian elites to control the people "below them" in clan, clientele, and tenancy lineages, and their continual tendency to control markets and stifle free enterprise, were blasted to smithereens. People could no longer be frozen in place in rural settings; two successive wars had set them loose, and they piled into the cities by the millions in succeeding years (South Korea is now more urbanized than the United States). In a country with such solidity of lineage and place, there now arrived the time of Thomas Hobbes's "masterless men," harbingers of anomie and modernity. Here is the deep meaning of the axiom that war is the great equalizer.

In place of the old aristocracy came entrepreneurs who had built up wealth through the auxiliary supply of warfare, a small but significant middle class of people engaged in commerce or attached to the enormous foreign presence and its many organizations, and rough people who had prospered at the nexus of human despair through money lending and corruption or simply the provision of services otherwise scarce in wartime (clothing, shelter, food, drink, sex). All these people were fertilized by the inconceivable amounts of U.S. cash that flowed into the country, down from the embassy and the presidential mansion through the civil and military bureaucracies, coursing through the PXs onto the black market and into the pockets of a horde of people who serviced the foreign presence: drivers, guards, runners, valets, maids, houseboys, black market operators, money changers, prostitutes, and beggars. Chông Chu-yông, later the billionaire chairman of the Hyundai Corporation, had run a small auto repair shop before the war but got his big break by ferrying supplies to U.S. bases on half-ton trucks or constructing troop billets. Many of the other *chaebôl* groups (sprawling conglomerates with many subsidiaries) got going at this time; there had been but a handful of big Korean enterprises before the war.

Standing above all the disorganization and human fragmentation of post-1953 Korea was a Korean military that had swelled from 100,000 in 1950 to well over 600,000 by 1953. It was now the strongest, most cohesive, best-organized institution in Korean life, and it soon made its political power felt. National conscription sent every male who could not bribe his way out through the ROK army's brand of education: boot camps, drills, discipline, patriotism, anticommunism, and an authoritarian practice that chilled even the most hard-bitten U.S. officers. The Korean military fought no more wars (save for some tens of thousands who went to Vietnam), but in the next thirty years it provided a school for industrial discipline. Max Weber, after all, once likened the modern factory to a military organization, so the relevance to Korea's economic development is abundant, as are the devastating consequences for Korean democracy.

Another bonanza came along in the form of the Vietnam War. Lyndon Johnson consistently escalated the war in Vietnam in 1965 and 1966 and sought to get an allied commitment like that which had accompanied the U.S. intervention in Korea. Park Chung Hee had already offered several times to send Korean troops to Vietnam, and after several months of negotiations the Koreans squeezed a large pile of cash and aid commitments out of Washington, estimated at $7.5 million per division. The operative document was the so-called Brown Memorandum of March 4, 1966, under which about $1 billion in U.S. payments went to Korea in the period 1965–1970. Scholars estimated that this arrangement accounted for between 7 and 8 percent of Korean gross domestic product annually in the period 1966–1969 and as much as 19 percent of total foreign earnings (Macdonald, 1992: 110; Woo, 1991: 93–96). Nearly 50,000 Korean soldiers fought in Vietnam, and by the time they withdrew in 1973, as many as 300,000 Koreans had served there. Vietnam also became a frontier for Korean enterprise, as many firms—especially construction companies like Hyundai—got contracts to support the American effort. For example, Vietnam absorbed 94 percent of Korea's total steel exports and 52 percent of its export of transportation equipment.[14] For Koreans it was a welcome irony, since Japan had gotten its economy going through U.S. procurements during the Korean War—something one scholar called "Japan's Marshall Plan" (C. Johnson, 1982). All this underlines the way in which warfare in East Asia was the handmaiden to economic growth in the period 1935–1975—and an overwhelming impediment to democratization.

South Korea's strong civil society of today cannot be attributed to U.S. beneficence and support for liberal democracy, nor is it simply a result of economic development, as Robert Putnam would argue. It is instead a perfect demonstration of the salutary contributions of conflict and struggle for strengthening civil society and for achieving democratic politics. Korea's democratic system is owed entirely to the bottom-up growth of a democratic movement that constituted itself in opposition to the authoritarian system—a system that is inexplicable apart from the multitude of urban student, labor, and middle-class protest groups that were the objects of its dictatorship.

Democratic struggles began in Korea the day Japan surrendered in August 1945 and have continued to the present. The popular forces of the late 1940s wanted both democracy and social justice—that is, a cleansing revolution that would wipe away the influences of Japanese imperialism. They got a cleansing in North Korea but no democracy and little if any cleansing democracy in South Korea. Within the constricted politics of the Rhee regime (1948–1960), where any sign of a leftist orientation meant a jail term if not death, a space for the intelligentsia cracked open enough so students, faculty, and intellectuals could be the vanguard for an overthrow of the First Republic in April 1960, albeit when Syngman Rhee was on his last legs and (most important) when the United States wanted him out.

The tepid opposition organized the Second Republic through a weak cabinet system of government, where for a year (April 1960–May 1961) civil society on the liberal model mushroomed rapidly. At this time South Korea had more college students per capita than Britain, more newspaper readers per capita than almost any country in the world, and a concentration of administrative, commercial, industrial, and educational energies in one great capital city—much like Paris.[15] A lively salon society animated the capital, publishers brought out thorough rewritings of modern Korean history, and students began to imagine themselves the vanguard of unification with the North.

General Park Chung Hee shut down civil society with his coup d'état in 1961 and the three-year emergency junta that followed and began to deploy the state as the initiator, guide, and financier of a classic type of "late" industrialization. Strong U.S. pressure from the Kennedy administration forced Park to drop his plans for instant heavy industrialization and to don mufti and run for election (in 1963), yielding "export-led development" and the contentious public sphere I still remember from my first encounter with it in 1967. The Nixon administration, however, enlarged the sphere of Korean autonomy through the Nixon Doctrine and Richard Nixon's neo-mercantilist New Economic Policy of August 1971, enabling Park to shut down democratic strivings completely in 1971–1972—with barely a murmur from Washington—with his Garrison Decree in October 1971 (at which time he sent tanks and troops crashing through the gates of Korea University, where they set up their bivouac on campus) and the "Yusin system" and martial law regime of autumn 1972.

What caused the turn toward full-blown, formal authoritarianism? Park justified the new course by reference to rapid changes in the international arena, and his reasons should not be dismissed as purely self-serving. In this period the Cold War in East Asia began to end, two decades before the fall of the Berlin Wall. Dramatic changes in U.S. foreign policy, beginning with Henry Kissinger's clandestine visit to Beijing in July 1971, deeply shocked Seoul and made it appear to be the last domino in Asia. The Nixon Doctrine clearly signaled a withdrawal without victory from the endless Vietnam War, thus jeopardizing Seoul's counterpart regime in Saigon. Furthermore, Nixon announced the withdrawal of a full division of U.S. troops from Korea, reducing the total number from 62,000 to 42,000. (Around this time a State Department official, Francis Underhill, "wrote a notorious memorandum" advocating "total military disengagement from South Korea" [Boettcher, 1980].) A sense of crisis afflicted Seoul within and without, and it reacted with a complex mixture of rigid authoritarianism, dramatic change in the political economy (the "big push" in heavy industry), and some quick footwork in foreign policy (e.g., high-level talks with P'yongyang).

To make a long and bloody story very short, we can say that Park misjudged the hidden strengths and growing maturity of the public sphere, which was overdeveloped in relation to the economy but still underdeveloped compared with the ubiquitous agencies of the expanding Yushin state: a vast administrative bureaucracy, huge armed forces, extensive national police, a Central Intelligence Agency with operatives at every conceivable site of potential resistance, and thorough ideological blanketing of every alternative idea in the name of forced-pace industrialization. Park's dictatorship thus set up an unending crisis of civil society that culminated in the urban disorders of Masan and Pusan in August and September 1979, in the most industrially advanced region of the country and leading to Park's assassination by his own intelligence chief in October—which led to the "coup-like event" mounted by Park protégés Chôn Tu-hwan and No T'ae-u in December 1979 and the denouement in the Kwangju Rebellion in May 1980. The period 1980–1987 will appear in history as a classic Brumairean event,[16] with the luckless "nephew" (Chôn) acting on behalf of the dispatched "uncle" (Park), using the jail and the gnout all the way but compounding into farce the tragedy of Park Chung Hee (who truly was Korea's industrial sovereign, if not its Napoleon). The real tragedy, of course, had taken place at Kwangju, where (as Habermas would put it) an aroused, self-organized, and intersubjective citizenry sought desperately to save itself from the new martial law regime Chôn had just announced, only to be slaughtered (a minimum of 600 killed, maximum of 2,000—like Tiananmen in 1989).

At the end of 1986 U.S. policy moved away from supporting the authoritarians in Seoul, however, as Washington began to worry about a popular revolution in South Korea and U.S. policy shifted on a world scale toward support for limited forms of democracy—something palpable in evidence William Robinson has brought to light. Robinson argues that the Philippines was a key test case for the Reagan administration after the murder of Benigno Aquino in 1983; a secret National Security Council directive approved in November 1984 called for U.S. intervention in Philippine politics—"we are urging revitalization of democratic institutions, dismantling 'crony' monopoly capitalism and allowing the economy to respond to free market forces." This was followed by personal meetings in Manila between Ferdinand Marcos and CIA director William Casey (May 1985) and Senator Paul Laxalt, Ronald Reagan's personal emissary (October 1985). Washington also vastly augmented the Manila Embassy's political staff (W. Robinson, 1996b: 91–92, 121–125). The same thing happened in late 1986 in Korea, as longtime CIA official James R. Lilley became ambassador to Seoul and began meeting with opposition forces for the first time since 1980.

Civil society began to awaken again with the February 1985 National Assembly elections, and by June 1987 the aroused, self-organized, and intersubjective citizenry had taken over the streets of the major cities—with latecoming but substantial middle-class participation—thus forcing Chôn from office. A few months later the always tepid opposition split again, allowing the emergence of an interim regime under the other, somewhat shrewder "nephew" (No T'ae-u)—a regime that first accommodated and then sought to suppress a newly energized civil society now including the liberated and very strong forces of labor (more strikes and labor actions occurred in 1987–1988 than at any point in Korean history or most national histories).

In 1995 a series of dramatic events and actions unfolded, with consequences no doubt unforeseen at the time but having the result of an audacious assault on the military dictators who ruled Korea from 1961 onward and their legacies, a reckoning that ultimately went beyond anything in the global transition from authoritarianism the world has witnessed since the end of the Cold War—beyond the Latin American cases, where (often at the urging of U.S. political scientists) the new regimes decided to let bygones be bygones and let the military go back to the barracks; beyond Rumania, where a rough summary justice dispatched dictator Nicolae Ceaușescu but let his system remain; and beyond East Germany, where Erich Honnecker was overthrown and expelled but where West Germany merely absorbed the old East German system rather than achieving a consensual merger between two rather different civil societies. Chôn and No ended up in prison, convicted of treason and monumental bribery; Kim Dae Jung arranged to pardon them in December 1997.

Kim Dae Jung, a former dissident (seven years in jail, six years of house arrest, several years in exile in the United States), was elected at the end of 1997 after a three-way split among ruling party and opposition candidates; he barely got 40 percent of the vote. The significance of his victory for my argument is that he could never have been elected during the Cold War; security agencies in Korea would have prevented it (and security people in Washington would have tacitly supported them). Kim moved quickly to end labor's exclusion from the system, adopting a tripartite peak bargaining arrangement among labor, business, and government. This master stroke in January 1998 allowed Korea's strong labor unions to help shape (rather than destroy) economic reforms necessitated by the 1997 Asian crisis, even as those reforms meant layoffs that boosted unemployment to a historic high in 1999 (8 percent; by late 2000 it was back to 3.9 percent). Korea thus finally arrived at the noncoercive, intersubjective public sphere it has long deserved and a democratic politics that went beyond the halting and temporary, jerry-built transitions to weak democracy in Latin America, the former Soviet Union and Eastern Europe, and the Philippines.

I conclude this brief consideration of recent Korean political history with the observation that the contribution of protest to Korean democracy cannot be overstated; it is a classic case of "the civilizing force of a new vision of society . . . created in struggle" (R. Williams, 1973: 231). A significant student movement emerged in Western Europe and the United States in the mid-1960s and had a heyday of perhaps five years. Korean students were central activists in the politics of liberation in the late 1940s, the overthrow of the Rhee regime and the politics of the Chang regime in 1960–1961, the repudiation of Korea-Japan normalization in 1965, and the resistance to the Park and Chôn dictatorships in the period 1971–1988. Particularly in the 1980s, through the mediation of *minjung* ideology and praxis (a kind of liberation theory borrowed from Latin America), Korean students, workers, and young people brought into the public space uniquely original and autonomous configurations of political and social protest— ones that threatened many times to overturn the structure of U.S. hegemony and military dictatorship (see in particular Lee, 2000). This was a classic example of Habermas's characterization of student protest in terms of a blurring of borderlines "between demonstration and civil disobedience, between discussion, festival, and expressive self-presentation" (Dews, 1992: 234). Many students also left the campuses to merge organically with the working class, often to find themselves jailed and tortured as "disguised

workers" and always at the risk of their careers. Even if that part of the Korean public sphere is relatively quiescent now, it made an indelible contribution to Korean democracy in the 1980s.

So far this comparative inquiry has argued that the limited pluralism of
U.S. politics is the outcome of an abortive development of civil society
under the pressures of the modern project itself over the past 200 years and
that the East Asian democracies are inextricably related to the regional security and economic networks in which they were enmeshed for most of the
twentieth century. Japan, South Korea, and Taiwan represent different outcomes for civil society and democracy, as each country reacted to its domestic and international milieu. What about the United States?

SECURITY AND DEMOCRACY IN THE UNITED STATES

The United States has not had warfare on its territory since 1865, and it is
a provider rather than a recipient of security services. Does this mean that
warfare and security have nothing to do with U.S. democracy? Quite the
opposite. Indeed, many of the ills of U.S. democracy and civil society can
be traced to the national security state that emerged coterminous with, and
in direct relationship to, the Korean War. I briefly examine the way in
which the militarized and externalized entity East Asians have dealt
with for more than fifty years emerged after 1945 and what it has meant for
U.S. democracy.

The postwar order was to be a liberal one, but in 1945 hardly anyone
knew what that meant since the world had been so illiberal for so long. But
as Robert Latham (1997) demonstrates, the meaning of liberalism was as
complex, heterogeneous, and varied as the meaning of democracy. The construction of a liberal world order was a problematic episode in the history
of a modern practice that had defined as liberal a Britain that had a sharply
inegalitarian class society, a highly restricted franchise (even after the Reform Act of 1867 only 30 percent of the adult population could vote), and
an empire—one that had included not just a host of disenfranchised colonial populations but, through its trading relations, cotton production by millions of slaves and sharecroppers in the American South. The liberal definition would also include a United States that in 1945 was a democracy for
the adult white population and an apartheid-like southern autocracy for the
black population. And during the Cold War a liberal world order led by the
United States included Chiang Kai-shek's Taiwan, Park Chung Hee's South
Korea, Molina Trujillo's Dominican Republic, Josie Broz Tito's Yugoslavia,
Suharto's Indonesia, and Sese Seko Mobutu's Zaire. In other words, a liberal
order was (and is) a complex, heterogeneous historical system that could not
be categorized simply as market driven or democratically governed.

The liberal world order U.S. planners constructed in the late 1940s, in interaction with other nations and peoples, has not been an empire of exclusively controlled territories. It has not been neoimperial, exploiting the economies of its members as if they were colonies, and it has not created onerous or inescapable dependencies. It has not dominated its constituent members. It has established boundaries of inclusion, but it has not necessarily punished exit, if that exit is to a middle ground of neutrality or irrelevance. But this order has been a hegemonic one, and it has had—and must have—a hegemonic leader. That hegemony is most effective when it is indirect, inclusive, plural, heterogeneous, and consensual—less a form of domination than of legitimate global leadership. This hegemony is nonetheless potent: in the 1940s it crushed one form of statist empire and in the 1980s another. Today it is eroding, if not erasing, the last formidable alternative system—the Japan-Korea model of state-directed neomercantilism (one undermined and made vulnerable by its inclusion in the postwar liberal order).

The postwar order took shape through positive policy and the establishment of distinct outer limits, the transgression of which was rare or even inconceivable, provoking immediate crisis—the orientation of West Berlin toward the Soviet bloc, for example. The typical experience of this hegemony, however, was a mundane, benign, and mostly unremarked daily life of subtle constraint in which (as we have seen) the United States kept allied states on defense, resource, and, for many years, financial dependencies. This penetration of allied nations was clearest in the front-line semisovereign states like Japan, West Germany, and South Korea; and it was conceived by people like George Kennan as an indirect, outer-limit control on the worst outcome—namely, orientation to the other side (Cumings, 1991: 57–58). Latham calls this structure the American "external state," an insight that leads him to examine the vast global militarization of this same liberal order (eventually encompassing 1.5 million U.S. troops stationed in hundreds of bases in thirty-five countries, formal security commitments to forty-three countries, the training and equipping of military forces in seventy countries)—a phenomenon often treated as an unfortunate by-product of the bipolar confrontation.

Latham is nonetheless correct to say that liberal modernity cannot be reduced to a mere capitalist modernity, a sly cloak for empire, or a libertarian empyrean where firms interact in the market and free individuals construct a civil society. Both states and markets existed long before capitalism and liberalism; liberalism may have transformed states and markets in distinct and decisive ways, but to stop with that (say, representative democracy as a liberal political form) would ignore the international dimension of liberal modernity. If for Karl Polanyi the self-regulating market had an inherent tendency to transcend national boundaries, for Latham the same is true about the emergence and ordering logic of liberalism. Most of those practices associated with liberalism—free trade, basic civil and political rights, universal suffrage, and national self-determination—can only be dated from the mid-nineteenth century as doctrine and (limited) practice, and only achieved global dominion after 1945.

Dictatorships like those in the Dominican Republic and South Korea were obviously not liberal, but their partial incorporation into a U.S.-organized world order (connoted as the "free world") was a commonplace aspect of a plural and diverse system that, as a whole, remained a central part of liberal modernity. The partial inclusion of a tyrant like Trujillo reflected an essential element of liberal hegemony: the demarcation of boundaries, of limits to the realm, which were most often expressed negatively. The best thing one could say about Trujillo was that he was not a communist, and Washington would support his overthrow only if it were assured that the Dominican Republic would not become communist as a result.

Like those of Russett and Weart, Latham's book has no index entries for the Korean War and just one for Vietnam. Yet it was the repositioning of Japan as a major industrial producer in the context of a raging anti-imperial revolution on the Asian mainland that explains most of East and Southeast Asian history for the next three decades (until the Indochina War finally ended in 1975). And the war in Korea was the lever through which Washington finally found a reliable method that would pay the bills for cold and hot wars on a global scale ("Korea came along and saved us," in Dean Acheson's memorable words): military Keynesianism, which floated economic boats and primed pumps not so much at home but in Japan and Western Europe.

The putative liberal world order U.S. statesmen sought to construct in the late 1940s thus experienced a completely unanticipated future that ran through bloody and disastrous wars in Korea and Vietnam, the ongoing reorientation of revolutionary China, and the more recent collapse of the Soviet Union—all experiences that would have flabbergasted a statesman seeking to chart the postwar order in 1945, should a clairvoyant have conjured them in a crystal ball. When the Cold War was over and the Soviet Union collapsed, one might have expected that the national security state at home and the external state abroad would also disappear. But defense spending is still hovering in the range of $280 billion per annum (albeit reduced by the effects of inflation in the 1990s), and in 1995 the Clinton administration committed the country to maintaining troops and bases in Europe and East Asia for at least the next twenty years. Furthermore, a new base and containment system emerged in the Middle East as a result of the Gulf War, requiring periodic military forays to keep Saddam Hussein "in his box," as Secretary of State Madeleine Albright frequently put it.

What about the implications of the U.S. global security role for domestic life? The effects of postwar security structures on U.S. democracy have been the subject of scholarship ever since Walter Lippmann's first critiques of the Cold War and Harold Lasswell's (1941) "garrison state." A brief list of these effects would include the absence of a U.S. labor party; the attenuation of the New Deal coalition and its more progressive policies, beginning in the late 1940s; the institution of government purges of security risks in 1947; McCarthyism in the 1950s, which resulted in a broad purge of progressives in government, academe, journalism, and popular culture (especially in Hollywood and the fledgling television industry) that effectively moved the perceived middle of the political spectrum sharply to the right; the role of the Korean War in shattering the Truman presidency and the role of the Vietnam War in shattering the Johnson presidency, resulting in no Democrat holding two terms in office from 1952 to 1996; the rise to influence within the Democratic Party of liberal Cold Warriors (Harry Truman, Hubert Humphrey, Henry Jackson); the rise to influence in the Republican Party of Western politicians like Nixon, Barry Goldwater, and Reagan, all lubricated by defense industry lobbying and campaign funds; and the lingering effects of McCarthyism down to the present, in which any hint or allegation of leftism is enough to exclude a person from power and which has shaped one academic field after another—especially the field of international relations, which remains the most conservative of the subfields in political science, with many of its members serving the national security bureaucracy at some point in their careers. No doubt I have missed many other ways in which the national security culture has influenced postwar American life.

CONCLUSION

Perhaps only in the United States would democratic theorists think so little about the external sources of and obstacles to democracy, and only here would a democratic peace literature emerge and flourish in the 1990s as if the interconnection between war and democracy in the long years of the Cold War, or the persistence of U.S. security structures around the world in spite of that "war" finally coming to an end, would have no relevance. The argument here is that the U.S. position in the world since 1945 should be a central consideration in any debate about a "democratic peace" as part of a larger focus on how international and regional relationships affect the possibilities of peace and democracy.

Japan provided us with a window into the ambiguities of the DP literature: the more Japanese industrial competition became a problem for Americans in the 1980s, the more analysts began to question whether Japan was really a democracy after all. Perhaps its political culture was in fact authoritarian, a heritage of Confucianism and ill-defined "Asian values." Yet through that period of trade conflict down to the present, Japan remained ensconced in the 1940s postwar settlement, and its semisovereign status and lack of security autonomy still do not allow a real test of the strength of postwar Japan's democratic institutions. South Korea provided a more interesting test because, on the argument here, its strong civil society and democracy emerged in the teeth of civil war, military dictatorship, and long-standing U.S. support for authoritarian rule; only the end of the Cold War provided a security milieu in which the dictators could be punished, the military could be put back in the barracks, and a genuine dissident and democrat, Kim Dae Jung, could finally come to power. This experience is difficult to reconcile with the Putnam–Huntington–Almond and Verba argument that democracy is the pot of gold at the end of the rainbow of economic development, and it gives the lie to stereotypes about Eastern and Western values. It also suggests the value of sharp social and political conflict to democratic outcomes.

In the end the argument comes full circle—from differing conceptions of democracy and civil society, to the role of imperialism, hegemony, and regional security structures in shaping domestic outcomes, to how three wars affected the possibilities of democratic development in East Asia and helped to create semisovereign states that we call allies, and finally to a national security state at home that was also a product of those wars and that has deeply influenced U.S. democracy, its political culture, and the contemporary civil society that Putnam and other analysts find so troubling. And as a result of this inquiry, I hope a relationship between two things called war and democracy now seems more vexed and complicated than one might gather from reading the contemporary democratic peace literature.

NOTES

1. See in particular Weart (1998), which I think is the best book in this growing literature; for a political science account, see Russett (1993). Both books provide extensive bibliographical guidance to the democratic peace literature.

2. See especially 1998: 78–87, where Weart makes many unwarranted assumptions about large categories of people, whether the Chinese people in the imperial epoch or communists in the modern era, while arguing against simple-minded assessments of national character and while understanding that political cultures can change dramatically—for example, in postwar West Germany.

3. Walter Kirp wrote in *The Nation* that the first book was "seminal, epochal, path-breaking . . . a *Democracy in America* for our times" (quoted on the back of the paperback edition).

4. In my reading, no reviewer of this book pointed out that many or even most northern Italian cities have had communist mayors in the postwar period. Putnam's colleague Michael Sandel says similar things about U.S. civil society (albeit from a more progressive position) (1996: 3–7, 124–133, 351).

5. Putnam disagrees with Almond and Verba, however, on consensus as a prerequisite for stable democracy. A profusion of disparities, cleavages, and fragmentations of various sorts was no bar to "good government" in northern Italy (1993: 116–117).

6. *The Civic Culture* makes interesting reading nearly forty years later. Seeking to quantify the Tocquevillean propensity of Americans to join voluntary associations, the authors found that 57 percent of Americans were joiners, compared with only 44 percent in West Germany. Union membership was at 14 percent in the stratified U.S. sample of 970 respondents and 15 percent among 955 West Germans. Today union membership in the United States is still at about 14 percent, whereas 40 percent of German workers are members of unions. No doubt a similar survey today would find that far more Germans than Americans are members of voluntary associations. If, for Almond and Verba, "weak democracy" is characterized by "the passive citizen, the nonvoter, the poorly informed or apathetic citizen," the United States would certainly qualify in the 1990s, according to Sandel and many others (Almond and Verba, 1963: 246–276, 338).

7. Habermas is eminently more sophisticated about such matters than Almond, Verba, or Putnam, however; for an interesting discussion of Habermas and Parsons, see Giddens, 1985b: 95–121.

8. Weber went on to contrast "the occident" not simply with "the Hindu and the Chinese," as was his wont, but with the three civilizations of East Asia. The "mandarin" was, according to Weber, "a humanistically educated literatus . . . but not in the least trained for administration"; furthermore, in China the mandarins were merely "a thin stratum of so-called officials," existing above "the unbroken power of the clans and commercial and industrial guilds." In Japan, "the feudal organization" led to a "complete exclusiveness as regards the outer world"; Korea, too, had an "exclusive policy," which was "determined" there on "ritualistic grounds" (M. Weber, 1981: 338, 344.) Of Weber's judgments here on China, Korea, and Japan, it need only be said that he was wrong on all counts. Mandarins were trained, not to mention highly skillful, in administration; Japan was more feudal before the Tokugawa isolation than after; Korea's isolation in the same period was "determined" by a devastating international war in the 1590s, just as was Japan's, with no precedent before that for a "Hermit Kingdom."

9. This book was published around the same time as Almond and Verba's *Civic Culture* and represents a profound (if unintended) critique of their project, but it was not translated into English until 1989.

10. See, for example, Przeworski and Limongi, 1995, and Giner, 1995: 24–27.

11. See Dahl (1989: 322–323), on political equality, and p. 264 where Dahl lists a number of conditions for democracy (or polyarchy, in his terms). The conditions listed barely go beyond the categories elaborated by Almond and Verba in their early 1960s work on civic culture.

12. Bertil Renborg (Principal Secretary to the UN Commission on Korea [UNCOK]) said that 80 percent of the national budget was spent on the national police and the army (UN Archives, Box Dag-1/2.1.2, box 3, report of March 31, 1950).

13. Woo (1991: 45–46) estimates $15 billion in economic and military aid from the United States and Japan from 1946 to 1976, a conservative figure.

14. The best book on the Korean effort is a novel, Ahn Junghyo's *White Badge* (1989). The figures are from Woo, 1991: 95–96.

15. A good source on this period is Henderson, 1968.

16. I am referring, of course, to the opening pages of Karl Marx, *The Eighteenth Brumaire of Louis Bonaparte*.

8

Democracy, Peace: What's Not to Love?

Mark Rupert

DEMOCRATIC PEACE OR DEMOCRATIZING PROJECTS?

After long years of wandering the wilderness in quest of theory (understood in terms of empirically falsifiable covering laws), today many scientifically minded students of international relations (IR) accept the proposition that states classified in some formal sense as "democratic" are unlikely to make war on one another. This so-called "democratic peace" (DP) thesis has been much celebrated among U.S. students of IR, and the hallowed phrase "empirical law" is now ritually invoked to describe it. Past articulations of the thesis have been problematic on a variety of grounds and have not gone unchallenged even within the mainstream of IR research (Lynn-Jones, 1996; Chan, 1997). Yet it seems the post–Cold War world may witness the emergence of a new postrealist IR orthodoxy, one that draws its core propositions from a liberal vision of the world but seeks to appropriate these liberal roots, as Andrew Moravcsik would have it, "in a nonideological and nonutopian form appropriate to empirical social science" (1997: 513).

The notion of a nonideological liberalism seems to me oxymoronic. I will argue here that this new liberalism—and the so-called democratic peace thesis that constitutes one of its core propositions—is quintessentially ideological insofar as it presupposes classical liberalism's ontology of abstract individualism (Lukes, 1973: chapter 11; Arblaster, 1984: chapters 2–4; Sayer, 1991: chapter 2) and thereby abstracts from the social relations that generate the possibility of liberal democratic state forms and the kinds of subjects (i.e., abstract individuals) who inhabit them. To the extent that it persuades its audience to accept as real these magical feats of abstraction (see, no wires!), the new liberalism obscures the social relations of domination that underlie the

153

historical forms of liberal democracy and impede realization of the democratic aspirations professed within modern liberal polities. If democracy is understood broadly to entail processes of social self-determination, then this neoliberalism appears actually antidemocratic; it occludes real material possibilities for the transformation of social dominance relations through the realization of unfulfilled promises of self-determination.

Reducing democracy to "polyarchy"—defined primarily in terms of more or less extensive franchise and competitive elections within particular territorial states (e.g., Russett, 1993: 14)—this literature articulates a hegemonic project wherein the scope of democratic self-determination is circumscribed within the electoral systems of liberal capitalist states. This results in forms of democracy "in which a small group actually rules and mass participation in decision-making is confined to leadership choice in elections carefully managed by competing elites" (W. Robinson, 1996a: 623–624). By defining "democracy" as a formal attribute of states—a condition that to one degree or another is either present or absent within a particular territorial political unit—the new liberalism constructs a world populated by democratic and nondemocratic entities, and privileges those designated as "democratic." The liberal capitalist state/societies of the West are represented in terms of the presence of democracy; within their boundaries, democracy is understood as having been achieved. In this way the project of democratization is effectively externalized.

To the extent that this vision has an explicit normative horizon, it is projected outside the boundaries of Western capitalist states. It imagines the possibility of a peaceful and democratic world, the realization of which seems to require the conversion of "nondemocratic" states into formal liberal democracies, as Michael Doyle (1995) warns. This kind of vision thus lends itself to self-justifying imperial projects such as Joshua Muravchik's *Exporting Democracy* (1992) and reproduces a logic of global power that has a long track record of doing violence to both democracy and peace (Kolko, 1988).

The mainstream DP literature, then, is ideological in the dual sense that it obscures social relations and processes from the view of their participants, and by disabling critical analysis it implicitly promotes the interests of groups privileged by those relations. Viewing the world in its terms, it becomes difficult to imagine radical democratizing projects that might seek to construct more participatory relations within and between capitalist social formations, transformative processes that might generate postliberal and conceivably postcapitalist forms of social life. Moreover, to the extent that practitioners of this newest liberalism bestow upon themselves the status of objective observers—inhabitants of an extraterrestrial realm of scientific value neutrality—they effectively absolve themselves from responsibility for the political consequences of their representations of the world.[1]

Having said that, I must register a caveat. I would not want to be understood as claiming to offer an alternative account of the politics of democratic peace that is somehow "nonideological." Rather, I would claim that by eschewing pretensions to scientific objectivity and grounding analysis in a critique of the ways in which liberal democracy is embedded in social relations of capitalism, accounts such as mine are less obfuscatory and more enabling of political dialogue and meaningful democratic discourse than those found in the mainstream literature. My purpose here is not so much to reject the democratic peace as an ideological scam or illusion of "false consciousness" but to re-present it as a potential reality and a political project that is unattainable within the bounds of liberal capitalist democracy and unknowable within the parameters of neoliberal empiricism.

I want to argue that some kinds of democratic peace might be potentially worthy political projects, but for that potential to be realizable a radical recasting of the terms in which the discussion is conducted will be required. In particular, we will need to be critically attentive to the historically specific social relations that have generated the possibility of the kinds of political visions we recognize as "democratic" and, at the same time, have circumscribed democracy within the narrow compass of the liberal state and reduced the meaning of democratic deliberation to the instrumental machinations of egoistic calculators. These relations include (but are not limited to) the capitalist social organization of production that presupposes particular forms and practices of "politics" (P. Thomas, 1994; Wood, 1995). Movement toward visions of democratic peace—that is, rearticulating the democratic peace in terms of democratizing projects—requires recasting these social relations of production and their political concomitants on a scale that is not circumscribed by conventional liberal boundaries demarcating state/society, politics/economics, and domestic/international. It requires the supercession of liberal capitalism's central subject—the abstract individual—and its replacement by forms of social subjectivity grounded in, but not reducible to, the social organization of production.[2] Realization of "democracy" and "peace" requires fostering participatory political communities in which groups presently subordinated to various forms of domination are enabled to effectively deliberate on the social relations in which they are embedded, on scales from the local to the global. It requires, that is, an expansion of political horizons and social self-understandings to make possible the realization of broader and deeper forms of democracy and a peace that is grounded in structures of social justice rather than simply emerging from discrete foreign policy decisions of statesmen. Various social movements are now actively pursuing transnational democratizing agendas that would contribute more or less directly to the realization of such visions (Rupert, 2000), but such actors, agendas, and visions are difficult to find in mainstream discussions of democratic peace. To my mind, this absence is an index of the narrowly ideological character of the DP debate.

CAPITALISM, LIBERAL DEMOCRACY, AND THE ABSTRACT INDIVIDUAL

A leading proponent of the democratic peace thesis understands democracy—in the idiom of this literature, the "independent variable"—in the following terms: "a voting franchise for a substantial fraction of citizens, a government brought to power in contested elections, and an executive either popularly elected or responsible to an elected legislature, often also with requirements for civil liberties such as free speech" (Russett, 1993: 14). Other scholars in this literature place greater emphasis on civil liberties or economic freedoms for individuals. What seems to be lacking, however, is a critical appreciation for the social relations that made possible such historically peculiar forms of "politics" and the subjects that practice them. Such an appreciation is a necessary (if not sufficient) condition for the realization of more profound forms of social self-determination.

John Dryzek presents such a contextualized vision of "democracy in capitalist times," which he sees as "a minimally authentic liberal democracy, which may be defined in terms of competitive parties, limited opportunities for public participation through voting and organized groups, constitutional constraints on government activity, the insulation of the economic sphere from democratic control, and a politics that mostly involves the pursuit and reconciliation of interests defined in private life" (1996: 9). At the heart of this limited and self-limiting version of democracy is an ontology—or vision of social reality—known as abstract individualism. This social self-understanding underlies modern theories of rational choice and has its roots in the atomistic theories of classical liberalism that arose along with modern capitalist social forms. Steven Lukes describes as follows this fundamental vision and the analytic strategy it entails:

> According to this conception, individuals are pictured abstractly as given, with given interests, wants, purposes, needs, etc.; while society and the state are pictured as sets of actual or possible social arrangements which respond more or less adequately to those individuals' requirements. Social and political rules and institutions are, on this view, regarded collectively as an artifice, a modifiable instrument, a means of fulfilling independently given individual objectives; the means and the end are distinct. The crucial point about this conception is that the relevant features of individuals determining the ends which social arrangements are held . . . to fulfill, whether these features are called instincts, faculties, needs, desires, rights, etc., are assumed as given, independently of a social context. (Lukes, 1973: 73)

Understanding social relations as an instrument of individual self-interest, assumed to be primordial and primary, this worldview effectively naturalizes a particular kind of social life and the subjects appropriate to it. Abstract individualism exempts from critical inquiry the social relations through which this worldview and these kinds of subjects are produced and obscures the politics that reproduces those social relations. Karl Marx was scathingly critical of abstract individualism as the ideology of the market, a social self-understanding that submerged and hid from view the relations of power and exploitation that inhere in the capitalist organization of production.

> The sphere of circulation or commodity exchange, within whose boundaries the sale and purchase of labor-power goes on, is in fact a very Eden of the innate rights of man. It is the exclusive realm of Freedom, Equality, Property and Bentham. Freedom, because both buyer and seller of a commodity, let us say labor-power, are determined only by their own free will. They contract as free persons who are equal before the law. Their contract is the final result in which their joint will finds a common legal expression. Equality, because each enters into relation with the other, as with a simple owner of commodities, and they exchange equivalent for equivalent. Property, because each disposes only of what is his own. And Bentham, because each looks only to his own advantage. The only force bringing them together, and putting them into relation with each other, is the selfishness, the gain and the private interest of each. Each pays heed to himself only, and no one worries about the others. And precisely for that reason, either in accordance with the pre-established harmony of things, or under the auspices of an omniscient providence, they all work together to their mutual advantage, for the common weal, and in the common interest. (Marx, 1977: 280)

Inhabitants of the capitalist market, the subjects of capitalist modernity, are then abstract individuals who, as such, are largely unable to discern—much less communally to govern—the social division of labor in which they are embedded. As Derek Sayer interprets Marx's theory of the modern subject, "People appear to be independent of one another because their mutual dependence assumes the unrecognizable form of relations between commodities" (1991: 64). In this view, the rise of capitalism and the commodification of labor (the rise of abstract labor, qualitatively undifferentiated labor power) made it possible to conceive of the individual independent of social context, the individual as such, the individual for whom all social bonds are external; and it is precisely this individual who is the presupposition and centerpiece of liberal theories of politics. "It is this solitary individual—'the individual' in the abstract, without any distinction of, or reference to, the 'accidental' peculiarities of concrete circumstance—who is the moral subject of the modern world. He is sanctified as such in the Rights of Man" (Sayer, 1991: 58).

Moravcsik's (1997) neoliberal theory of IR is exemplary of such reasoning. Moravcsik proposes to recast IR theory such that the preferences of individuals and groups and their constrained choices determine the values, strategies, and policies pursued by state actors and hence are constitutive of IR. Yet Moravcsik wants to understand the social identities of these individuals and groups, their social self-understandings and powers, as somehow outside of and prior to politics. "Liberal theory," he explains, "rests on a 'bottom-up' view of politics in which the demands of individuals and societal groups are treated as analytically prior to politics. . . . Socially differentiated individuals define their material and ideational interests independently of politics and then advance those interests through political exchange and collective action" (Moravcsik, 1997: 517). But it is precisely the social differentiation of individuals and groups—the production of their social identities, interests, and powers and the social dominance relations implicated here—that liberals characteristically elide. This elision leaves them with a shallow and implicitly conservative vision of politics that represents those forms of social life historically bound up with the social relations of capitalist modernity as if they were natural, necessary, and beyond the reach of politics (see Sayer, 1991: chapter 2).

As Ellen Wood has consistently argued, the historical structures of capitalism effect a formal separation of politics from economics and in so doing privilege the putatively private powers exercised by capital in the economy and simultaneously evacuate from the explicitly political sphere any real capacity for democratic deliberation and communal self-determination in and through social relations, particularly the social organization of production. "It is capitalism that makes possible a form of democracy in which formal equality of political rights has a minimal effect on inequalities or relations of domination and exploitation in other spheres" (Wood, 1995: 224). In this view, then, democracy is an unfulfilled promise of liberal capitalism—a promise that could not be fulfilled without calling into question the privileged status of private property, the powers of the class that owns it, the apparently apolitical economy within which it is ensconced, and the social self-understandings of abstract individualism that are attendant upon all of these.

LIBERAL DEMOCRACY AND CLASS POWER

Since Western liberal capitalist societies, especially the United States, are presumed by the new liberalism to be the avatars of democracy, it may be useful to examine concretely the extent to which democracy—broadly understood as deliberative and open-ended processes of social self-determination (Arblaster, 1987; Dryzek, 1996)—is constrained by the existence of democratically unaccountable concentrations of private power grounded in class relations. Despite the triumphalist liberalism of the post–Cold War era, with its noisy pronouncements of the bankruptcy of Marxian socialism, the classical Marxian concept of class based on relationship to the means of production surely has some purchase in the contemporary U.S. political economy. Ownership of the means of production is concentrated within the wealthiest 10 percent of U.S. families; according to Federal Reserve data for 1995, this top decile held 84 percent of the stock and 90 percent of the bonds owned by individuals (including indirect ownership through mutual funds), as well as 92 percent of business assets. And ownership of these assets is even more highly concentrated in the upper reaches of the top decile: the richest 1 percent of the population owned over 42 percent of stocks, almost 56 percent of bonds, and more than 71 percent of business assets (Federal Reserve data reported in Henwood, 1997c: 3).

In the classical Marxian view, the private ownership of the means of production (and appropriation of its product by the owning class) presupposes the existence of a class of people who are from day to day dependent on the sale of their labor power to secure the necessities of life. Samuel Bowles and Richard Edwards report that in 1988, the richest 1 percent of U.S. families (enjoying annual incomes of more than $1 million) received almost three-quarters of their income from property ownership in the form of profit, interest, capital gains, rents, and royalties. This contrasts markedly with the great majority of families who are primarily dependent upon wage labor to enable them to meet their needs and who are therefore more or less fully subject to the manifold relations of power and domination that inhere in the capitalist wage relation. In 1988 the 46 million families whose incomes fell between $20,000 and $75,000 received almost 84 percent of their income from labor (Bowles and Edwards, 1993: 105).

To these relations of class correspond particular kinds of social power. Owners of the means of production may be socially empowered as employers and as investors.

As employers, capitalists and their managerial agents attempt to assert direct power over the quantity and quality of work performed by those whose labor power is being purchased: "the capitalist forces the worker where possible to exceed the normal rate of intensity, and he forces him as best he can to extend the process of labor beyond the time necessary to replace the amount laid out in wages" (Marx, 1977: 987). This workplace power can be as simple and direct as the "drive system" under which foremen cajoled and coerced workers to greater levels of output, or it can take the form of enormously complex organizations of production such as that commonly referred to as "Fordist."

Displacing predominantly craft-based production in which skilled laborers exercised substantial control over their work conditions, Fordist production entailed an intensified industrial division of labor; increased mechanization and coordination of large-scale manufacturing processes (e.g., sequential machining operations and converging assembly lines) to achieve a steady flow of production; a shift toward the use of less skilled labor performing, ad infinitum, tasks minutely specified by management; and the potential for heightened capitalist control over the pace and intensity of work. In the mid-1920s one production worker described as follows the relentless pace and intense effort his job required and the consequences of failing to meet that standard on a daily basis: "You've got to work like hell in Ford's. From the time you become a number in the morning until the bell rings for quitting time you have to keep at it. You can't let up. You've got to get out the production . . . and if you can't get it out, you get out" (quoted in Rupert, 1995: 111). At the core of the Fordist reorganization of production, then, was the construction of new relations of power in the workplace; to the extent that those relations of power could become established parameters of the work process, capital would reap the gains of manifold increases in output per hour of waged labor. The promise of massive increases in productivity led to the widespread imitation and adaptation of Ford's basic model of production throughout the industrial core of the U.S. economy. The institutionalization of such a system of production required a combination of force and persuasion: a political regime in which trade unions would be subdued, workers might be offered a higher real standard of living, and the ideological legitimation of this new kind of capitalism would be embodied in cultural practices and social relations extending far beyond the workplace (Rupert, 1995).

As limited as the "industrial democracy" of Fordist unionism may have been (see Rupert, 2000: 28–30), most people today are even less able to have any meaningful voice in their working lives. There has been a shift in the correlation of forces within the workplace and a recasting of the historical structures in which capitalist production relations are instantiated. After decades of deunionization, restructuring and layoffs, downsizing and outsourcing, and transnationalized production, workers in post-Fordist America are effectively disempowered and less able to lay claim to the fruits of their growing productivity.

That employers are fully aware of the fearful dependence of working people upon their jobs and in an era of transnationalized production are prepared to exploit this economic insecurity as a source of workplace power is demonstrated by the fact that employers commonly threaten to close plants and eliminate jobs when faced with unionization drives or new collective bargaining situations. According to one of the most comprehensive and systematic studies of unionization campaigns in the post-NAFTA period, this type of workplace extortion has taken a variety of forms: "specific unambiguous threats ranged from attaching shipping labels to equipment throughout the plant with a Mexican address, to posting maps of North America with an arrow pointing from the current plant site to Mexico, to a letter directly stating that the company will have to shut down if the union wins the election." One firm shut down a production line without warning and "parked thirteen flat-bed tractor-trailers loaded with shrink-wrapped production equipment in front of the plant for the duration" of the unionization campaign, marked with large hot-pink signs reading "Mexico Transfer Job." Between 1993 and 1995, such threats accompanied at least half of all union certification elections (Bronfenbrenner, 1997: 8–9). In the words of one auto worker contemplating his future in a transnationalized economy, the threat of runaway jobs "puts the fear in you" (quoted in Rupert, 1995: 195), and indeed, it is intended to do so.

These shifting relations of power have had measurable effects. During the peak decades of postwar Fordism, real wages rose steadily along with productivity (Rupert, 1995: 179). That relationship has since been severed; productivity continues to rise (albeit more slowly than during the high Fordist period), but real wages have been declining over the long term, and total compensation (wages + benefits) has stagnated (Mishel, Bernstein, and Schmitt, 1997: 131–138). Doug Henwood, editor of *Left Business Observer,* explains:

> We're constantly told by economists and pundits that the key to getting wages up again is raising productivity. But over the last several decades, productivity—the inflation-adjusted value of output per hour of work—has risen much faster than real compensation (wages plus fringe benefits adjusted for inflation). . . . Here's another way to think about the growing gap between productivity and wages. According to the World Bank, in 1966, U.S. manufacturing wages were equal to 46 percent of the value added in production (value-added is the difference between selling price and the costs of raw material and other inputs). In 1990, that figure had fallen to 36 percent. (Henwood, 1997b)

Much celebrated have been recent wage gains that, between 1996 and 1999 reached down to even low-income workers and seem to have lent renewed credibility to the capitalist-friendly metaphor that a rising tide floats all boats. The Economic Policy Institute (EPI) puts this wage growth in perspective, however: "Historically, increases in productivity have meant growth in real compensation for much of the workforce. . . . However, the gap between productivity and the median wages of both males and females grew through the 1989–96 period, and, despite the stronger wage growth since 1996, this gap between the economy's growth and the growth of workers' wages remains significant. Even with the recent growth spurt in wages, the economic fortunes of the median worker continue to diverge from the overall growth in the economy" (Bernstein and Mishel, 1999: 3). Moreover, recent wage gains are largely attributable to a conjuncture of tight labor markets at the peak of a long business cycle upswing, low inflation, and the federally mandated minimum wage increase. These conjunctural gains do not portend a significant shift in what we might call the "underlying fundamentals" of the U.S. political economy—the relative disempowerment of people who depend on wages to live.

This intensified exploitation of workers is a large part of the explanation for higher corporate profits, a roaring stock market, and extravagant growth in executive compensation. According to EPI economist Lawrence Mishel (1997), whereas "labor's share of corporate sector income rose from 79.2 percent in 1959 to 83.9 percent in 1979," it had declined to about 81 percent by 1996. In the manufacturing sector, the reversal has been even sharper (Mishel, 1997). Correspondingly, the EPI reported that over the last business cycle, corporate profit rates have hit record peaks, up over 50 percent from the profit peak of the previous cycle—substantially higher, that is, than the profit peak of the rabidly pro-business Reagan-Bush years:

> Corporate profit rates reached a new peak in 1996 and are now at their highest level since these data were first collected in 1959. . . . In no previous period in U.S. history have profit rates experienced such a rapid sustained rise. . . . The rise in profit rates results from two factors: a shift in income from wages to profits, and a decline in the relative size of the capital stock due to low levels of investment. . . . In 1988, 14.07 percent of corporate income went to profits. In 1996, this proportion had risen by more than a full percentage point to 15.16 percent. This shift from wages to profits created a gap between wage growth and productivity growth, and took away approximately one quarter of the wage gain that workers would have realized over the last eight years if their wages had kept pace with productivity. (Economic Policy Institute, 1997)

Conditions favoring extraordinary levels of corporate profitability have translated into rich rewards for investors. According to Henwood, recent record highs on Wall Street represent the crest of a wave that has been building for years: "Over the last 15 years, the real (inflation-adjusted) Standard & Poor's 500 index, a proxy for blue-chip corporate America, is up 574 percent, by far the biggest 15-year real rise since good statistics start in 1886; in 1964, it was 434 percent; in 1929, 205 percent. By most conventional measures of whether stocks are reasonably priced, the market is at or near historic extremes" (1997a: 1). Not only have investors made out like bandits on the appreciation of their assets, but they have also been receiving generous dividends: "firms are paying out near-record shares of their profits to their stockholders—70 percent of after-tax profits since 1982, [almost] twice historical averages." Henwood suggests that, Alan Greenspan notwithstanding, this "exuberance" in the markets is not altogether "irrational," but rather "stock markets are celebrating the political triumph of capital worldwide" (Henwood, 1997a: 1–2). It is sometimes claimed that growing participation in mutual funds and pension plans has "democratized" the ownership of capital, implying that the benefits of a booming stock market might trickle down at least as far as the "middle class." It is important to remember, however, that ownership of financial and business assets remains highly concentrated among the very rich, as I demonstrated earlier.

If the 1990s were good to members of the investor class, who derive the bulk of their income from the ownership of financial and business assets, they were also happy times for corporate executives (who, as recipients of large stock options, are also members of the investor class). In 1978 the average American corporate CEO earned about 60 times as much as the average worker; by 1995 the average CEO was pulling down 172 times as much as his or her workers. The compensation of the average CEO grew by 152 percent between 1978 and 1995, rising to more than $4.3 million annually (Mishel, Bernstein, and Schmitt, 1997: 226).

In an environment where the rewards to corporate managers and investors have far outstripped the wages of working people, it should not be surprising to discover that inequalities of income and wealth are at historically high levels. According to the U.S. Census Bureau, income inequality increased markedly between 1968 and 1994, such that the income gap between rich and poor was wider in 1994 than at any time since 1947 when they began collecting such data (U.S. Census Bureau, 1996; see also Mishel, Bernstein, and Schmitt, 1997: 52–64). Inequality of wealth is even more stark than the income gap. According to Federal Reserve data for 1995, the top 1 percent now controls more wealth than the bottom 90 percent of the population. Although unequal ownership of wealth is nothing new in the U.S. political economy, such inequality is now more extreme than at any time since the 1920s (Henwood 1997a; also Mishel, Bernstein, and Schmitt, 1997: 278–281).

Clearly, employers and investors in the United States have enjoyed the fruits of their enhanced social power. But that power is not confined within the boundaries of the "economy"; it has broader political manifestations as well. "Even in a society whose government meets the liberal democratic ideal, capital has a kind of veto power over public policy that is quite independent of its ability to intervene directly in elections or in state decision making" (Bowles and Gintis, 1986: 88). Even if members of the owning class were somehow unable or unwilling to access political influence through massive campaign contributions, private coffees with the president, or nights spent in the Lincoln bedroom, they would nonetheless be uniquely privileged by virtue of their structural situation and social powers. Insofar as the state under capitalism depends for its economic vitality on the investment activities of a class of "private" owners of the social means of production, it is effectively subject to their collective blackmail. If a state fails to maintain conditions of "business confidence" (Block, 1977: 16), or if it enacts policies that appear threatening to the interests of the owning class, investors responsible only to their own pocketbooks may decline to invest there. In effect, they may subject the state to a "capital strike"—driving up interest rates, depressing levels of economic activity, throwing people out of work, exacerbating the fiscal crisis of the state, and endangering the popular legitimacy of the incumbent government. Thus are market values enforced on governments that claim to be responsive to popular democratic pressures. "The presumed sovereignty of the democratic citizenry fails in the presence of the capital strike" (Bowles and Gintis, 1986: 90).

The power of transnationally mobile capital to override democratic processes and public deliberations has increased manifoldly along with the growth of international liquidity and the sophistication and speed of exchange in the world's financial markets. According to Howard Wachtel, "Some $650 billion in foreign exchange transactions are completed each day in New York, Tokyo, and London. Only about 18 percent support either international trade or investment. . . . The other 82 percent is speculation" (1995: 36). Responding to short-term differences in perceived conditions of profitability and variations in business confidence between one place and another, these huge speculative flows are highly volatile. Massive amounts can be shifted from one currency (or assets denominated in one currency) to another literally at the speed of light through computer modems and fiber optic cables that link the world's financial markets. The volume and speed of this trading have heightened the potential disciplinary effect of a threatened capital strike, and governments are increasingly obliged to weigh carefully their welfare, fiscal, and monetary policies against the interests of investors who may exit en masse in response to expectations of lower relative interest rates or higher relative inflation rates. This disciplinary power has the effect of prioritizing the interests of investors, who as a class are effectively able to hold entire states/societies hostage. Moreover, the particular interests of the owning class are represented as if they were the general interests of all: "since profit is the necessary condition of universal expansion, capitalists appear within capitalist societies as bearers of a universal interest" (Adam Przeworski, quoted in P. Thomas, 1994: 153). In this ideological construction the social and moral claims of working people and the poor are reduced to the pleadings of "special interests," which must be resisted in order to secure the conditions of stable accumulation. In William Greider's apt summary,

> Like bondholders in general, the new governing consensus explicitly assumed that faster economic growth was dangerous—threatening to the stable financial order—so nations were effectively blocked from measures that might reduce permanent unemployment or ameliorate the decline in wages. . . . Governments were expected to withdraw more and more benefits from dependent classes of citizens—the poor and elderly and unemployed—but also in various ways from the broad middle class, in order to honor their obligations to the creditor class. (1997: 298, 308)

This disciplinary power was reflected in Bill Clinton's speedy transformation from a candidate advocating "putting people first" (through job creation and public investment strategies) to an incumbent deficit hawk whose eyes were glued to the bond markets (Greider, 1997: chapter 13).

But the antidemocratic ramifications of liberal capitalism are not exhausted by cataloguing the ways in which capital and its interests are privileged within putatively democratic liberal states, for capitalism and its politics have never been confined within the boundaries of states. Capitalism is a social order premised upon accumulation for its own sake, endless accumulation, and as such it recognizes no boundaries. As Marx and Engels famously declared, "The need of a constantly expanding market for its products chases the bourgeoisie over the whole surface of the globe" (in McLellan, 1977: 224). Although there is considerable debate on the substance and significance of the current phase of "globalization," it seems clear that the postwar world order—and the historic bloc whose project this was—has fostered the growth of transnational capitalism along with institutions and ideologies to support worldwide accumulation (see Rupert, 2000: 43–49).

Ian Robinson (1995) has been an outspoken critic of the latest rounds of transnational liberal institutionalization, arguing that NAFTA and the WTO empower transnational capital at the expense of democratic self-government at national and local levels. They do this in two ways. First, these "free capital agreements" directly impose legal restrictions on the policies governments may enact—for example, prohibiting performance requirements that might otherwise be used to impose some measure of social responsibility on transnational investors and limiting public provision of goods and services that might circumvent the market imperatives of private profit. Second, by subjecting established political communities to intensified competitive pressure, investors will be able to seek out the most congenial environment in terms of wages, labor and environmental regulations, tax burdens, and so forth. In this way, the imperatives of market competition are focused on the public sphere, compelling governments to reduce to the world economy's lowest common denominator the burdens and social responsibilities placed on investors—fostering a "race to the bottom." Together, these two effects have a devastating impact on the bargaining power of democratic communities. "The ban on performance requirements protects corporations from competing against one another to give governments concessions in return for the right to invest. There is nothing to prevent governments from competing to offer concessions to corporations in return for their investment, and much that encourages it" (I. Robinson, 1995: 376).

In the 1999 edition of its annual *Human Development Report,* the United Nations Development Program (UNDP) notes the dramatic worsening of global inequalities that have been attendant upon neoliberal globalization. By the late 1990s the fifth of the world's population living in the highest-income countries had 86 percent of world GDP, 82 percent of world market exports, 68 percent of foreign direct investment, and 74 percent of the world's telephone lines; the poorest fifth had only about 1 percent of each of these items (United Nations Development Program, 1999: 3). According to UNDP, these inequalities have been deepening as the neoliberal project has unfolded; the wealthiest 20 percent of the world's people received 74 times as much income as the poorest 20 percent in 1997, up from a ratio of 60 to 1 in 1990 and 30 to 1 in 1960. It is frequently claimed that the current period of economic internationalization is little different from that around the turn of the twentieth century, but UNDP claims the income gap was 7 to 1 in 1870 and 11 to 1 in 1913. If these figures are even remotely indicative, the inequalities fostered by the current processes of globalization are manifoldly more intense than anything witnessed during its nearest historical analog. Arguably, then, liberal capitalist democracy is not all that democratic, and the contemporary liberalizing world appears actually to be moving away from the cosmopolitan vision of self-determination and mutual respect presented in the more normative versions of the democratic peace. Instead, transnational liberalization is bringing with it an unprecedented global hierarchy of wealth and power.

Indeed, it is the presumption of democracy in the democratic peace thesis I most wish to challenge here. But as Jutta Weldes usefully reminded workshop participants with specific reference to gendered violence deployed in support of patriarchal social hierarchies, neither can liberal states/societies be presumed to be "zones of peace" wherein conflicts are settled without the use of coercive force. Within liberal capitalist democracies, social power relations are maintained through shifting combinations of coercion and consent, but the former is never entirely absent. In the United States, there is a long tradition of repressing political forces perceived as alien, radical, un-American: recall, for example, the Haymarket affair, the executions of Sacco and Vanzetti, the Red Scare and Palmer raids of the post–World War I years, and the McCarthyite purges of government, academia and education, labor, and the entertainment industry during the early Cold War (Heale, 1990). Local and federal law enforcement have also engaged in the surveillance and infiltration of civil rights and antiwar groups and, more recently, of the Committee in Solidarity with the People of El Salvador (CISPES). Most recently, mass movements protesting against neoliberal globalization have been subject to police infiltration, surveillance, and preemptive action, in addition to barrages of rubber bullets and streams of pepper spray unleashed on protesters in the streets. In Britain—homeland of parliamentary democracy—the powerful, militant, and socialist-led miners union was the object of a secret campaign of infiltration, disruption, and public disinformation by the government's security forces as part of a wider strategy to destroy the social power of labor unions in Britain (Milne, 1994).[3]

If straightforward political repression is not alien to the exemplars of liberal democracy, then neither is coercion that upholds a social order based on stark inequalities of wealth and power. The U.S. "justice system" is overcrowded with more than 2 million prisoners: overrepresented relative to their proportion of the population are African Americans and Latinos, many from deindustrialized and impoverished U.S. urban areas; underrepresented are investors and corporate CEOs whose decisions contributed to the production of these landscapes of desperation. You do not have to be Lenin to conclude that liberal democratic societies are underpinned by coercive power; indeed, it was Adam Smith who wrote, "civil government, so far as it is instituted for the security of property, is in reality instituted for the defense of the rich against the poor, or of those who have some property against those who have none at all" (1993: 413). Liberalism's defense of property and privilege is also evident on a global scale, explaining in large part why—despite the absence of any credible threat to U.S. national security—the United States continues to keep military expenditures at near Cold War levels, to maintain a global military presence, and to plan for the contingency of simultaneous engagements in multiple armed conflicts in different parts of the world.

REDEEMING DEMOCRACY

As Ellen Wood has it, then, "Liberal democracy leaves untouched the whole [historically specific] sphere of domination and coercion created by capitalism, its relocation of substantial powers from the state to civil society, to private property and the compulsions of the market" (1995: 234). Moreover, even the relatively tepid democracy that is thereby enabled to exist in the public, political sphere of liberal capitalist societies is subject to corruptions and structural constraints that dramatically narrow the range of possible outcomes and effectively institutionalize class-based powers and privileges. Yet as Jeffrey Isaac usefully reminds us, the reproduction of social power relations "is always problematic," embedded in relations that are reciprocal if not necessarily symmetrical: "the successful exercise of power is always a contingent and negotiated outcome of interaction. The interpretation of social norms, the struggle over their meaning, is a crucial ambit of this negotiation" (1987: 93, 101). Thus struggles over the meaning of "democracy" may serve to reproduce or contest the relations of power and domination embedded within liberal capitalism. To the extent that the "private" powers of employers and investors are understood to inhibit communal self-determination, popular aspirations for democracy can become a potentially transformative force.

The journalist William Greider has emerged as one of the public intellectuals of the global economy. Greider sees the post–Cold War world as deeply contradictory: "The historic paradox is breathtaking: At the very moment when western democracies and capitalism have triumphed over the communist alternative, their own systems of self-government are being gradually unraveled by the market system" (1993: 212). In a highly suggestive formulation, he has argued for a broadening of political horizons in order to combat the rise of "offshore politics" that institutionalizes the power of transnational capital and further distances citizens from possibilities for democratic self-determination:

> For ordinary Americans, traditionally independent and insular, the challenge requires them to think anew their place in the world. The only plausible way that citizens can defend themselves and their nation against the forces of globalization is to link their own interests cooperatively with the interests of other peoples in other nations—that is, with the foreigners who are competitors for the jobs and production but who are also victimized by the system. Americans will have to create new democratic alliances across national borders with the less prosperous people caught in the same dilemma. Together, they have to impose new political standards on multinational enterprises and on their own governments. The challenge, in other words, involves taking the meaning of democracy to a higher plane. (Greider, 1993: 196)

As I read Greider, he is suggesting that Americans move away from social self-understandings revolving around U.S. liberal exceptionalism and privilege and begin to see themselves as enmeshed in webs of transnational economic and political relationships, webs structured around the social powers of capital. A reorientation of this kind is a condition of possibility for the construction of common interests with others similarly (if not identically) subordinated to transnational capital.[4] "Genuine reform will require a new and unprecedented form of cross-border politics in which citizens develop continuing dialogues across national boundaries and learn to speak for their common values. Only by acting together can they hope to end the exploitation . . . across the global production system" (Greider, 1993: 203).

Although not altogether unproblematic, Greider's vision holds enormous appeal for me.[5] In passages such as these, he is imagining the possibility of new kinds of political identity and action emerging from public deliberations among those located in similar structural circumstances in the global economy. This vision implies the dereification of liberal dichotomies separating economics from politics, society from state, and domestic from international and a democratic renegotiation of the social relations of capitalist modernity. If democracy is to be understood as a process of deliberative social self-determination, then Greider's vision seems to me a major step beyond the procedural democracy of liberal capitalism. It is a step onto a path of popular empowerment that leads toward challenging the institutionalized powers of transnational capital but in so doing opens up a range of possible futures that are inaccessible from within the fixed horizons of liberal capitalism. For me, it is this democratizing vision that redeems Greider's calls for global Keynesianism and redistribution (see especially Greider, 1997), for that could become little more than a "passive revolution," disempowering popular movements by granting limited concessions that leave intact the political forms of capitalism and the social powers of capital. The project of democratization, it seems to me, provides critical resources with which to put pressure on any such accommodation.

How might such a democratizing politics be translated into a strategy for attacking the powers of transnational capital? Jeremy Brecher and Tim Costello are also politically engaged public intellectuals committed to furthering democratic self-determination in a transnational political economy. They describe their project as "globalization from below" and explain that it rests on "the fundamental premise of democracy, that people should be able to make the decisions that affect their lives." This project, then, requires "that global institutions be democratic, transparent, accountable, and accessible to the public" (1994a: 78). Their "Lilliput strategy" seems to me a useful metaphor for imagining such a new global politics:

> Facing powerful global forces and institutions, people need to combine their relatively modest sources of power with often very different sources of power available to participants in other movements and locations. Just as the tiny Lilliputians captured Gulliver by tying him with many small pieces of thread, the Lilliput strategy weaves many particular actions designed to prevent downward leveling into a system of rules and practices that together force upward leveling. (Brecher and Costello, 1994b: 758)

Brecher and Costello envision "a multilevel system of democratic governance" (1994a: 79): networks of overlapping grassroots social movements—encompassing "working people, women, marginalized groups and their communities" (1994b: 758)—that would produce democratically constructed demands for social responsibility in economic life, enacted and institutionalized at multiple levels from local to global. The vehicles for achieving this popular empowerment and upward leveling might include corporate codes of conduct, social charters in international trade agreements, transnational labor rights, and environmental campaigns; and Brecher and Costello embrace Jorge Casteneda's call for a "grand bargain" between the global North and South whereby citizens of the North would actively support imports from the South so long as they were produced in accordance with democratically determined social, labor, and environmental standards (1994a: 110–111, 121–140). This vision presupposes "a dialogue among First and Third World popular movements and organizations" (1994a: 110). Accordingly, Brecher and Costello acknowledge the crucial importance of supplanting liberal individualism with a more contextualized

social self-understanding as a basis for political action: "To link self interest with common global interests, the first step is to clarify the connections
between the immediate conditions people face and the global processes that
are affecting them." They call on their readers to "resist downward leveling
where you are and help others resist it where they are" (Brecher and
Costello, 1994b: 758–759). In contrast to the antidemocratic "corporate
agenda," they call for "a virtual democratic revolution" but insist that this
cannot be confined within liberal capitalist understandings of the political
sphere: "the movement to expand democracy will mean little to most people
unless democracy gives them the opportunity to reshape the economic, social and environmental conditions of their daily lives" (1994b: 760). So they
too imagine new forms of boundary-crossing political practice and new
kinds of subjects to enact them, inconsistent with those of liberal capitalism.

Kim Moody, veteran labor activist and editor of *Labor Notes,* antici-
pates the emergence of a new international "social movement unionism" in
response to the hardships and rigors imposed transnationally by neoliberal
regimes and lean production systems—"a rebellion against capitalist globalization" that begins with a rejection of the ideology of cooperation with
employers in the interest of international competitiveness (1997: 53). In
place of this strategy of capitulation to market forces, Moody envisions
"social movement unionism [as] an active strategic orientation that uses the
strongest of society's oppressed and exploited, generally organized workers, to mobilize those who are less able to sustain self-mobilization: the
poor, the unemployed, the casualized workers, the neighborhood organizations" (1997: 59). This strategy implies that unions must work toward
broader social agendas, in which the interests of the "working-class public"
may be reflected, and the linkage of those movements across borders. Thus
he calls for transnational campaigns to spread employment by reducing
work weeks, to reduce or forgive third world debt, and to reestablish social
safety nets. All of these would effectively strengthen the position of working classes by reducing the vulnerability of those who must sell their labor
power in order to survive. As important for Moody, such campaigns could
foster a self-transformative process as social forces coalesce and struggle
around common agendas and overlapping social visions.

All of this may sound wildly utopian, but such visions continue to an-
imate transnational grassroots movements formulating more egalitarian,
democratic, and sustainable visions of globalization. For example, the 1998
Peoples' Hemispheric Agreement was drafted by coalitions from Canada,
Quebec, Chile, Mexico, and the United States, and embodies many of the
social values and commitments expressed in earlier, trinational documents
such as the Just and Sustainable Trade and Development Initiative (Kamel
and Hoffman, 1999: 114–115). In consultation with a number of the activists

and nongovernmental organizations involved in these multinational dialogues, congressional progressives led by Bernie Sanders (Independent, Vermont) in 1999 drafted a document envisioning far-reaching reforms of the global economy. In its opening pages, The Global Sustainable Development Resolution declared as its overriding purpose that "the people of the United States and the people and governments of the other nations of the world should take actions to establish democratic control over the global economy" (Sanders, 1999: 2). The resolution declared that unregulated economic globalization has produced the following consequences: heightened financial volatility and instability; intensified competitive pressures driving a race to the bottom in labor, environmental, and social standards; tendencies toward inadequate aggregate demand and underemployment; increased poverty; massive increases in economic inequality; intensification of discriminatory burdens borne by women, ethnic and racial minorities, and indigenous peoples; and the degradation of democracy. In contrast to this situation, the resolution envisioned a global economy framed by such principles as "democracy at every level of government from the local to the global," human rights (including "labor, social, environmental, economic, and cultural rights") for all people, environmental sustainability, and "economic advancement for the most oppressed and exploited parts of the population, including women, immigrants, racial and ethnic minorities, and indigenous peoples" (Sanders, 1999: 9).

Sanders and his collaborators propose reforming international economic institutions so that voting rights are based on population rather than wealth, increasing the openness of their decisionmaking procedures, and explicitly including in their deliberations "labor unions, environmental groups, women's organizations, development organizations, and other major sectors of civil society in each affected country" (Sanders, 1999: 16). Further, the drafters call for the creation of Commissions on the Global Economy at national and transnational levels to encourage broad public debate (explicitly including the various elements of civil society) on globalization and alternative possible futures. The drafters further envision measures to re-regulate capital and tax foreign exchange transactions in order to reduce short-term speculative capital flows and encourage long-term investment in socially accountable and sustainable development. They call for the cancellation of debts owed by the poorest countries and the reorientation of international financial institutions toward domestic economic growth and full employment rather than domestic austerity and export-led growth. And they propose enforceable codes of conduct designed to "establish public control and citizen sovereignty over global corporations" (Sanders, 1999: 41). Labor, environmental, and social standards would be inscribed in these codes of conduct, as well as in the governing principles of international financial institutions and trade agreements. According to Sanders's office, the resolution was endorsed by at least seventy non-governmental organizations, including many that have been active in resistance to neoliberal globalization.

In Seattle and around the globe, progressive visions such as these have been articulated, insisting that we need not accept the delimitation of political horizons embodied in neoliberal institutions of global governance. Ideological struggles currently under way will determine whether it is possible to develop, clarify, and anchor firmly within popular common sense conceptions of politics, democracy, and political agency that transcend the narrow scope of liberal democracy as it is practiced within capitalist social formations and imagined within the literature of the democratic peace. Unless the question of democratic peace is recast to consider these struggles and say something meaningful to ongoing projects of grassroots democratization, the democratic peace debate will remain the peculiar preoccupation of U.S. IR scholars, unwilling or unable to see the global politics of the twenty-first century even as it unfolds before them.

NOTES

This chapter developed arguments that were subsequently incorporated into my book, *Ideologies of Globalization* (Routledge, 2000). The latter, however, was published before this chapter. I therefore acknowledge that Routledge/Taylor and Francis has granted permission for me to reproduce here material for which it is the formal holder of copyright.

1. Not all proponents of the DP thesis are so reluctant to make normative claims; for example, Doyle, 1995.

2. For more on an open-ended historical materialism in which various forms of social subjectivity might be grounded in, but not reducible to, social relations of production, see Hall, 1988, and the chapters in Morley and Chen, 1996.

3. I am grateful to Hazel Smith for making me aware of this.

4. I make no presumption of a simple and unproblematic class identity such as "global proletariat." Rather, I would argue that people in different social and historical settings have been incorporated into global capitalism in a variety of ways, articulating their own historical relations and cultures with those of core capitalism. I believe the various forms of subordination to transnational capital nonetheless entail structural commonalities that create the *possibility* for the negotiation of common political horizons, common interests, and a transnational democratizing project.

5. I am troubled by Greider's apparent alternation between a democratizing vision that points toward an open-ended process of social reconstruction and one that focuses more narrowly on underconsumptionist tendencies in the global economy and points toward a macroeconomic regime of global Keynesianism that might stabilize global capitalism (compare Greider 1993, 1997).

9

Democracy and Peace in the Global Revolution

Martin Shaw

Since the 1980s there has been, as James Rosenau (1990) proclaimed, a new "turbulence" in world politics. Fundamental processes of change have affected both the internal politics and external relations of nation-states. Although these processes have been complex and contradictory, two major trends have been widely welcomed by liberal and democratic opinion: democratization within states and the pacification of relations between them. Even before but especially since 1989, the number of formally democratic—or at least democratizing—states has increased rapidly on any criterion. At the same time, interstate war—at least between central states in the international system—has become increasingly unlikely.

In this new situation, some political and international scholars have proclaimed a specific kind of deep connection between these two trends. Democratic states, it is argued, do not fight each other. Jack Levy (1988: 88) has even claimed this tendency as the nearest thing to an "empirical law" political science has yet produced. In this chapter I do not enter into a close critical discussion of this literature. This is not because I doubt either the credibility or the desirability of these trends or indeed the plausibility of some kind of connection between them. It is because numerous critics (see the survey in MacMillan, 1996) have already shown that the debate about the "democratic peace" (DP), as it has come to be called, has posed these issues in very partial ways.

The democratic peace literature made an interesting move beyond realist international theory in bringing the domestic politics of states back into the international equation. It represented, however, distinctly limited progress, since although linking these hitherto separated spheres, it preserved their structural distinctiveness as the basis of analysis. In this sense, it failed to address the blurring of these analytical categories, which Rosenau (with his idea of "postinternational" relations) and many "global" theorists had begun to suggest. In restricting the relations of democracy and peace to the correlation of domestic structures and foreign policy, democratic peace arguments bypassed much more profound attempts to restructure the categories of international relations that were developing in the discipline. They largely ignored the question of how to grasp the relations of democracy and peace as aspects of the global changes of our times. This question has been raised in various ways by many different contributions, all the way from the long-standing debate about interdependence in international relations, begun by Robert Keohane and James Nye (1977), to David Held's (1992, 1995) conceptualization of "cosmopolitan" democracy.

The more interesting issue is therefore how to develop a more holistic conception of contemporary worldwide social and political change in which the relations of democracy and peace can be understood. One direction from which this may be attempted is that of historical-sociological understanding, reflected in the serious attention paid in international relations to the work of social theorists such as Theda Skocpol (1979), Anthony Giddens (1985a), and Michael Mann (1993). In this chapter, I do not have space to discuss the general meaning (or problems) of this approach, which I have done elsewhere (Shaw, 1994, 2000a). Instead, I suggest its desirability by first outlining the pitfalls of *a*historical and *non*sociological modes of analysis. Second, I enter into a substantive discussion of what a historical and sociological approach to the question of democracy and peace might look like, offering a schema that raises some of the questions with which the new debate on the democratic peace might be concerned. Third, I examine the meaning of this historical and sociological approach to democracy and peace in the global transformation of the present period.

HOW NOT TO ANALYZE DEMOCRACY AND PEACE

It is an obvious but important starting point to remember that democracy and peace are not timeless but historical social concepts. Indeed war itself—the negation of peace—is a historical product. Although some seek to explain war as a product of instinctive aggression, as *organized* violence it presupposes socially controlled use and originates in definite historical forms. Similarly, although there is reason to suppose war and democracy might be opposites—war is clearly the negation of a democratic relationship between two parties—historically, war has always been compatible with forms of democratic relationship *within* one of the organized parties to war (Shaw, 1997b). Indeed the "Western way of war" is generally held to have originated in the same time and place as Western democracy: in classical Athens, citizens were also warriors.

The democracy with which we are concerned today is, of course, very different from that of Athens. It is taken for granted that democracy involves an open representative system based on elections through universal suffrage, with entrenched freedom of expression and association, within a nation-state. This is indeed the dominant model of the Western bloc of states, approximated in a number of other states worldwide. It is rapidly becoming (since the end of the Cold War) the norm to which most states pay lip service, as well as the object of U.S. and general Western policy throughout the world (W. Robinson, 1996b).

Even if we agree on some such definition of modern democracy, however, it tells us relatively little about the nature and changing role of democracy in the emerging twenty-first-century world, including its relation to peace. Democracy has always been both an institutional form and a social movement—often even a revolutionary movement. In the contemporary world, although democracy is becoming normal, it is also contested—notably between those who wish to use democratic forms to maintain largely authoritarian elite rule and those who wish to enlarge popular freedoms and control. Democracy is part of the great changes of our times and as such is often partial and compromised, as well as insecure and unstable.

Today's wars are also very different from those not only of classical Greece but also of the recent historical past. We can define warfare as organized violence between two parties in which each seeks to compel the other to submit to its will. We can operationalize this (as most have done since the Correlates of War project; see Small and Singer, 1982) to count conflicts in which there are a thousand or more battle deaths. But even with such a definition it is by no means clear that we can find a normal model of contemporary warfare, since any such model, like that of democracy, is challenged by contemporary developments.

Warfare has undergone such huge transformations in modern times and has taken so many diverse forms that even regarding its standard modern form it is difficult to agree. The distinctive form is sometimes taken to be "Clausewitzian" (van Creveld, 1991; Kaldor, 1997), but I have argued that, given the conjunction of total mobilization with total destruction in the warfare of the industrial era, it is better understood from a sociological perspective as "total war" (Shaw, 1988). All agree, however, that the very idea of "modern" war is under great pressure. New forms of war are emerging, seen either as "post-Clausewitzian" (Kaldor, 1997, 1998) or in terms of "degenerate" forms of total war (Shaw, 1999).

In these circumstances it is even less clear that we know what we mean by peace. Many defined the Cold War, despite its perpetual war-preparation and proxy wars, as a form of peace. Although nonwarlike relations have clearly been consolidated between the former Cold War adversaries and war appears to be in the process of abolition between the major states or groups of states, the worldwide extent of warfare (let alone war preparation broadly defined) is still alarming. Are we really to understand the post–Cold War order as peaceful—except when the growing lawlessness within the states of the Balkans, Caucasus, or central Africa actually takes the form of fighting?

Finally, at the heart of these uncertainties about democracy, peace, and war lies the conundrum of the modern state. We may agree on some version of Max Weber's general definition of states as organizations claiming monopolies of violence in given territories (Mann, 1993: 55, offers an improved, suitably qualified variation of this; see also the discussion in Shaw, 2000b: chapter 6). We may even agree that modern states have increasingly taken the *form* of nation-states. This does not mean, however, that we can adequately define contemporary states as national institutions. On the contrary, the national character of states has been undergoing a critical transformation.

The classic modern embedding of national forms of state in the nineteenth and early twentieth centuries was within imperial relations. More recently, nation-states were embedded in the bloc relations of the Cold War. Today's unprecedented number of nation-states is implicated in a new constellation: the emergent power relations of a global world. On the one hand, many so-called nation-states are hardly able to guarantee the internal pacification Giddens (1985a), following Weber, saw as the hallmark of the modern nation-state, let alone the external projection of violence he saw as its corollary. On the other hand, even today's most powerful national centers—including the sole remaining superpower—are actually embedded in pan-Western and emergent global structures of state power (Shaw, 1997a; 2000b).

What these uncertainties tell us is that democracy, war and peace, and state or nation-state are all concepts that need to be grasped historically, in the context of successive changes in social and political relations in general. If our own time is agreed to be one of considerable flux—indeed I shall argue more strongly that it is one of historic upheaval—then this is the wrong time to try to fix the terms of debate in concepts of democratic nation-states and interstate war inherited even from the recent past.

In particular, we should avoid three major traps of contemporary social science, all of which seem to be implicated in the democratic peace debate. Two of these are problems of the social sciences as a whole: the "methodological nationalism" (Scholte, 1996), according to which national states and societies are regarded as the units of social analysis, and the corresponding idea that generalizations in social science should be established principally through the "comparative method," which examines variations across national cases. Both of these ideas embed the idea that national units are the given structures of modern social order.

Following from these two general traps is a third, the favorite notion of international relations theory: the idea that the world is primarily structured in distinct "domestic" and "international" spheres. By assuming the separation of these spheres, we can then proceed to "correlate" the tendencies within them, as has been done in democratic peace analysis. But the notion that this is a frontier to be penetrated belongs to a particular historical epoch. This period, in which the world can be defined in national and international terms, is drawing to a close. Before we can develop a historical account of democracy and peace, we need to overcome these inherited flaws of modern social science in general and international relations in particular.

A HISTORICAL FRAMEWORK: STATE RELATIONS IN THE NATIONAL AND INTERNATIONAL ERA

In this chapter I can only summarize the general framework in which I propose we may understand the relations of democracy, war, and peace. The core of my argument is that we can grasp these issues by locating them within the developing social relations of state power (which I call for short *state relations*) throughout modernity. My argument, which I have developed more fully elsewhere (Shaw, 2000b), is that the history of the modern period has been structured critically by the emergence, transformation, and eventual decline of particular social relations and forms of state, most generally characterized as national and international.

My core assumption is that the pivotal historical changes within this modern era are not, as Marxists have proposed, changes in the mode of production as such, important as those have been, but changes in these state relations. In this era, in which state power has typically been fragmented among many major centers, it has been "Janus-faced" (Skocpol, 1979), pointing both inward toward society and outward toward other states. Following Skocpol, Giddens (1985a), and Mann (1993), I take for granted that the capacity of particular states to mobilize power is developed simultaneously in relation to society and to other centers of state power.

The central issues in state relations have been two-way, however. State relations are not only about the control of state over society—its capacity for surveillance or mobilization of social relations in general. They are also, in contrast, about the ability of society outside the state—individuals, groups, and society as a whole—to survey, limit, and ultimately control the state. The question of democracy has been, in this way, one side of the political dynamics of the entire modern, or national-international, era.

I now introduce another key concept: *state forms*. In the modern period, states have tended increasingly to be centered socially on nations, so the forms of the state have been in general simultaneously national (relations between state and nation or groups within it) and international (relations between centers of state power). In this context, democracy has been defined primarily in relation to the nation-state (Held, 1995).

The fragmentation of state power within modern society has meant the key to state relations has been war between major state centers, which has increasingly shaped the relations of state to society. Inherently linked to the state's growing capacity for surveillance and mobilization of society, war has been a central dynamic in the development of modern state relations. The democratic side of these relations has also been bound up in war: as a result of war mobilization, society often becomes aroused for political change, and in return for that mobilization democratic states often offer or are forced to concede extensions of democratic rights.

This is particularly true with total war, which we can identify (following Mary Kaldor's [1982] definition) as the dominant "mode of warfare" in which war as a social activity was organized in the twentieth century. In this mode, warfare has come to be the organizing principle not just of state power but of economy and social relations in general. Thus I have suggested (Shaw, 1988) that the prime sources of change in twentieth-century society were the contradictions of the way in which the expanded mode of warfare impacted society. And whereas Giddens (1985a) tended to write out *revolution* from developed modernity, I argued that definite revolutionary processes could be identified within the "dialectics of war" (Shaw, 1989).

If democracy has been a key question within all these political dynamics of the national-international era, particularly within the dialectics of war, it has not conformed to a single pattern but has been constantly transformed and reposed by each successive historical shift. In Table 9.1 I try to suggest (in a schematic way) the parameters of these changes and the corresponding changing relations of democracy with war and peace, which are explored in this discussion.

A major problem for the hypothesis of pacific democracy lies in its articulation with dominant paradigms in international relations theory. If democratic governance explains at all the absence of war in interstate relations within what international relations generally characterizes as a "Westphalian" state system, it can clearly be at best only a very partial explanation of war and its absence. That is, it can only explain the contrasting patterns of interstate relations between democratic and nondemocratic states. It cannot explain particular cases of relatively pacific or warlike relations *within* these groups.

In particular, the question of democracy can tell us little about relations between states in the early Westphalian system, since no state could be called democratic at that time. And yet Westphalia is generally supposed to have inaugurated a period of relative peace in interstate relations in Europe compared to the period of general continental war that preceded it. Ironically, some of the earliest democratic movements (e.g., the radical movements in the English civil war of the 1640s) had been implicated in that period of war.

Table 9.1 War and Democracy in the National-International Era and the Global Transition

World Order Period	Interstate System	Mode of Warfare	State Relations	State Forms	Democracy for War	Democracy for Peace
Pre-national era, 1648–1793	Westphalian European state system	Limited, mainly colonial, wars	Limited mobilization capacity	Prenational monarchical and imperial	Democratic movements revolutionary	New constitutional orders?
Early national-international era, 1793–1870	Early interimperial	Revolutionary and counterrevolutionary national/imperial (pretotal)	Political mobilization, but weak economic and social control	Revolutionary national, predemocratic imperial state	Popular nationalism feeds war mobilization; settlers attack indigenous peoples	Origins of liberal democratic internationalism
High national-international era, 1870–1914	High interimperial	Pretotal war—infrastructures created (industrialization, mobilization); limited wars	Becoming bordered power containers; growing economic and social control	Nation-state empires; semidemocratic core, colonial peripheries	Growing democracy as infrastructure for nationalist-imperialist mobilization	Socialist internationalism
Crisis of national-international order, 1914–1945	Politicized interimperial	Total war, including guerrilla war; society as target of war, genocidal world wars	Statist, emerging total control of economy and society	Politicized nation-state empires; democratic vs. totalitarian	Used to seize power and launch war (totalitarians); war mobilization (democracies)	Victory of democratic allies creates stable democratic order in West
Preglobal transitional era, 1945–1989	Cold War bloc system	Nuclear arms race and worldwide conflict; wars of national liberation, new interstate and civil wars	Greater horizontal integration, vertical disintegration; slow loosening of state control	Bloc states, Western democratic and communist; Third World nation-states, democratic and authoritarian	Cold War mobilization; democracies back Third World wars; settler nationalists resist liberation	Western bloc internally pacified, but communist bloc fragments into wars
Global revolution and early global age, 1989–	Emergent global order	Genocidal wars of state disintegration; Western-UN global state vs. "rogue" states and genocidal nationalists	Increasing interstate integration and regulation, decline of traditional welfarism and planning	Emergent global democratic UN-legitimated dominance of Western bloc	More stable among new democracies slowly integrated into pacified West	Democratic forms harnessed by nationalist nomenklatura, even genocidists

The early post-Westphalia period, roughly up to the American and French Revolutions at the end of the eighteenth century, is best character-ized as a "prenational" and "predemocratic" era. Although elements of modern nationality and democracy began to develop together in the core of the emerging world order of European empires in this period, states were generally monarchical and increasingly imperial. They also still possessed, by later standards, very limited mobilization capacity in either political or economic terms. Wars, mostly relating to colonies, were generally limited compared with those of the subsequent and even preceding periods.

Democracy was very much a subordinate theme in these developments, although by the late eighteenth century it was part of a larger movement to-ward the growth of a distinctively modern, rational, secular, scientific world. In this movement the possibility of new constitutional orders was linked to world peace in the most enlightened thought (e.g., Kant, 1991 [1796]). The emergence of democracy as a revolutionary movement and a form of gov-ernment, however, was hardly a peaceful process. The classic modern revo-lutions, of 1776 and 1789, proclaimed universal liberal principles in order to create a modern basis for nation and empire. Because of their double threat (internal and interstate) to the old world order, they unleashed counterrevo-lutionary wars that spread across the European world system.

This was not a historical accident but something intrinsic (as Skocpol [1979] argued) to the character of revolution within an interstate system. Moreover, as Karl von Clausewitz's classic work observed (1976), a new form of war was clearly linked to developments within these early modern revolutions. In his trinitarian definition of war, therefore, the people repre-sented its quintessentially violent character (generals were linked to state-craft, governments to policy). Since then, military thinkers like Michael Howard (1983) have seen the democratic aspect of modern war—the peo-ple in arms—as a source of its prospensity to total violence.

Clearly, the early revolutionary states were hardly stable constitutional democracies by contemporary criteria, so it might be supposed that demo-cratic peace theorists could breathe a sigh of relief. They would be mis-taken, however, to see this point as of limited significance. The forms of democracy have been harnessed to authoritarian, militarist, and ultimately undemocratic purposes throughout subsequent history. Indeed, the tension between pacific and warlike tendencies remains pivotal to the modern his-tory of democracy.

Only by severely restricting the nature of the linkage between democ-racy and peace, as well as the relevance of cases, can a one-sided account be sustained. French revolutionary nationalism turned, with Napoléon, into an imperial venture in which democratic tendencies were extinguished. Even relatively democratic settler colonists in North America, Australasia, and Africa were distinguished by their brutal—even genocidal—military campaigns against indigenous peoples. Indeed Mann (1996, 2000) has argued that the more democratic the settlement, the greater its genocidal tendencies.

In the high interimperial period at the end of the nineteenth century, the development of parliamentary democracy went hand in hand with that of imperialism and militarism. It is a questionable historical logic that legitimates the case of Western "democratic defenders" (Britain, France, the United States) against German "imperialist" and "militarist" "aggressors" in the Great War. A more balanced judgment would surely recognize the real democratic elements alongside the imperialism in each state's war making, even while recognizing the differences between them. German social democracy was notoriously mobilized to support the kaiser, just as its British and French sister parties supported their governments.

To make this case is not to ignore the important antimilitarist tendencies of democratic movements, particularly liberal and socialist internationalist. It is to argue that democracy often had a double-edged significance for peace. The triumph of the Western allies in the Great War led to democratic revolutions in Russia, Germany, and Italy, as well as other states. But within these newly democratized nation-states, democracy was neither stable nor pacific. In Russia, the counterrevolutionary mobilization by neighboring states—similar to that after 1789, and whose backers included Western "democracies"—led to a civil war in which the Bolsheviks quickly extinguished the revolutionary democracy of the soviets. In Germany and Italy, the new, unstable postwar democratic conditions spawned fascist and national-socialist movements that glorified militarism.

Fascist movements are perhaps the archetype of the aggressive, antidemocratic militarism, the supreme negative confirmation of the democratic peace hypothesis. We should not forget, then, their exploitation of democratic forms and legitimacy in the seizure of power. Nor should we see the Western democracies as exponents of purely defensive war making. Only by a historical sleight of hand could we dismiss as defensive (for example) the antidemocratic, counterrevolutionary violence with which the "democratic" European empires (France, Holland, even Britain) tried to retain their colonial possessions in and after 1945.

The point of this polemic is that throughout the emergence, consolidation, heyday, and decline of the European nation-state-empires, military violence and culture were structural conditions of democracy. There may be some truth in the idea that the most aggressive empires were the least democratic and that the most democratic were less aggressive. But no safe generalizations can separate democracy and militarism throughout this era. Only a profoundly limited theory and methodology would seek to simplify their complicated linkages in this way.

Moreover, in the great crisis of the interimperial system, from World War I to World War II, democracy took on a new significance in state relations. As the great imperial powers moved toward renewed and intensified total war, with much more total control over society, interstate conflict became much more highly ideologized. Nazi Germany, Italy, and the Soviet Union were controlled by regimes with (counter)revolutionary ideologies that denounced parliamentary democracy. Under these conditions the democratic states mobilized their own populations by intensifying their democratic ideology. Through this process the meaning of democracy came to be understood, first in Britain and then throughout much of the West outside the United States, in terms of socioeconomic as well as political rights. There was democratic reform—a social democratic extension of democracy—as democratic claims became more central to the total war confrontation and mobilization.

The democracies were successful in World War II, not alone—since they were allied with the Soviet Union—and probably less because they were democratic (although that was a factor) than because, with the U.S. economy behind them, they possessed by far the more powerful war machine. The claim that this was a victory "for democracy" was meaningful, however, since the most extreme antidemocratic model—fascism—was fundamentally defeated and discredited. But even more apparent was that this was a victory for two states, the United States and the Soviet Union, above all others. The secondary victors, such as Britain and France, were subordinate through military and financial dependence if not, as in the case of Japan and Germany, through defeat.

The significance of the embedding of democracy in the Western military alliance became clear in the evolution of this situation into clear-cut opposition between two Cold War blocs. The bloc order was a major evolution beyond the classic state relations of the old national-international world order, since it boiled down the rivalries of numerous major centers of state power to two superpowers and their dependent blocs. It was also a major evolution in that, within the Western bloc at least, alliance spawned integration among nation-states, and the bloc became an increasingly interdependent single conglomerate of state power (Shaw, 1997a, 2000b).

State relations underwent fundamental changes. In the Cold War, military mobilization diminished rapidly and was no longer so extensive (or "total") because the nuclear transformation of warfare increasingly made the mass army redundant. Mobilization, so far as it still occurred, was no longer simply national because of the bloc system. In these circumstances, although states became more integrated horizontally, they became less integrated vertically. States no longer needed to control economy and society in the same way they had done in the era of total war.

With shrinking state sectors—even the powerful military-industrial complex mobilized a smaller section of the economy and workforce over the decades—came the revival of liberal market economics. Within increasingly integrated Western bloc state structures, with global reach—and in Europe a particularly tight form of integration—new state relations developed that provided the framework for the increasingly worldwide, globalized economy of the late twentieth century.

The relations of war and democracy in the Cold War flowed from these realities of bloc competition. Democracy became a line of division and an ideology of the Cold War. The Soviet Union extinguished the transitional democracies of Eastern Europe to better control its satellites—the misnamed "people's democracies." The United States developed the Western alliances as a bloc of parliamentary democratic states, notably imposing new democratic constitutions in West Germany and Japan, although some nondemocratic states (Turkey, Portugal, and Greece) were welcomed as members of the North Atlantic Treaty Organization (NATO) as long as their regimes were anticommunist.

Not surprisingly, democracies in this era did not fight each other, but that was hardly *because* they were democracies. Rather, they did not fight and they were democracies for a common set of reasons: their mutual subordination to the major victor of the war (the United States) and their common rivalry with the Soviet bloc. As the Cold War period lasted for over forty years, Western-bloc integration developed apace, encompassing many sorts of economic and political as well as military institutionalization so that war between the component nation-states became less and less likely. Again, although democracy was a factor in institutionalizing this integration, it was hardly the principal independent reason for it.

An ambiguous relationship among democracy, peace, and war ran through the Cold War West. Democracy was undoubtedly a mobilizing principle in the rivalry with the Soviet bloc. But as such, it was hardly an unambiguously peaceful ideology, since it threatened to lead to nuclear war—including the threat of aggressive "first use," which would have destroyed the people on all sides. Nor, as Cold War ideology, was democracy consistently practiced even in the Western heartlands. On the contrary, the Cold War was a justification for secret, even authoritarian state institutions and practices, from the McCarthyism of the early years through the continuing machinations of Western security services and the secrecy surrounding nuclear weapons developments. The security apparatuses were the highest level of power in the Cold War West but the level least open to any kind of accountability to democratic publics (Mills, 1956, 1958).

Even within the Western bloc, as I have noted, openly authoritarian states remained welcome, if generally marginal, members. Outside the bloc, in the so-called Third World, Western and especially U.S. power frequently—indeed generally—backed authoritarian, corrupt, and military rulers, including apartheid South Africa, against democratic movements. This cannot, moreover, be represented as a peaceful process. Not only did the internal repression practiced by Western-backed states frequently cross the line into civil war; the United States in particular also intervened directly or indirectly by military means to install, support, or restore authoritarian rule. European democracies used military power to oppose colonial liberation movements. Western client states—such as "democratic" Israel—launched numerous wars.

During the Cold War period, therefore, democratic states were hardly unambiguously peaceful in orientation. The military conflict with the Soviet Union constrained the quality of democratic culture and institutions within the West. It restricted support for democratic movements in the Third World and also in the Soviet bloc, since the West could hardly give effective support to democratic resistance if that would threaten interbloc war.

The Cold War was a preglobal, transitional period in world order in which a major change occurred in state relations. The replacement of the interimperial world system, in which a number of major independent centers of state power functioned increasingly more or less as "bordered power containers," by a bloc system was a very fundamental change. The democratic structures and ideology of the dominant Western bloc state undoubtedly conditioned the post–Cold War evolution of state relations in more global and democratic directions. During the Cold War, however, democratic movements within both the Soviet bloc and the Third World—and even social movements for democratic change within the West—often came up against the limits of the democratic Western state.

DEMOCRACY IN THE GLOBAL REVOLUTION

The end of the twentieth century saw the emergence of several narratives of transition. Most pervasive in the late 1980s was the idea of postmodernity, according to which all historically given forms were in unprecedented flux and relativity. At the end of the decade and the beginning of the 1990s, this was succeeded (although obviously postmodernist ideas continued to hold much sway) by the idea of a post–Cold War world. By the mid-1990s this had given way in turn to globalization as the dominant narrative. The shifting dominance of these narratives reflected the pattern of historical development, from widely diffused cultural senses of transformation in the 1980s to political-military change in 1989–1991 and economic and communications changes in the mid-1990s, as the political dust began to settle.

What is notable about these narratives is that they have tended to emphasize different processes of change (cultural, political-military, economic-communications) and that whereas the first two are defined in essentially negative terms ("post-"), only globalization proposes a new content (the global). On examination, moreover, this content dissolves into largely technical changes (time and space relations), with once again a dominant negative motif (undermining of the nation-state).

The global is not to be understood in this way. The current transition should be understood as a fundamental change that encompasses all the processes identified—cultural, political-military, and economic-communications. Global means something different from simply world or worldwide, let alone international; "globality" (this term for the global is defined by Martin Albrow [1996]) is about a fundamental unification or commonality of human social relations. The global transition is a *revolutionary* change, not just in the loose sense of major transition but in a specific sense of a fundamental change in state relations accompanied by major popular upheavals.

Clearly, the meaning of global change I propose here is very different from that commonly indicated by globalization. It differs in three major ways. First, it represents a change in which conscious, purposeful human action plays an important role rather than the relatively mechanical process indicated by globalization. Second, it is very much defined by political relations, which determine the context of economic and cultural change rather than vice versa. Third, it is a set of radical and relatively sharp changes rather than simply a gradual process. Furthermore, the *global* revolution differs from previous revolutionary transformations. It is not merely a more or less simultaneous international movement across a number of different nation-states. Rather, it involves the beginnings of a transformation in world order, from the national-international order of the last two centuries to a specifically global order.

The global revolution is essentially a development from two major processes of the Cold War era, which I defined earlier as the final stage of national-international order and which contained many preglobal aspects. First, it is a further transformation of state relations and forms in the Western bloc state through the development of distinctively global relations and forms of state power. Second, it is a continuation of the democratic revolution, overcoming many of the constraints imposed on it in the Cold War period. These two trends come together to the extent that global state forms are defined in democratic terms, and democratic change increasingly shows a global dimension.

Recognition of the depth of global revolution is limited because—in this unprecedented worldwide political transformation, just as in any revolutionary change—there are many continuities (notably the national and international forms of state power). There are also many conflicts; like every previous revolutionary transformation the change is an uneven, contradictory, and contested set of processes, meeting new obstacles that arise from remnants of old relations and forms. It is also, at the beginning of the twenty-first century, very much an *unfinished* revolution.

The transformation of state relations and forms centers on processes whereby the Western state bloc—harnessing the globally legitimate institutions of the UN system, as well as the wide range of more specifically Western international institutions—has established itself as the effective center of worldwide state power. Secondary centers of power, notably the weakened successors of the former rival Soviet bloc and the relatively more powerful Chinese state, are increasingly (but still problematically) integrated into a larger, Western-centered conglomerate of state power. Tertiary centers, the major states of all continents and regions, are also increasingly but very unevenly integrated. Some states remain largely on the margins: Iraq, Libya, Iran, North Korea, and Serbia, which have come into conflict with the West, are defined as "rogue" states—although even in these cases there is some acceptance in principle of international authority.

This transformation has generated a new name for globally legitimate authority, the "international community," which is applied to the various manifestations of global and Western state power. These, of course, are shifting and variable—polymorphous crystallizations of the global state rather in the way Mann (1993) saw national power as fluid in form. There are two apparently contradictory sides to this legitimation of global state power. On the one hand, there is the assertion of Western and especially U.S. power, the confirmation of NATO as the dominant international military structure, and the preference of Western leaders for ad hoc alliances such as "contact groups" rather than for strong, enhanced permanent international institutions with clear legitimacy. On the other hand, there is the embedding (de facto as well as de jure) of Western and even U.S. policy in wider international coalitions, the centrality of the United Nations as a legitimate institutional framework for Western power, and the real development of that framework. The conflict between these two sides came into the open in the 1999 Kosovo war. It remains a central tension in U.S. foreign policy.

Alongside, and also in tension with, this global state development is the unprecedented worldwide democratic revolution. The paradox of this revolution is that, of course, in form it is national and international as well as global. As the Soviet bloc unraveled from the late 1980s—especially in the decisive period from the East German, Czechoslovak, and Romanian revolutions in late 1989 to the collapse of the USSR in 1991—many states and republics were reconstituted on a democratic and national basis. But although the disintegrative tendency was clear, so was the integrative tendency. The new states emerging from the Soviet collapse were mostly not—although some were and others tried to be—nation-states in the sense of effective, autonomous centers of military power. The more advanced and geographically Western of them, especially in Eastern and Central Europe, sought early membership in the European Union and NATO. Most, including even Russia, embraced key elements of Western ideology, worldwide political economy, international institutions, and leadership.

Above all, almost without exception they embraced democracy. The democratic transition varied hugely from those states in which there were democratic revolutionary movements to the many in which the old nomenklatura embraced democratic forms in order to restructure their power. However real or unreal the substance, democratic change was for both people and rulers alike—but often for very different reasons—a means of admission to and recognition by the new Western-dominated global world order.

The post–Cold War democratic revolution has not been confined to the former Soviet bloc. An early signal was the 1980s transformation of the majority of Latin American states from authoritarian and military to parliamentary-democratic rule and the overthrow of Ferdinand Marcos in the Philippines. In the 1990s it embraced large numbers of states in Africa and especially Asia. It included such notable national changes as the ending of apartheid, the establishment of multiracial democracy in South Africa, and the democratic upheavals in South Korea and (very problematically) Indonesia. The Middle East is the major world region least touched by this movement, although interestingly the Palestinian authority has been a forerunner of change toward elected authority, and postrevolutionary Iran has also developed genuine electoral processes.

In all regions, democratic change has been linked to an increased if often critical orientation, by popular movements as well as governments, toward international institutions and the Western-defined global order. Some major states, above all China, have to date resisted formal democratization, and there has been brutal repression. Nearly all states are involved to a greater or lesser extent, however, in closely linked global tendencies; no states have been immune to the social changes behind democratization. It is not easy to envisage, therefore, the long-term exclusion of many states from at least limited or token involvement in democratic reform. There is considerable momentum behind continuing democratic change, which state elites will find increasingly hard to resist.

Democratization is linked to global change particularly because of the new policies of the Western bloc and especially the United States. In the 1980s, after decades of supporting undemocratic regimes and promoting wars in the struggle with their Soviet rivals, Western leaders finally proclaimed democracy and peace to be appropriate worldwide. (Even in the early 1980s, under Ronald Reagan and Margaret Thatcher, the West was still willing to support or condone authoritarian, antidemocratic regimes and forces as long as they were anti-Soviet—although European governments were not always prepared to go along with these policies.) The conversion of the United States to "promoting polyarchy" (W. Robinson, 1996b) was therefore both a recognition that popular pressures for democratic change were inevitable in many regions and an attempt to manage them.

In the 1990s, especially under Bill Clinton, the West adopted an increasingly clear rhetorical stance of support for democratic change, pulling the rug from under old dictators rather as Mikhail Gorbachev did from under the Stalinist rulers of some eastern-central European states. Although the United States especially often retains close relations with those authoritarian rulers who manage to cling to power, again notably in China, it is usually clear that this is a pragmatic stance that does not preempt support for change, as was demonstrated in the Indonesian upheaval of 1998. The European Union, moreover, has reinforced this trend by imposing relatively clear democratic conditions on new entrants from eastern, central, and southern Europe.

Related to these trends have been two more clearly globalist democratic developments. On the one hand, democratic social movements for social justice, environmental reform, and democracy have emerged; and a "global civil society" has been increasingly recognized by interstate international institutions. The idea of "international community," although primarily understood in interstate terms, has also been broadened increasingly to include such civil society organizations. On the other hand, formal global democratic institutions have become something more than a dream. The European Parliament has provided the first working model of an elected transnational parliamentary body. This has encouraged the idea of a formally based "cosmopolitan democracy" (as advocated, for example, by Held [1992]).

DEMOCRACY IN THE
NEW RELATIONS OF WAR AND PEACE

Following realist (or, for that matter, Marxist) assumptions, we might have expected the Western bloc to disintegrate once the discipline of the Cold War was gone. The post–Cold War years have indeed been ones of heightened economic competition—not only among national economies but among emerging regional economic blocs in Europe, North America, and Pacific Asia. Military rivalry has been limited, however, to the disputes between the United States and Britain and France over NATO policy in the Balkans and with Japan over "burden-sharing" in the Pacific. These are hardly omens of fundamental new military rivalries between nation-states or between imperialisms.

In the global era, established liberal democratic states do not fight each other. But once again it is obvious that this is not simply because they are democracies but because they are embedded in the raft of common Western and global state institutions. Indeed it is not just established liberal democracies that do not fight each other; major non-Western states—although like Russia and China still quasi-imperial and semi, if not openly, authoritarian—are not likely to fight with the dominant Western power.

Outside the Western core of global state power, however, national centers are more weakly integrated with institutional structures, and regional institutions that might inhibit local conflicts are much weaker than they are in the core. In the Cold War era, interstate rivalries between major regional powers—such as Russia and China, India and Pakistan and China, Indonesia and Malaysia, Iran and Iraq, Israel and the Arab states—led to wars and border incidents. Although integrative tendencies in the emerging global polity, including democratization, may increasingly inhibit wars, it clearly remains possible that such interstate rivalries will generate new wars.

Democratization in itself is not a guarantee of war avoidance in such conficts. Israel, the only internally democratic state in the Middle East, has also been the most belligerent; Indian democracy has been quite compatible with bellicosity toward Pakistan. Democratic as well as military governments may see war, as long as it can be kept limited and relatively cost free, as a means of boosting popularity. Thus Boris Yeltsin's Russia sought a military solution in the breakaway republic of Chechnya, despite the lessons of the former Soviet failure in Afghanistan. Only in defeat did Russia's weak democracy penalize the regime for the new disaster, and then not decisively. The lesson learned by Yeltsin's successor, Vladimir Putin, was that a more streamlined and ruthless military campaign would be more likely to deliver the electoral goods.

Manipulating democracy is the new trade of the nomenklatura throughout the Soviet bloc, and especially in the successor states of the Soviet Union. In the Caucasus and central Asia, from Armenia and Azerbaijan to Georgia, Moldova, and Tadjikistan, ruling elites—mostly but not exclusively staffed from the old regime—have won elections while, and through, waging war against neighboring states or internal minorities. In contemporary democratizing states, authoritarian-inclined regimes are likely to use electoral and military processes simultaneously to produce and reproduce their power.

Thus in the new nation-states of Serbia (and the rump federal Yugoslavia, which it dominates) and Croatia, governing elites have used "democracy" to legitimate war and genocide and used war and genocide to legitimate their national authority and electoral success. In both cases, of course, democratization has been far from complete; particularly in Serbia, electoral rigging has been blatant, and in both states the freedom of opposition parties and the media has been drastically restricted. Formal democracy has not seriously impeded war making, and war making has not weakened electoral legitimation.

Indeed Kaldor (1998) explains that democratic forms have become part of the genocidal process of the "new wars" of the global era. Whether waged by recognized states or breakaway centers of power, electoral legitimation is actually part of the process of genocide. Knowing that in the global era democratic legitimation is the path to international recognition, power mobilizers seek to create ethnically homogeneous territories in which they use coercive identity politics to ensure electoral majorities. Minorities or even majorities who do not fit with the rule they seek to impose are expelled from their houses and land, villages and towns. Although intimidation and low-grade violence often account for much of the process, physical abuse and even large-scale killing are also essential ingredients. After the expulsions—so-called ethnic cleansing—elections or referenda confirm the new majority's exclusive right to the territory.

The acquisition of territory by ethnic exclusion has been supported by democratic means in earlier periods, as Michael Mann's contribution to this collection shows. We easily forget that Hitler's accession to power had a substantial electoral base. More recently, Israel's expulsion of the majority of the Palestinian population was legitimated by elections held among an overwhelmingly Jewish electorate; the remaining Arab population was too numerically weak and politically cowed to pose a serious problem to the state's legitimacy.

In contemporary state making and annexation, electoral legitimation through universal suffrage has become almost compulsory, no longer an option of convenience for nationalists. Excluded groups cannot be simply disenfranchised. Unless they are very small minorities in the population, they must at least be confined to territories outside the electoral base—on the model of the Bantustans in apartheid South Africa. Often they cannot be tolerated even as powerless minorities. Hence the process of homogenization has frequently been taken to the point at which these groups are virtually wiped from the territory to be annexed. Up to 90 percent of non-Serbs may have been forced from Serbian-occupied territories in Bosnia in the early 1990s. Abkhazian separatists in Georgia, claiming to represent the less than one-fifth of the region's population who were ethnically Abkhaz, managed to expel the majority in their quest for an ethnically homogeneous state.

The contemporary global revolution, although universalizing democracy, has generated a counterrevolution that utilizes democratic forms. Democracy even becomes a cloak for its antithesis, genocide. Global democratic norms actually generate incentives to those who seek to gain power through war to perpetrate it in a genocidal manner. As interstate war has declined, the dominant forms of warfare have become genocidal, directed—like the Nazi war against the Jews—against unarmed civilian populations. But whereas the Nazi campaign was one component of the interstate war across Europe, in contemporary wars genocide is often the principal form of violence, with civilians the prime victims. In World War II, civilian victims were still an overall minority; in contemporary wars, they are the vast majority. Thus democratic principles are cruelly inverted in the new wars.

Where ethnic exclusion and genocide take place, they are rarely reversed even through globally legitimate international interventions. Intervention usually occurs (if at all) after the main phases of war and genocide, not at a point when prevention is possible. Thus large-scale intervention in Bosnia did not take place until 1995, after three years of cleansing. Serious intervention was avoided in Rwanda in 1994, even though it was obvious that a relatively small force could have stemmed the mass killings. After the event, UN-sponsored (in Bosnia, NATO-organized) forces eventually arrived, supporting in principle the processes of returning victims and bringing criminals to international justice. All of this was far too little and too late, as President Clinton and Secretary-General Annan acknowledged in their apologies to the Rwandan people and government for international inaction.

Western states—as well as the UN Security Council, in which less democratic states like Russia and undemocratic states like China have major voices—are often more concerned with the forms of democracy than with the content. For example, although the Serbian genocide in Bosnia implicated virtually the entire Serbian elite and all forms of state institution, the Dayton Accords of 1995 legitimated Republika Srpska, the Serbian entity produced by the genocide. The West then supported "moderate" Serbian nationalists, led by Biljana Plavsic, former deputy of the indicted war criminal Radovan Karadzic who was herself to surrender to the International War Crimes Tribunal in 2001. She was prepared to cooperate with the international community. The West thus condoned and legitimated this acceptable Serbian nationalism with its ethnically cleansed electorate.

Such cases emphasize more than ever the ambiguities in the relationships among democracy, war, and peace. The global revolution is doubly unfinished. First, democratic change is only partially accomplished. In some major states it has either not developed very far or been blocked. Even at the beginning of the 1989–1991 revolutionary period, democratic change in China was defeated through military repression. Democratic reform in the Soviet Union was pursued hesitantly by Gorbachev, who fatally failed to secure electoral legitimation for his reforms. The fragmentation of the Soviet Union under Yeltsin resulted largely in a seizure of power by a new set of semiauthoritarian republican elites, who were mostly wise enough to wrap themselves in the forms of democracy while conceding minimal parliamentary control. Even in Central Europe, where parliamentary democracy had more content than in the former Soviet Union or former Yugoslavia, some authoritarian trends remained. A balance sheet of the period 1989–1991 in the former communist states reveals a very partial and uneven advance for democratic reform.

Elsewhere in the world, democratic change has similar problems. Essentially, there are three specific limitations. Many authoritarian states have still seen little significant reform. In many, if not most, of those where reforms have taken place, there is often little institutional or cultural embedding of democracy, so authoritarianism can be maintained or re-created in "democratic" guise. Finally, in most states, although civil society has been strengthened, it remains weak compared with the established democracies and thus is a poor counterweight to state power.

The second way in which the global revolution remains unfinished is the weak development of globally legitimate authority and institutional frameworks. The United Nations has recovered some of its standing, which was highly compromised during the Cold War, but it is poorly developed as a global authority system. The West—especially the United States, which remains at the center of power—refuses to invest resources or authority in legitimate global institutions. There is a deep structural contradiction in a global order that rests not just on national and international forms in general but so disproportionately on a particular nation-state. U.S. superiority sustains the deeply embedded nationalist ideology that sees U.S. interests as the arbiter of global change.

The rest of the West, even the rapidly developing European Union, remains incapable of articulating globalist strategies, institutions, and ideologies in a way that can spur the development of a more coherent and legitimate global order (although at the end of the 1990s the world economic crisis and the new ascendancy of social democratic parties in Europe were slightly raising the profile of this agenda). The legitimacy of the Western-UN bloc among non-Western elites and even more populations is highly variable and problematic. This is not just because of the continuing authoritarianism and nationalism in many states but also because globally dominant interests and actually existing global institutions offer so very little to most of the world's people.

In particular, the renewed global institutions remain far too accommodating to states and parties that launch wars. They largely failed to manage the outbreak of new, genocidal wars in the 1990s and have managed aftermaths in ways that have offered little to victimized populations. The development of international legal institutions, especially the International Tribunal for Yugoslavia and Rwanda and the proposed permanent International Criminal Court, has been important but slow and uncertain. (The United States has scandalously refused to cede even minimal authority to the proposed court.) Although there is some evidence that the numbers of wars in Europe and the former Soviet area are declining with the stalemating of post–Cold War conflicts (D. Smith, 1998), the progress of global order to date offers little hope of any fundamental advance in the control of violence.

The unfinished character of the global revolution is part of the explanation for the problems more commonly associated with globalization in the literature. The growing integration of the world economy, especially in sectors like finance and communications, poses new problems of management and regulation that are only partially amenable to the control of national state apparatuses and that the Western state bloc and its institutions are tackling too slowly. The failure to recognize that a partially global economy requires correspondingly strong global institutions is another sign of the inability of Western elites to provide leadership for worldwide change, despite their pivotal position in the emergent global order. Instability in the world economy is another factor in the instability of state relations and forms in the new era.

This analysis suggests that the global revolution will be consolidated only when a stronger, more coherent new structure of state relations and forms replaces those of the disintegrating national-international order. Further major upheavals are inevitable before the global revolution can be consolidated in anything like a stable order in which conflict is managed institutionally rather than erupting in widespread violence. In this sense, the contradictory relations of democracy and war are likely to continue to mark the history of the early twenty-first century.

On the one hand, forces in both state institutions and civil society that are pushing toward the creation of a genuine, stable democracy—both within national units and in expanded global state institutions. On the other hand, powerful forces in national states and societies will continue to use war to counter this democratic revolution and will abuse democratic forms to create and legitimate their power. On the evidence to date, the dominant Western state bloc and its U.S. center will continue to vacillate between these contending forces, often much more concerned with their own local interests than with global principles. The demonstration of a causal link between democratic government within states and peaceful relations between them may support the reorientation of Western—especially U.S.—foreign policy toward the belated promotion of democracy, but it neatly returns the primary responsibility for a peaceful world order to local state elites. In an era when Western leaders are more willing to talk global and democratic than to commit real resources and effort to the construction of global democratic institutions, this doctrine may be reassuring.

This is a situation in which the equation of democracy and peace is more a historic promise, which we are beginning to realize through global movements and institutions, than a settled pattern we can identify with established democratic nation-states and their interrelations. The given historic pattern, which continues to this day, is one in which democracy has been implicated too often in war, violence, and even genocide. Overcoming this legacy, rather than complacently affirming the superiority of Western democratic states, is the real challenge.

10

The International Relations of Democracy, Liberalism, and War: Directions for Future Research

Raymond Duvall and Jutta Weldes

Human beings have long demonstrated their capacity and willingness to engage in organized violence against one another. All too often, one or another political entity—band, gang, tribe, empire, principality, nation, modern state, confederation, transnational military alliance—has inflicted organized violence on another political entity in an effort to compel, or sometimes to destroy or eliminate, the latter. War is a very human phenomenon.

But so, too, is the effort to organize social relations in ways that control, reduce, or at least mitigate warring. Innumerable institutional arrangements—from a monopoly of coercive authority in a Hobbesian leviathan to a dispersal of popular sovereignty in competitive elections and unregulated markets, from a balance of power to a rule of law, from collective security to arms control—have attempted to solve or at least mitigate the problem of war. And hope seems to spring eternal, at least for some, that one or another such institutionalized system of social relations will permit an end to organized violence. In that respect, John Lennon's entreaty to "imagine . . . nothing to kill or die for" also represents a very human phenomenon—the social imagining of, and the working to create, a world free from war, a world of "perpetual peace."[1]

Academics evince the full range of human propensities in their scholarship. Hence they support and abet various instances of warfare, as well as imagining and promoting institutional arrangements designed to establish a world of peace. Sometimes the same scholarly work does both, even simultaneously. In attempting to demonstrate the war-mitigating aspects of a particular institutional arrangement, for example, academic research may legitimate assumptions and practices that themselves foster organized violence, if only inadvertently.[2] Could that be the case for the literature that purports to establish the validity of a lawlike relationship now widely referred to as the "democratic peace" (DP) proposition? Could the proponents of that proposition, in their very human social imaginings of and efforts to foster a world of peace, simultaneously be contributing to the conditions of possibility of large-scale organized violence?

The contributions to this volume engage the literature of the democratic peace proposition at the level of questions such as these. The volume thus offers a critique, but not in the terms of the ongoing debate between proponents of the proposition and its (mostly realist) opponents. That debate largely concerns the existence and causal interpretation of an empirical pattern in which interstate wars between liberal democracies have been extremely rare. By contrast, this volume seeks to move research beyond the empirical pattern and its causal interpretation. It is not quibbling with the democratic peace proposition at that level, nor does it charge that the empirical pattern on which its proponents say the validity of that proposition rests is meaningless. Instead, the works assembled here start from a different ground. Collectively, they assert that the empirical pattern cannot sustain the weight of argument built on it, or the implications generally taken to flow from it, by its proponents. Specifically, the empirical pattern does not constitute a transhistorically valid causal law; it is merely an empirical pattern. Although they do not claim that this pattern is meaningless, the authors here concur that its meaning is substantially different from that at stake in the existing debate. Accordingly, rather than calling for research to focus on further documenting the pattern, on directly challenging its existence, or on the now more common agenda of seeking to establish *the* causal mechanism responsible for generating it, this collection promotes research in very different directions.

The chapters in this book have not produced final, definitive answers to questions about liberalism, democracy, war, and peace. They have not settled research agendas (except perhaps to terminate that of the democratic peace proposition per se). Instead, this collection opens up an array of new agendas by viewing the empirical pattern underlying the DP proposition in a different light. Specifically, this volume directs attention to the historical and systemic contexts that provide both the meaning of and conditions of possibility for the empirical pattern, as well as to the multiple and complex other ways in which liberalism, democracy, war, and peace are interrelated and co-determined.

In this chapter we highlight some of the emerging research questions raised by contributions to this volume. We also suggest additional questions that, although not explicated in this collection, are in the spirit of its critical engagement with the DP proposition. Our aim in building on the other chapters here is to sketch the outlines of new research agendas for the international relations of democracy, liberalism, and war. Those agendas, we hope, will propel research well beyond a fixation on a simple, bivariate empirical pattern of dubious transhistorical causal significance.

We organize the development of this outline in three sections, each of which concerns questions primarily about the possibility conditions for some phenomenon. The questions that we propose to guide research, then, are first and foremost constitutive rather than causal questions.[3] The three sections suggest a progressive expansion beyond the narrow confines of the DP proposition. In the first, we address the possibility conditions for "seeing" the empirical pattern that is at the heart of the existing debate and propose a critical engagement with the taken-for-granted assumptions in the scholarly establishment and its validation of that pattern. In the second, we turn our attention to the historical and systemic conditions of possibility for the democratic peace itself, encouraging consideration of how liberal democracy and a "zone of peace" have been made jointly possible. (Note that this is *not* asking, "What feature of liberal democratic states 'causes' them not to engage one another in intense, direct military combat?") Finally, in the third section we consider the historical and systemic possibility conditions for multiple and complex relations among liberalism, democracy, war, and peace. Here we explicitly encourage a research shift away from the predominant fixation on a single, bivariate empirical pattern.

SEEING THE DEMOCRATIC PEACE

What makes it possible for scholars of international relations to claim a lawlike relationship between democracy and peace? How must they view the world in order to discern a strong empirical pattern? Why, in the current historical context, have liberal scholars and policymakers in various parts of the world been so accepting of the import of the pattern while realists and critical theorists have remained skeptical? These are a first set of questions toward a new research agenda. They concern the conceptual foundations of the DP proposition, the concepts in terms of which a pattern is seen. Few participants in the ongoing DP debate would disagree that the empirical evidence is heavily dependent on the precise "operational definitions" of the two key concepts, democracy and peace (or, more correctly, war, the absence of which is taken to define peace). But even fewer seem to be concerned about the work being done by this conceptual dependence. We are not referring here to matters of coding—whether one or another case meets or fails to meet the criteria of this or that operational definition—about which much has already been written. Instead, we are pointing to a far more basic question, which asks, "What kind of world, with what relations of power and in whose interests, is being taken for granted, or made to seem natural, through these conceptual definitions, and what kinds of worlds are ruled out?" This is a question of ideology. It grows out of the recognition that social scientific concepts are not neutral data containers, but rather are elements in broader discourses that are productive of differentially interested and empowered social relations. A first step beyond the limitations of the DP debate, then, is to turn a critical eye toward the discursive, ideological foundations of the proposition around which it revolves. This, we suggest, should be approached in two ways.

First, critical research is needed on the discourses of democracy and war in which the concepts of the democratic peace proposition are embedded. As Tarak Barkawi and Mark Laffey propose in the introduction to this volume, this calls for something of a genealogy, examining how and why the specific conceptual meanings of that proposition came to be taken for granted. How is it that "democracy" has come to be understood unproblematically as a system of competitive elections, executive accountability, and political-legal rights for individuals, with the result that the United States stands as the model of a liberal democratic state? And how has "war" come to be viewed as intense deadly combat between the regular armed forces of two sovereign states? What ideological work has gone into the production of these dominant discourses of democracy and war? These are not issues of mere words, nor are they arcane or navel-gazing questions. Rather, they lie at the heart of what the democratic peace proposition *means*. After all, as Tarak Barkawi shows in Chapter 6, democracies do in fact fight each other, but these cases are ruled out—with profound ideological effects—by the conceptual underpinnings of the DP proposition. The DP proposition, in other words, is an ideological artifact of specific definitional practices. Such academic practices and their ideological effects should therefore be further investigated because they are central to an understanding of what relations of power and what interests are privileged in the celebration of that proposition as a putatively transhistorically valid causal law, as well as in efforts to deploy it as a guide for practical action.[4]

These issues lead in turn to questions about the broader worldviews or theories implicit in the taken-for-granted conceptions underlying the DP proposition. For example, the conception of war as intense deadly combat between the regular armed forces of two or more sovereign states entails, among other things, a particular set of assumptions about the state and the military and their relationship. Those kinds of assumptions, the implicit theorizations underlying the DP proposition, need to be examined critically. As Timothy Kubik demonstrates very effectively in Chapter 5 on the militarization of imperial Germany, doing so can lead to a radically different understanding of the proposition. So a first part of a new research agenda suggested by this volume is a careful, critical analysis of the "democracy" and "war" that frame the ongoing DP debate. This is a call not for a critique of coding rules and coding decisions but for an excavation of the theories and ideologies that such rules and decisions entail.

Second, this issue should be approached as well, we believe, through explicit attention to conceptions of democracy, war, and peace that are ruled out by the naturalizing of the concepts of the democratic peace proposition. If one understands democracy and peace differently and draws on different discourses, the strong claims that have been made on behalf of this empirical pattern are disrupted. Specifically, does one still see the zone of democratic peace as either a zone of democracy or a zone of peace? In Chapter 8, Mark Rupert—highlighting the lack of democracy in actually existing liberal democratic states—indicates that the answer to that question may well be no. If liberal democracies are not democratic in important ways, then what is the democratic peace really about? Perhaps it is about something other than democracy. Moreover, actually existing liberal democracies are not in fact peaceful domestically. For instance, the United States, the exemplar of liberal democracy, is rife with the internal use of force (both by the state directly and indirectly sanctioned by the state); it appears, for instance, in the pervasive domestic violence against women and children, in the increasing use of violence against a burgeoning prison population, and in the long and painful histories of labor and racial violence. As more attention to the analytical categories of race, class, and gender would highlight, for many who are marginalized within liberal democracy it might be insulting to call this a "zone of peace." And if liberal democracies are not internally pacific, what of the normative claim for the global promotion of liberal democracy that typically accompanies the DP proposition?

A fruitful avenue for research, then, would be a systematic exploration of the representations of the putative zone of democratic peace generated in the light of alternative understandings of democracy, war, and peace.[5] Pursuing that avenue will highlight clearly and explicitly the narrowly circumscribed meaning and significance of the democratic peace proposition.[6] Failing to do so risks making a fetish of specific conceptions, which in turn can contribute to the scientific legitimation of a range of practices otherwise seen as undemocratic, antidemocratic, or warlike. Barkawi's critique in Chapter 6 of the DP proposition in light of some of the violent practices of power politics by the United States, particularly in the so-called Third World during the Cold War, provides a pointed reminder of this. He and Mark Rupert (Chapter 8) give strong impetus to a research agenda that self-consciously works against the fetishizing of the narrow conceptualizations of democracy and war that, when adopted, permit analysts to see a zone of democratic peace.

CONTEXTUALIZING THE DEMOCRATIC PEACE

If a first significant research step beyond the democratic peace proposition is a critical engagement with its conceptual foundations, a second important step suggested by this volume is to direct attention away from atomistic and behavioralist commitments. Needed instead is a focus on the historical and systemic contexts that have made the observed empirical pattern possible and have shaped the social meaning of a zone of democratic peace.

The logic of explanation employed predominantly by analysts of the democratic peace is reductionist and causal (in the Humean sense). That is, researchers seek to account for the observed phenomenon—in this instance, the behavioral regularity that liberal democratic states have rarely engaged one another's regular armed forces in intense deadly combat—by identifying properties or attributes of the entities whose behaviors are at issue—in this instance, properties of liberal democratic states such as institutional arrangements, decisionmaking style, a culture of compromise, or acceptance of norms of reciprocity. This is reductionist, or atomistic, in that it defines the phenomenon purely in behavioral terms *and* locates the explanation in properties or attributes of the behaving entities. It is causal (in the Humean sense) in that explanation is taken to be a matter of identifying some variable antecedent condition(s), the occurrence of which is uniformly associated with the behavioral regularity. This reductionist, causal logic of explanation leads to the potentially dangerous and definitely problematic conclusion that some (virtually magical) feature of liberal democracies—invariant across time, space, and cultural context—prevents them from being belligerent in relation to one another.

The current volume pushes in a different direction. It accepts that when democracy and peace are defined in very specific ways, there is (or, since the future is uncertain, it is probably better to say there has been) an empirical pattern of democratic peace.[7] In dispute is how to view and understand that pattern. The contributions here suggest the radical alternative of seeing it as a historically contingent, systemic condition. This calls for a new research agenda focused on the conditions of possibility of the coproduction of (a particular form of) liberal democracy and (a specific expression of) a zone of peace, rather than searching for causes among the attributes of liberal democratic states. What might such a research agenda entail? At least three strands of research are necessary, we believe.

First, since a (frequently hidden or unacknowledged) premise of the DP proposition is that two states must recognize each other as democracies, inquiry is called for into the possibility conditions for such mutual recognition.[8] This means asking how a shared discourse of democracy has been socially constructed in international relations. It also means asking what that discourse produces—what the social identity of liberal democracy means, and what kinds of social relations are effected through the performance of that identity. These may seem like rather pedestrian, even trivial matters; that is, it might be assumed that there is no great mystery in democracies recognizing one another as such. But these issues are far from trivial. Identity production is always a historically contingent cultural process that draws on and is productive of particular social relations. To be a democracy is not simply to have certain structural features; nor is it primarily a matter of self-identity, of calling oneself a democracy. Instead, it is to be *socially* recognized (by other states, for example) as such and, accordingly, *not* to be deemed to be something outside of or "other" to the democratic world. David Blaney in Chapter 2 and Martin Shaw in Chapter 9, each in his own way, suggest the dependence of the liberal democratic zone of peace on the relations of that zone of peace to an "outside." We propose that such suggestions be followed up by a research agenda that focuses on the historically shifting boundary between the democratic world and its outside as among the possibility conditions for a democratic peace. How is that boundary produced, and with what implications for conditions of inclusion in a world of mutually recognized democracies?

Two contemporary examples may help to make this point. Although definitive answers to counterfactual questions will always elude social scientists, it is worth asking whether Yugoslavia under Slobodon Milosevic's rule would not have been identified as part of the democratic world if its domestic political institutions and practices of 1998–1999 (e.g., competitive elections, relatively uncensored press, reforms toward a more open economy, efforts to suppress the "radical" insurrection) were set in the historical, systemic context of fifteen years earlier. Have the social practices of recognition of democratic identity in international relations not changed over the past 25, 50, 100, 200 years? Another example is provided by Himadeep Muppidi in Chapter 3: the long-term adversarial relationship between India and Pakistan over Kashmir has varied in intensity over time but involves a nearly continuous engagement of forces in combat, regardless of changes in the formal institutional status of democracy in either or both. As Muppidi argues, this may reflect the fact that democratic identity plays a limited, perhaps even irrelevant role in the mutual recognition of the two states. Related to this second example is the noteworthy point that most, if not all, of the ambiguous, borderline, or controversial cases much discussed in the DP debate can be understood in terms of the limited salience of mutual recognition as democracies per se. Rather than quarrel over the degree to which these cases fit precise criteria of fixed operational definitions, researchers would be well advised to direct attention to the historically and systematically variable discourses of democracy that have shaped the possibility of a democratic peace.

Second, an important line of research is to investigate the coupling of the socially produced identity boundary to the social constitution of a zone of peace. In short, how did the democratic world also get produced as a noncombat zone among the regular militaries of its members? This is not a question of the attributes of individual democracies that prevent them from making war against each other. Instead, it is a matter of specific understandings and practices of war and peace as culturally connected to—or articulated with—social recognition of a democratic identity. We are not subtly imposing the causal argument here that the democratic peace is caused by some transcendent normative consensus or even assuming that a normative consensus exists. Instead, we are saying that a zone of peace is made possible only by virtue of a set of understandings and knowledgeable practices through which it is constituted, even if the democratic peace is an unintended consequence of them. How is it, we ask, that the mutual recognition of democracies is linked to some social understandings and practices such that direct military combat is not how disputes are settled? A normative consensus, if it exists, could provide that linkage. But so could a variety of different practices: the structural integration of militaries, or the expansion of liberal capitalism, or the exercise of control by a hegemonic power in the informal empire of a democratic world. What is needed is research concerning the historically shifting and systemically variable meanings and practices of war and peace and the grafting of a distinct subset of those understandings onto democracy and democratic practices. In Chapter 9, Martin Shaw nicely hints at such arguments, as he points explicitly to historical changes in the understandings and practices of war. Additional research could usefully ask at least the following questions: What are the social understandings of war and peace that in different historical contexts have been articulated with democracies and democratic practices? What relations of power and privilege do they effect? What is the character of the democratic zone of peace? That is, what kind of peace, and for whom, is produced in and by it? These issues are at the heart of the social constitution of the democratic peace. They concern how the empirical pattern is possible and what it means.

Again, the recommendations we are making here can be clarified through an example. At the start of the twenty-first century, an elaborate discourse has become solidly entrenched through which an international politics of violence is justified. This discourse pivots around notions of humanitarian intervention,[9] peacekeeping, preventing genocide, protecting human rights, countering terrorism, and fighting internationally organized crime as a collective military responsibility of the established democracies. Somewhat akin to the doctrine of the White Man's Burden a century earlier, this discourse locates a center of responsibility for providing a stable, just, and peaceful world order. This center is defined by articulating "war as responsibility" with the established democracies as a collectivity. This discursive construction is a potentially important condition of possibility for the constitution of the democratic peace in the early twenty-first century, just as the partial integration of militaries under NATO to maintain perpetual vigilance against communist aggression was a similar but distinct condition of possibility for democratic peace during the Cold War era. Also in the context of the early twenty-first century, there has become established a prominent discourse of war as an especially difficult undertaking for democracies but easy for and expected of nondemocracies. This discourse has often been joined with the discourse of humanitarian war to graft war and peace onto the social identities of democratic and nondemocratic worlds in complex ways. Simply consider the pronouncements of U.S. pundits and policymakers alike commenting on NATO's war against Serbia regarding Kosovo. One could hear a claim that wanton violence by "the democracies" was just; at the same time one could hear assertions that "our democratic character" makes it more difficult than ever before to engage in violence that might result in casualties for "our" troops. This involves the articulation of a complex, historically contingent understanding of war with a similarly contingent understanding of democracy and its "other." Careful research on such articulations is called for in order to understand the constitution of a democratic peace.

Third, with the democratic peace contextualized in terms of the social understandings and practices that constitute the observed empirical pattern, it is imperative that attention be directed to the broader systemic conditions—material and ideational—that underpin and make possible the historically specific couplings of democracy and peace it entails. This, of course, is a very large research agenda, one that almost certainly can never be brought to closure. The current volume suggests at least one major avenue, however, that merits highlighting: to focus explicitly on the basis of the democratic peace in liberal modernity. The DP proposition is cast in terms of a conception of *liberal* democracy, the implications of which are generally not adequately probed. By contrast, a major contribution of this volume is to bring to the fore the substantial work performed by its liberal foundations. In Chapter 2, David Blaney, for example, makes the compelling point that liberal modernity sets the terms of the democratic peace. As a historical project, liberal modernity is manifested in capitalism, as well as in a citizenry in specific relation to the modern state, including its administrative and military arms. Pursuing Blaney's lead, then, gives rise to questions of the following kinds: How is capitalism, as the economic face of liberalism, expressed in internationally integrated free markets, internationally recognized property rights, and the virtually global commodification of all facets of life, bound up with the making of a world in which liberal democratic states do not engage one another in intense deadly military combat yet do so engage "others"? How are the distinct discourses of war and peace articulated with democracy rooted in the modern liberal administrative state form and the specific ways it is internally related to citizens as individuals with rights and interests?[10] And to return to the kind of question with which we began this chapter, does the project of liberal modernity foster the legitimacy of organized violence against the illiberal other?

For instance, what some have called "America's longest war"—the U.S. government's sustained campaign of violence to displace, subjugate, and "pacify" nations of indigenous peoples of North America—stands as an important case for consideration. That war does not figure in the DP debate. Many of the indigenous nations were highly democratic but not in a liberal form. And the war against them was not about democracy. It was instead about the social extension of the project of liberal modernity and the violent transformation of the illiberal other into an (inferior) image of the liberal self. As such, this war presaged late-nineteenth-century imperialism and late-twentieth-century crusades for human rights, individual liberty, and free markets. An issue for research, then, is how the project of liberal modernity itself has been simultaneously productive of a zone of peace among liberal democratic states and connected to practices of large-scale organized violence. Such questions are among the issues that must be addressed through careful research by scholars of the international relations of democracy and war in order to develop an adequate understanding of the meaning and significance of the democratic peace. Delimiting the contextual scope of applicability of the DP proposition, more than any other issue, calls for systematic research.

ABANDONING FIXATION ON THE DEMOCRATIC PEACE

Perhaps the most unfortunate feature of the ongoing DP debate is that it fixes attention on a single, simple, bivariate empirical pattern. It is time to abandon that fixation, which, even if only as a subtle subtext in the guise of scientifically objective inquiry, far too readily fosters a self-congratulatory celebration of liberal democratic states' (read "our") passivity, at least in relation to one another. As this volume effectively proclaims, it is time instead to expand the gaze. The historically and systemically conditioned relations among liberalism, democracy, war, and peace are multiple and complex. They are not reducible to the contextually highly limited proposition that the regular armed forces of liberal democratic states have rarely engaged one another in intense deadly combat. A research agenda for the international relations of democracy, liberalism, and war must be attentive to those multiple and complex relations. It would be impossible for us to give a complete accounting of all the research directions that would be entailed in making such a move. We can, however, point to three important lines of research that follow from several contributions to this book.

We already hinted at one of these lines. If there have been and are multiple meanings-in-use of liberalism, democracy, war, and peace, it is important to understand how specific combinations have been and are articulated together. For example, in the context of the Cold War, how did the maintenance of peace within the democratic (or, in the preferred language of the time, free) world articulate with the necessity of always ongoing war with Soviet communism *through* Third World clients irrespective of the democratic aspirations of those clients' opponents? Political movements struggling for popular empowerment and economic democracy routinely met intensely violent responses led by one or another liberal democratic state—liberal democracy was regularly at war with other forms of democracy. Or for a more contemporary example, how is a zone of democratic peace sustained through collective or integrated violence against rogues under the banner of promoting liberal democracy? How do intervention and peacekeeping come to be associated with the established democracies while aggression, terrorism, and genocide are attached to nondemocracies? How is the sometimes brutally repressive policing of domestic challenges to state authority that are rooted in capitalist society (e.g., drug dealers, gangs, organized crime) articulated to an international zone of peace? Much remains to be learned about the many ways in which the social constitution of liberal and/or democratic identities affects the form of knowledgeable practices of war and peace that are connected to the presence or absence of those identities.

A second line of research would follow the lead, but neither the explanatory logic nor the empirical focus, of the DP proposition in investigating how democratic practices shape the meaning and waging of war. It is frequently assumed that in liberal democracies, popular constraints limit war-making abilities. The practical relevance of that assumption, however, has varied across historical and systemic contexts. In the post–Vietnam War era, among NATO members, for example, it is of pronouncedly greater salience than it was in the mid–twentieth century. That enhanced importance has dramatically affected the conduct of war, as well as institutional arrangements for war making. The 1990s' wars against Iraq and Serbia, in which violence was delivered overwhelmingly from air power, provides vivid testimony to this. But the shaping of the meaning and practice of war through democratic practices is not limited even to such relatively simple and direct effects. It includes as well the ways in which broader discourses of democracy, entailing families of closely interconnected concepts such as popular sovereignty and "the people," are implicated in the social-political organizing of relations of violence. In Chapter 3, Himadeep Muppidi's analysis of the democratic pressures that stimulated war between the democratic states of India and Sri Lanka provides a case in point. In Chapter 4,

Michael Mann's exposition of the downside of democracy in making genocide and ethnic cleansing possible is also powerfully illustrative, as well as
suggestive of research avenues. One might ask how genocide, a form of
war made possible through a discourse of democracy, comes to be the object of justification for war making by democratic states. "They" (nondemocracies) engage in genocide and ethnic cleansing, which must be opposed, even violently if necessary, by democracies acting responsibly; but
genocide and ethnic cleansing themselves are made possible through discourses of democracy. Research on the international relations of democracy
and war needs to be systematically attentive to such complex, contextually
conditioned relations. There is no timeless, general relationship between
liberal democracy and the making of war and peace.

A third line of work would reverse the causal arrows, if you will, and
focus on ways in which war has affected democracy. This, too, is a complex
and contextually conditioned set of relations. In Chapter 7, Bruce Cumings
very effectively highlights the profound importance of war in establishing
the institutional arrangements of liberal democracy in East Asia (and more
generally). This raises the crucially important question, just how dependent
has the making and maintenance of liberal democracy been on war making?
Here, to point to just one example, it seems worth reflecting on the fact that
each of the major extensions of the franchise in the United States in the
twentieth century (to women, to African Americans, and to adults between
the ages of eighteen and twenty-one) was rooted in a major international
war. What is the character of the democracy that is generated and sustained
through modern warfare? For example, one could usefully ask what the
meaning of democracy in the United States such that World War II and the
Cold War fostered the creation of a vast national security apparatus that was
sometimes at "war" with some U.S. citizens. Are the contemporary military
interventions and incursions by established democracies under the banner
of promoting and safeguarding liberal democracy productive of a more effectively democratic world? And how do those interventions and the myriad other forms of war engaged in routinely by at least some liberal democracies, such as the United States, shape the practices of democracy at
home? For example, one could study the many ways in which the U.S. military defeat by the Vietnamese had profound and complex effects on the
practices of democracy in the United States. If, as Mark Rupert argues in
Chapter 8, contemporary liberal democracy is not very democratic, are new
forms of warfare, as popular struggles, called for? What kinds of democracy
do those alternative forms of war produce? Are such democratic worlds
more effectively peaceful worlds? And if contemporary liberal democracy is
not very peaceful internally, are new forms of democracy called for? What
forms of democracy might the pursuit of internal peace produce?

The list of questions could go on. But we fear we may be verging on being as guilty as democratic peace proponents of letting our imaginings of a desirable world blind us to the great complexities of the international relations of democracy, liberalization, war, and peace. It is to those complexities more than specific imaginings that we believe it is time for research to be directed.

NOTES

1. We use the term "world" to denote any large-scale social system, although we do wish to include the possibility of reference to "the whole world." One could substitute the currently popular term "zone" without loss of meaning and hence could speak of the social imagining of a zone free from war or a zone of perpetual peace as long as such language, too, includes the possibility of reference to the whole world. Some of the contributions to this volume, such as David Blaney's, suggest, however, that the latter condition does not hold in democratic peace theory because in the assumptions underlying that theory, the zone of peace is bound up intimately and necessarily with a zone of war. There is no possibility in this view of imagining a liberal democratic peace for the whole world. In this regard, consider also the chapters by Martin Shaw and Bruce Cumings (Chapters 9 and 7, respectively).

2. For example, a putative Munich Syndrome is frequently invoked by critics of scholarship that promotes institutional practices of negotiation among adversaries in an effort to remind that the concessions and appeasement that are part and parcel of negotiation can energize a would-be aggressor. If this "syndrome" has validity, the scholarly proponents of a negotiated peace may simultaneously foster the conditions of possibility of a war of aggression. Or more generally, since at least the second edition of E. H. Carr's *The Twenty Years' Crisis* (1946), realists have maintained, whether rightly or wrongly, that the utopian images of peace through international institutions are counterproductive. For Carr, the crisis that set the stage for the deadliest of modern international wars was very much a product of liberal, utopian thought. It is interesting to note, however, that Carr's realism did not in fact see concessions and appeasement as utopian. The original edition of *The Twenty Years' Crisis* expressed support for the wisdom of the Munich agreements and indeed praised Neville Chamberlain's policy as "a reaction of realism against utopianism" (1939: 14, note 1).

3. For an elaboration of this distinction and a strong justification of a research focus on the former, see Wendt, 1999.

4. In terms of implications for practical action, pronounced differences can arise depending on what the DP proposition is understood to mean. For example, it might be interpreted by some as legitimating a crusade, whereas for others it implies a "rally the wagons" effect. The bases of these important differences cannot be brought effectively to light except through critical examination of the ideological foundations of the DP proposition.

5. Obviously, limits would have to be placed on the range of alternative conceptualizations and discourses of democracy, war, and peace. It seems sufficient, in our view, to limit analysis to identifiable meanings-in-use among participants in arenas of politically organized violence or engaged in democratic or democritizing practices. That is, we propose that researchers take seriously actors' self- and

social understandings of democracy, war, and peace. These action-relevant understandings are clearly not currently restricted to the specific, narrow operational definitions of the democratic peace proposition, nor have they been so limited throughout history. In that respect, we are calling for research that relaxes rigid scientism and its fixing of meanings in favor of at least some appreciation of an interpretive methodology's sensitivity to the meanings-in-use among actual practitioners in different contexts. Certainly, some powerful actors currently understand democracy, for example, in terms very similar to those of the democratic peace. But just as certainly, other actors have engaged in often difficult struggles to effect democracy in radically different terms. It is analysis around just such *significant* meanings that we are proposing here.

6. In more positive terms, it will also permit the kinds of analyses proposed in the last section of this chapter—namely, investigations of the multiple and complex relations among liberalism, democracy, war, and peace.

7. Although Himadeep Muppidi in Chapter 3 does point out that even on these terms the democratic states of India and Pakistan went to war several times.

8. Lacking this premise, the DP proposition would have no ability to account for the frequency with which democracies make war against nondemocracies. There must be mutual recognition through which each sees the other as fundamentally like itself—that is, a democracy. Otherwise, the empirical pattern would be accidental.

9. In the context of NATO's war against Serbia concerning Kosovo, the notion of humanitarian intervention was even replaced by the term "humanitarian war." The meaning of that apparent oxymoron is sensible only in the context of the liberal discourse of just war doctrines.

10. The notion of internal relations refers to structural or mutual constitution. The elements of an internal relation do not exist as such except by virtue of their relation to each other. Classic examples are master-slave and parent-child structures. Our point is that the liberal state and a citizenry of individuals with rights and interests are similarly internally related, or structural, elements.

Bibliography

Abish, Walther. 1980. *Wie Deutsch Ist Es? A Novel.* New York: W. W. Norton.
Abrams, Philip. 1982. *Historical Sociology.* Ithaca: Cornell University Press.
Adler, Emanuel. 1997. "Seizing the Middle Ground: Constructivism in World Politics." *European Journal of International Relations* 3(3): 319–363.
Agnew, John. 1994. "The Territorial Trap: The Geographical Assumptions of International Relations Theory." *Review of International Political Economy* 1(1): 53–80.
Agnew, John, and Stuart Corbridge. 1995. *Mastering Space: Hegemony, Territory and the International Political Economy.* London: Routledge.
Ahmad, Aijaz. 1994 [1992]. *In Theory: Classes, Nations, Literature.* London: Verso.
———. 1995. "Postcolonialism: What's in a Name?" in Roman de la Campa, E. Ann Kaplan, and Michael Sprinker, eds., *Late Imperial Culture.* London: Verso, pp. 11–32.
Albrow, Martin. 1996. *The Global Age: State and Society Beyond Modernity.* Stanford: Stanford University Press.
Almaguer, Tomas. 1994. *Racial Fault Lines: The Historical Origins of White Supremacy in California.* Berkeley: University of California Press.
Almond, Gabriel, and Sidney Verba. 1963. *The Civic Culture: Political Attitudes and Democracy in Five Nations.* Boston: Little, Brown.
Andreas, Peter. 2000. *Border Games: Policing the U.S.-Mexico Divide.* Ithaca: Cornell University Press.
Anzaldua, Gloria. 1990. "Hacienda caras, una entrada," in Gloria Anzaldua, ed., *Making Face, Making Soul: Hacienda Casas.* San Francisco: Aunt Lute, pp. xv–xxviii.
Appadorai, A., and M. S. Rajan. 1985. *India's Foreign Policy and Relations.* New Delhi: South Asian Publishers.
Arblaster, Anthony. 1984. *The Rise and Decline of Western Liberalism.* Oxford: Blackwell.
———. 1987. *Democracy.* Minneapolis: University of Minnesota Press.
Aron, Raymond. 1968. *On War.* New York: W. W. Norton.
———. 1974. *Imperial Republic: The United States and the World, 1945–1973.* Englewood Cliffs, NJ: Prentice-Hall.
Arrighi, Giovanni. 1999. "Globalization, State Sovereignty, and the 'Endless' Accumulation of Capital," in David A. Smith et al., eds., *States and Sovereignty in the Global Economy.* London: Routledge, pp. 53–73.

Bader, Veit. 1995. "Citizenship and Exclusion: Radical Democracy, Community, and Justice. Or What Is Wrong with Communitarianism?" *Political Theory* 23(2): 211–246.

Bald, Detlef. 1977. *Der deutsche Generalstab, 1859–1939: Reform und Restauration in Ausbildung und Bildung.* Wolfenbüttel: Rock.

Bald, Detlef, Gerhild Bald-Gerlach, and Eduard Ambros. 1985. *Tradition und Reform in militärischen Bildungswesen: Von der preuischen Allgemeinen Kriegsschule zur Führungsakademie der Bundeswehr: Eine Dokumentation, 1810–1985.* Baden-Baden: Nomos Verlagsgesellschaft.

Banuri, Tariq. 1990. "Modernization and Its Discontents: A Cultural Perspective on the Theories of Development," in Frederique Apffel-Marglin and Stephen A. Marglin, eds., *Dominating Knowledge: Development, Culture, and Resistance.* Oxford: Clarendon, pp. 73–101.

Barkawi, Tarak. 1998. "Strategy as a Vocation: Weber, Morgenthau and Modern Strategic Studies." *Review of International Studies* 24(2): 159–184.

Barkawi, Tarak, and Mark Laffey. 1999. "The Imperial Peace: Democracy, Force and Globalization." *European Journal of International Relations* 5(4): 403–434.

Barraclough, Geoffrey. 1967. *An Introduction to Contemporary History.* London: Penguin.

Bell-Fialkoff, Andrew. 1996. *Ethnic Cleansing.* New York: St. Martin's.

Berghan, Volker. 1982a. *Militarism, 1861–1979.* Leamington Spa: Berg.

———. 1982b. *Modern Germany: Society, Economy and Politics in the Twentieth Century.* Cambridge: Cambridge University Press.

Bernstein, J., and L. Mishel. 1999. "Wages Gain Ground," Washington, DC: Economic Policy Institute.

Bickford, Susan. 1996. *The Dissonance of Democracy: Listening, Conflict, and Citizenship.* Ithaca: Cornell University Press.

Biersteker, Thomas, and Cynthia Weber, eds. 1996. *State Sovereignty as Social Construct.* Cambridge: Cambridge University Press.

Blackbourn, David, and Geoff Eley. 1984. *The Peculiarities of German History: Bourgeois Society and Politics in 19th Century Germany.* New York: Oxford University Press.

Blackbourn, David, and Richard J. Evans. 1991. *The German Bourgeoisie: Essays on the Social History of the German Middle Class from the Late Eighteenth to the Early Twentieth Century.* New York: Routledge.

Blaney, David L., and Naeem Inayatullah. 1994. "Prelude to a Conversation of Cultures in International Society? Todorov and Nandy on the Possibility of Dialogue." *Alternatives* 19(1): 23–51.

Block, Fred. 1977. "The Ruling Class Does Not Rule." *Socialist Revolution* 33: 6–28.

Blum, William. 1995. *Killing Hope: U.S. Military and CIA Interventions Since World War II.* Monroe, ME: Common Courage Press.

Boettcher, Robert, with Gordon L. Freedman. 1980. *Gifts of Deceit: Sun Myung Moon, Tongsun Park, and the Korean Scandal.* New York: Holt, Rinehart, and Winston.

Bohman, James. 1997. "The Public Spheres of the World Citizen," in James Bohman and Matthias Lutz-Bachmann, eds., *Perpetual Peace: Essays on Kant's Cosmopolitan Ideal.* Cambridge, MA: MIT Press, pp. 179–200.

Bohman, James, and Matthias Lutz-Bachmann, eds. 1997. *Perpetual Peace: Essays on Kant's Cosmopolitan Ideal.* Cambridge, MA: MIT Press.

Bowles, Chester. 1954. *Ambassador's Report.* New York: Harper and Brothers.

Bowles, Samuel, and Richard Edwards. 1993. *Understanding Capitalism: Competition, Command, and Change in the U.S. Economy,* 2d ed. New York: HarperCollins.

Bowles, Samuel, and Herbert Gintis. 1986. *Democracy and Capitalism.* New York: Basic.

Brands, H. W. 1993. *The Devil We Knew: Americans and the Cold War.* Oxford: Oxford University Press.

Brass, Paul R. 1997. *Theft of an Idol.* Princeton: Princeton University Press.

Brecher, Jeremy, and Tim Costello. 1994a. *Global Village or Global Pillage.* Boston: South End.

———. 1994b. "The Lilliput Strategy: Taking on the Multinationals." *The Nation* (December 19): 757–760.

Bremmer, Stuart. 1993. "Democracy and Militarized Interstate Conflict." *International Interactions* 18(3): 231–249.

Bridgman, Jon, and Leslie J. Worley. 1997. "Genocide of the Herreros," in Samuel Totten et al., eds., *Century of Genocide: Eyewitness Accounts and Critical Views.* New York: Garland, pp. 3–24.

Bronfenbrenner, Kate. 1997. "We'll Close! Plant Closings, Plant-Closing Threats, Union Organizing and NAFTA." *Multinational Monitor* (March): 8–13.

Broszat, Martin. 1981. *The Hitler State: The Foundation and Development of the Internal Structure of the Third Reich,* trans. John W. Hiden. London: Longman.

Brown, Chris. 1992. "'Really Existing Liberalism' and International Order." *Millennium* 21(3): 313–328.

Buchholz, Arden. 1991. *Moltke, Schileffen, and Prussian War Planning.* New York: Berg.

Bueno de Mesquita, Bruce, James D. Morrow, Randolph M. Siverson, and Alastair Smith. 1999. "An Institutional Explanation for the Democratic Peace." *American Political Science Review* 93(4): 791–807.

Bukhari, Shujaat. 1997. "Defending Siachen at All Costs." *The Hindu,* July 24: 14.

Bull, Hedley, and Adam Watson, eds. 1984. *The Expansion of International Society.* Oxford: Clarendon.

Bundesminister der Verteidigung. 1985. *Weissbuch: zur Lage und Entwicklung der Bundeswehr.* Bonn: Im Auftrage der Bundesregierung herausgegeben von Bundesminister der Verteidigung.

Bundy, McGeorge. 1988. *Danger and Survival: Choices About the Bomb in the First Fifty Years.* New York: Vintage.

Büsch, Otto. 1962. *Militarsystem und Sozialleben im alten Preussen, 1713–1807.* Berlin: De Gruyter.

Cable, Larry E. 1986. *Conflict of Myths: The Development of American Counterinsurgency Doctrine and the Vietnam War.* New York: New York University Press.

Campbell, David. 1992. *Writing Security: United States Foreign Policy and the Politics of Identity.* Minneapolis: University of Minnesota Press.

Carr, E. H. 1939. *The Twenty Years' Crisis, 1919–1939: An Introduction to the Study of International Relations.* New York: Harper and Brothers.

———. 1945. "Democracy in International Affairs," Nineteenth Cust Foundation Lecture. Nottingham: University College. Pamphlet.

———. 1946. *The Twenty Years' Crisis, 1919–1939: An Introduction to the Study of International Relations,* 2d ed. London: Macmillan.

Castle, Timothy N. 1993. *At War in the Shadow of Vietnam: U.S. Military Aid to the Royal Lao Government 1955–1975.* New York: Columbia University Press.

Champagne, Duane. 1992. *Social Order and Political Change: Constitutional Governments Under the Cherokee, the Choctaw, the Chickasaw and the Creek.* Stanford: Stanford University Press.

Chan, Steve. 1997. "In Search of Democratic Peace: Problems and Promise." *Mershon International Studies Review* 41(suppl. 1): 59–91.

Chatterjee, Partha. 1986. *Nationalist Thought and the Colonial World: A Derivative Discourse?* London: Zed.

———. 1993. *The Nation and Its Fragments.* Princeton: Princeton University Press.

———. 1995. "Religious Minorities and the Secular State: Reflections on the Indian Impasse." *Public Culture* 8(1): 11–39.

Chay, Jongsuk, ed. 1990. *Culture and International Relations.* New York: Praeger.

Churchill, Ward. 1997. *A Little Matter of Genocide: Holocaust and Denial in the Americas, 1492 to the Present.* San Francisco: City Lights.

Clausewitz, Karl von. 1976. *On War*, ed. by Peter Paret and Michael Howard. Princeton: Princeton University Press.

Clinton, William. 1994. "Excerpts from President Clinton's State of the Union Message," *New York Times,* January 26: A17.

Cohen, Raymond. 1994. "Pacific Unions: A Reappraisal of the Theory that 'Democracies Do Not Go to War with Each Other.'" *Review of International Studies* 20(3): 207–223.

Conboy, Kenneth, and James Morrison. 1999. *Feet to the Fire: CIA Covert Operations in Indonesia, 1957–1958.* Annapolis, MD: Naval Institute Press.

Connolly, William. 1991. "Democracy and Territoriality." *Millennium* 20(3): 463–484.

———. 1995. *The Ethos of Pluralization.* Minneapolis: University of Minnesota Press.

———. 1998. "Rethinking *The Ethos of Pluralization.*" *Philosophy and Social Criticism* 24(1): 93–102.

Cox, Robert. 1981. "Social Forces, States and World Orders: Beyond International Relations Theory." *Millennium* 10(2): 1–20.

Craig, Gordon A. 1955. *The Politics of the Prussian Army.* Oxford: Oxford University Press.

———. 1978. *Germany, 1866–1945.* Oxford: Oxford University Press.

Creasy, Edward Shepherd. 1995 [1852]. *Fifteen Decisive Battles of the World.* New York: Random House.

Creveld, Martin van. 1991. *The Transformation of War.* New York: Free Press.

Crozier, Michael, Samuel P. Huntington, and Joji Watanuki. 1975. *The Crisis of Democracy: Report on the Governability of Democracies to the Trilateral Commission.* New York: New York University Press.

Cruise O'Brien, Donal. 1999. "Does Democracy Require an Opposition Party? Implications of Recent African Experience," in H. Giliomee and C. Simkins, eds., *The Awkward Embrace: One-Party Domination and Democracy.* Cape Town, South Africa: Tafelberg Press, pp. 119–136.

Cullather, Nick. 1999. *Secret History: The CIA's Classified Account of Its Operations in Guatemala, 1952–1954.* Stanford: Stanford University Press.

Cumings, Bruce. 1981. *The Origins of the Korean War,* Vol. I. Princeton: Princeton University Press.

———. 1991. *The Origins of the Korean War,* Vol. 2. Princeton: Princeton University Press.

———. 1993. "'Revising Postrevisionism,' or, the Poverty of Theory in Diplomatic History." *Diplomatic History* 17(4): 539–569.

———. 1999. *Parallax Visions: Making Sense of American–East Asian Relations at the End of the Century.* Durham, NC: Duke University Press.

Dadrian, Vahakn N. 1995. *The History of the Armenian Genocide.* Providence, RI: Berghahn.

Dahl, Robert. 1989. *Democracy and Its Critics*. New Haven: Yale University Press.

Dahrendorf, Ralf. 1967. *Society and Democracy in Germany*. New York: Norton.

Dallmayr, Fred. 1996. *Beyond Orientalism: Essays in Cross-Cultural Encounter*. Albany: SUNY Press.

Dawisha, Karen, and Bruce Parrott. 1997. *Conflict, Cleavage, and Change in Central Asia and the Caucasus*. Cambridge: Cambridge University Press.

Demeter, Karl. 1965. *The German Officer Corps in Society and State, 1650–1945*. New York: Praeger.

Deudney, Daniel, and G. John Ikenberry. 1999. "The Nature and Sources of Liberal International Order." *Review of International Studies* 25(2): 179–196.

Deutsch, Karl W. 1964. "External Involvement in Internal War," in Harry Eckstein, ed., *Internal War: Problems and Approaches*. New York: Free Press of Glencoe, pp. 100–110.

Dews, Peter. 1992. *Autonomy and Solidarity: Interviews with Jurgen Habermas*. New York: Verso.

Diamond, Larry. 1990. "Beyond Authoritarianism and Totalitarianism," in Brad Roberts, ed., *The New Democracies: Global Change and U.S. Policy*. Cambridge, MA: MIT Press, pp. 227–249.

Dobbs, Michael. 2000. "'Critical' Foreign Expertise Helped Set the Stage for Milosevic's Defeat." *International Herald Tribune* (London), December 13: 2.

Dolan, Frederick M. 1998. "Paradoxical Responsiveness." *Philosophy and Social Criticism* 4(1): 83–91.

Doyle, Michael W. 1983. "Kant, Liberal Legacies, and Foreign Affairs, Part 1 and 2." *Philosophy and Public Affairs* 12(3, 4): 205–235, 323–353.

———. 1986. "Liberalism and World Politics." *American Political Science Review* 80(4): 1151–1163.

———. 1995. "Liberalism and World Politics Revisited," in Charles Kegley, ed., *Controversies in International Relations Theory*. New York: St. Martin's, pp. 83–106.

———. 1996. "Kant, Liberal Legacies, and Foreign Affairs," in Michael Brown, Sean M. Lynn-Jones, and Steven E. Miller, eds., *Debating the Democratic Peace*. Cambridge, MA: MIT Press, pp. 3–57.

———. 1997. *Ways of War and Peace: Realism, Liberalism and Socialism*. New York: W. W. Norton.

Drechsler, Horst. 1980. *"Let Us Die Fighting": The Struggle of the Herrero and the Nama Against German Imperialism*. London: Zed.

Dryzek, John. 1996. *Democracy in Capitalist Times*. Oxford: Oxford University Press.

Dugger, Celia. 1999. "India Holds Fire in Kashmir as Enemy Forces Pull Out." *New York Times*, July 13.

Duiker, William J. 1995. *Sacred War: Nationalism and Revolution in a Divided Vietnam*. New York: McGraw-Hill.

Dulles, Allen W. 1965. *The Craft of Intelligence*. New York: New American Library.

Dutt, V. P. 1984. *India's Foreign Policy*. New Delhi: Vikas.

Duvall, Raymond. 1976. "An Appraisal of the Methodological and Statistical Procedures of the Correlates of War Project," in Francis W. Hoole and Dina A. Zinnes, eds., *Quantitative International Politics: An Appraisal*. New York: Praeger, pp. 67–98.

Economic Policy Institute (EPI). 1997. *Profits Fax: Corporate Profit Rates Hit New Peak*. Washington, DC: EPI <http://epinet.org/pr970328.html>.

Eden, Lynn. Forthcoming. *Constructing Destruction*. Ithaca: Cornell University Press.

Eley, Geoff. 1996. "German History and the Contradictions of Modernity: The Bourgeoisie, the State, and the Mastery of Reform," in Geoff Eley, ed., *Society, Culture and the State in Germany, 1870–1930*. Ann Arbor: University of Michigan Press, pp. 67–103.

Elman, Miriam Fendius. 1999. "The Never-Ending Story: Democracy and Peace." *International Studies Review* 1(3): 87–103.

————, ed. 1997. *Paths to Peace: Is Democracy the Answer?* Cambridge, MA: MIT Press.

Elshtain, Jean Bethke. 1993. *Public Man, Private Woman: Women in Social and Political Thought*, 2d ed. Princeton: Princeton University Press.

Falk, Richard A., Robert C. Johansen, and Samuel S. Kim, eds. 1993. *The Constitutional Foundations of World Peace*. Albany: SUNY Press.

Fall, Bernard B. 1969. *Anatomy of a Crisis: The Laotian Crisis of 1960–1961*. Garden City, NY: Doubleday.

Farber, Henry S., and Joanne Gowa. 1995. "Polities and Peace." *International Security* 20(2): 123–146.

Feaver, Peter D. 1996. "The Civil-Military Problematique: Huntington, Janowitz, and the Question of Civilian Control." *Armed Forces and Society* 23(2): 149–178.

Fein, H. 1984. "Scenarios of Genocide: Models of Genocide and Critical Responses," in Israel W. Charny, ed., *Toward the Understanding and Prevention of Genocide*. Boulder: Westview, pp. 3–31.

Fishkin, James S. 1991. *Democracy and Deliberation: New Directions for Democratic Reform*. New Haven: Yale University Press.

Forsythe, David P. 1992. "Democracy, War, and Covert Action." *Journal of Peace Research* 29(4): 385–395.

Freeman, M. 1995. "Genocide, Civilization and Modernity." *British Journal of Sociology* 46(2): 207–223.

Friedberg, Aaron L. 1992. "Why Didn't the United States Become a Garrison State?" *International Security* 16(4): 109–142.

Fukuyama, Francis. 1989. "The End of History." *National Interest* 16 (summer): 3–18.

Gaddis, John Lewis. 1982. *Strategies of Containment: A Critical Appraisal of Postwar American National Security Policy*. Oxford: Oxford University Press.

Gagnon, V. P. 1997. "Ethnic Nationalism and International Conflict: The Case of Serbia," in Michael E. Brown et al., eds., *Nationalism and Ethnic Conflict*. Cambridge, MA: MIT Press, pp. 132–168.

Gellner, Ernest. 1983. *Nations and Nationalism*. Oxford: Blackwell.

Gerschenkron, Alexander. 1962. *Economic Backwardness in Historical Perspective*. Cambridge, MA: Harvard University Press.

Geyer, Michael. 1986. "German Strategy in the Age of Machine Warfare," in Peter Paret, ed., *Makers of Modern Strategy: From Machiavelli to the Nuclear Age*. Princeton: Princeton University Press, pp. 527–597.

————. 1990. "The Past as Future: The German Officer Corps as Profession," in Geoffrey Cocks and Konrad Jarausch, eds., *German Professions*. Oxford: Oxford University Press, pp. 183–212.

Giddens, Anthony. 1985a. *The Nation-State and Violence*. Cambridge: Polity.

————. 1985b. "Reason Without Revolution? Habermas's Theorie des kommunikativen Handelns," in Richard J. Bernstein, ed., *Habermas and Modernity*. Cambridge, MA: MIT Press.

Gilbert, Alan. 1999. *Must Global Politics Constrain Democracy? Great-Power Realism, Democratic Peace, and Democratic Internationalism*. Princeton: Princeton University Press.

Gill, Lesley. 2000. *Teetering on the Rim: Global Restructuring, Daily Life, and the Armed Retreat of the Bolivian State*. New York: Columbia University Press.

Gillard, Michael Sean, Melissa Jones, Andrew Rowell, and John Vidal. 1998. "BP in Colombia: A Tale of Death, Pollution and Deforestation." *The Guardian*, August 15, pp. 4–5.

Gillis, John R., ed. 1989. *The Militarization of the Western World*. New Brunswick: Rutgers University Press.

Giner, Salvador. 1995. "Comment," in Amiya Bagchi, ed., *Democracy and Development*. New York: St. Martin's, pp. 24–27.

Gleijeses, Piero. 1991. *Shattered Hope: The Guatemalan Revolution and the United States, 1944–1954*. Princeton: Princeton University Press.

Goldgeier, James, and Michael McFaul. 1992. "A Tale of Two Worlds: Core and Periphery in the Post–Cold War Era." *International Organization* 46(2): 467–491.

Gong, Gerritt W. 1984. *The Standard of "Civilization" in International Society*. Oxford: Clarendon.

Gopal, Sarvepalli. 1984. *Jawaharlal Nehru: A Biography*, Vol. 3. Cambridge, MA: Harvard University Press.

Gowa, Joanne. 1999. *Bullets and Ballots*. Princeton: Princeton University Press.

GPD. 1992. "Indo-Pak Relations: Getting to the Roots." *Economic and Political Weekly* 36: 1889–1890.

Gray, John. 1998. "Where Pluralists and Liberals Part Company." *International Journal of Philosophical Studies* 6(1): 17–36.

Greider, William. 1993. "The Global Marketplace: A Closet Dictator," in Ralph Nader et al., eds., *The Case Against Free Trade*. San Francisco: Earth Island, pp. 195–217.

———. 1997. *One World Ready or Not*. New York: Simon and Schuster.

Gupta, Karunakar. 1956. *Indian Foreign Policy*. Calcutta: World Press.

Gurr, Ted Robert. 1990. *Polity II: Political Structures and Regime Change (Codebook)*. Ann Arbor: ICPSR No. 9263.

———. 1993. *Minorities at Risk: A Global View of Ethnopolitical Conflict*. Washington, DC: United States Institute of Peace.

Habermas, Jürgen. 1968. "Technik und Wissenschaft als 'Ideologie,'" in *Technik und Wissenschaft als "Ideologie."* Frankfurt: Suhrkamp Verlag.

———. 1984. "Toward a Reconstruction of Historical Materialism," in Jurgen Habermas, *Communication and the Evolution of Society*, trans. Thomas McCarthy. Boston: Beacon, pp. 130–177.

———. 1987. *The Philosophical Discourse of Modernity*, trans. Frederick Lawrence. Cambridge, MA: MIT Press.

———. 1989 [1961]. *Strukturwandel der Öffentlichkeit*. Darmstadt and Neuwied, FRG: Hermann Luchterhand Verlag; trans. Thomas Burger as *The Structural Transformation of the Public Sphere*. Cambridge, MA: MIT Press.

———. 1997. "Kant's Idea of Perpetual Peace, with the Benefit of Two Hundred Years' Hindsight," in James Bohman and Matthias Lutz-Bachmann, eds., *Perpetual Peace: Essays on Kant's Cosmopolitan Ideal*. Cambridge, MA: MIT Press, pp. 113–153.

Hagtvet, Bernt. 1980. "The Theory of Mass Society and the Collapse of the Weimar Republic: A Reexamination," in Stein Ugelvik Larsen et al., eds., *Who Were the*

Fascists? Social Roots of European Fascism. Bergen: Universitetsforlaget, pp. 66–117.

Hall, Stuart. 1988. "The Toad in the Garden: Thatcherism Among the Theorists," in Charles Nelson and Lawrence Grossberg, eds., *Marxism and the Interpretation of Culture.* Urbana: University of Illinois Press, pp. 35–73.

Halliday, Fred. 1994. *Rethinking International Relations.* Vancouver: University of British Columbia Press.

Halperin, Morton H., et al. 1976. *The Lawless State: The Crimes of the U.S. Intelligence Agencies.* New York: Penguin.

Hamilton, Alexander, James Madison, and John Jay. 1961. *The Federalist Papers,* with an introduction by Clinton Rossiter. New York: New American Library.

Harff, Barbara, and Ted Robert Gurr. 1988. "Toward an Empirical Theory of Genocides and Politicides: Identification and Measurement of Cases Since 1945." *International Studies Quarterly* 32(3): 359–371.

Heale, M. J. 1990. *American Anticommunism: Combating the Enemy Within, 1830–1970.* Baltimore: Johns Hopkins University Press.

Hegel, Georg Wilhelm Friedrich. 1952. *The Philosophy of Right,* trans. T. M. Knox. Oxford: Oxford University Press.

Held, David. 1987. *Models of Democracy.* Cambridge: Polity.

———. 1992. "Democracy: From City-State to Cosmopolitan Governance." *Political Studies,* Special Issue: September.

———. 1995. *Democracy and the Global Order: From the Modern State to Cosmopolitan Governance.* Stanford: Stanford University Press.

———. 1997. "Cosmopolitan Democracy and the Global Order: A New Agenda," in James Bohman and Matthias Lutz-Bachmann, eds., *Perpetual Peace: Essays on Kant's Cosmopolitan Ideal.* Cambridge, MA: MIT Press, pp. 235–251.

Held, David, Anthony McGrew, David Goldblatt, and Jonathan Perraton. 1999. *Global Transformations: Politics, Economics and Culture.* Cambridge: Polity.

Henderson, Gregory. 1968. *Korea: The Politics of the Vortex.* Cambridge, MA: Harvard University Press.

Henwood, Doug. 1997a. "Dow 7000." *Left Business Observer* 76 (February 18): .

———. 1997b. "Earnings," posted on *Left Business Observer* website: <http://www.panix.com/~dhenwood/Stats _earns.html>.

———. 1997c. "Measuring Privilege." *Left Business Observer* 78 (July 17): .

Hermann, Margaret G., and Charles W. Kegley Jr. 1995. "Rethinking Democracy and International Peace: Perspectives from Political Psychology." *International Studies Quarterly* 39(4): 511–534.

Herz, John. 1950. "Idealist Internationalism and the Security Dilemma." *World Politics* 2(2): 157–180.

Hettne, Bjorn. 1997. "The Double Movement: Global Market and Regionalism," in Robert W. Cox, ed., *The New Realism: Multilateralism and World Order.* Tokyo: United Nations University Press, pp. 223–242.

Hintze, Otto. 1975. "Military Organization and the Organization of the State," in Felix Gilbert, ed., *The Historical Essays of Otto Hintze.* New York: Oxford University Press, pp. 178–215.

Hobsbawm, Eric. 1990. *Nations and Nationalism Since 1780: Programme, Myth, Reality.* Cambridge: Cambridge University Press.

Holsti, Kalevi J. 1996. *The State, War and the State of War.* Cambridge: Cambridge University Press.

Honneth, Axel. 1997. "Is Universalism a Moral Trap? Presuppositions and Limits of a Politics of Human Rights," in James Bohman and Matthias Lutz-Bachmann, eds., *Perpetual Peace: Essays on Kant's Cosmopolitan Ideal.* Cambridge, MA: MIT Press, pp. 155–178.

Horowitz, Donald L. 1985. *Ethnic Groups in Conflict.* Berkeley: University of California Press.

———. 2000. "Constitutional Design: An Oxymoron?" in Ian Shapiro and Stephen Macedo, eds., *Designing Democratic Institutions.* New York: New York University Press, pp. 253–284.

Horowitz, Irving Louis. 1982. *Taking Lives: Genocide and State Power,* 3d ed. New Brunswick, NJ: Transaction.

Howard, Michael. 1983. *The Causes of Wars.* London: Temple Smith.

Human Rights Watch. 1995. *Slaughter Among Neighbors.* New Haven: Yale University Press.

Huntington, Samuel P. 1957. *The Soldier and the State.* Cambridge, MA: Belknap.

———. 1996. *The Clash of Civilizations and the Remaking of World Order.* New York: Simon and Schuster.

Inayatullah, Naeem. 1996. "Beyond the Sovereignty Dilemma: Quasi-States as Social Construct," in Thomas Biersteker and Cynthia Weber, eds., *State Sovereignty as Social Construct.* Cambridge: Cambridge University Press, pp. 50–80.

Inayatullah, Naeem, and David L. Blaney. 1996. "Knowing Encounters: Beyond Parochialism in International Relations Theory," in Yosef Lapid and Friedrich Kratochwil, eds., *The Return of Culture and Identity in IR Theory.* Boulder: Lynne Rienner, pp. 65–84.

Isaac, Jeffrey. 1987. *Power and Marxist Theory.* Ithaca: Cornell University Press.

Jalal, Ayesha. 1995. *Democracy and Authoritarianism in South Asia: A Comparative and Historical Perspective.* New Delhi: Cambridge University Press.

James, Patrick, and Glenn E. Mitchell II. 1995. "Targets of Covert Pressure: The Hidden Victims of the Democratic Peace." *International Interactions* 21(1): 85–107.

Janowitz, Morris. 1960. *The Professional Soldier: A Social and Political Portrait.* Glencoe, IL: Free Press.

Jenkins, Rhys. 1987. *Transnational Corporations and Uneven Development: The Internationalization of Capital and the Third World.* London: Routledge.

Jessop, Bob. 1997. "Capitalism and Its Future: Remarks on Regulation, Government, and Governance." *Review of International Political Economy* 4(3): 561–581.

Johnson, Chalmers. 1982. *Miti and the Japanese Miracle: The Growth of Industrial Policy, 1925–1975.* Stanford: Stanford University Press.

Johnson, U. Alexis. 1984, with Jef Olivarius McAllister. *The Right Hand of Power.* Englewood Cliffs, NJ: Prentice-Hall.

Jonassohn, Kurt. 1998. *Genocide and Gross Human Rights Violations in Comparative Perspective.* New Brunswick, NJ: Transaction.

Junghyo, Ahn. 1989. *White Badge.* New York: Soho.

Kacowicz, Arie. 1998. *Zones of Peace in the Third World: South America and West Africa in Comparative Perspective.* Albany: SUNY Press.

Kahin, Audrey R., and George McT. Kahin. 1995. *Subversion as Foreign Policy: The Secret Eisenhower and Dulles Debacle in Indonesia.* New York: New Press.

Kaldor, Mary. 1982. "Warfare and Capitalism," in E. P. Thompson et al., eds., *Exterminism and Cold War.* London: New Left, pp. 261–287.

———. 1997. "Introduction," in Mary Kaldor and Basker Vashee, eds., *New Wars.* London: Cassell, pp. 3–33.

———. 1998. *Organised Warfare in a Global Era.* Cambridge: Polity.

Kamel, R., and A. Hoffman, eds. 1999. *The Maquiladora Reader.* Philadelphia: American Friends Service Committee.

Kant, Immanuel. 1970. *Political Writings,* ed. Hans Reiss. Cambridge: Cambridge University Press.

———. 1983. *To Perpetual Peace, a Philosophical Sketch.* Indianapolis: Hackett.

———. 1991 [1796]. *On Perpetual Peace,* reprinted in *Kant's Political Writings.* Cambridge: Cambridge University Press.

Kaviraj, Sudipta. 1992. "The Imaginary Institution of India," in Partha Chatterjee and Gyanendra Pandey, eds., *Subaltern studies VII.* Delhi: Oxford University Press, pp. 1–39.

———. 1995. "Democracy and Development in India," in Amiya Kumar Bagchi, ed., *Democracy and Development.* New York: St. Martin's, pp. 92–130.

Kelsey, Jane. 1997. *The New Zealand Experiment: A World Model for Structural Adjustment?* 2d ed. Auckland: Auckland University Press.

Keohane, Robert O., and Joseph S. Nye. 1977. *Power and Interdependence: World Politics in Transition.* Boston: Little, Brown.

———. 1989. *Power and Interdependence,* 2d ed. New York: HarperCollins.

Khatak, Saba Gul. 1996. "Security Discourses and the State in Pakistan." *Alternatives* 21: 341–362.

Klare, Michael. 1991. "The Pentagon's New Paradigm," in Micah L. Sifry and Christopher Cerf, eds., *The Gulf War: History, Documents, Opinions.* New York: Times Books, pp. 466–476.

———. 1995. *Rogue States and Nuclear Outlaws: America's Search for a New Foreign Policy.* New York: Hill and Wang.

Kolko, Gabriel. 1988. *Confronting the Third World: United States Foreign Policy 1945–1980.* New York: Pantheon.

Koshar, Rudy. 1986. *Social Life, Local Politics, and Nazism: Marburg, 1880–1935.* Chapel Hill: University of North Carolina Press.

Kothari, Rajni. 1997. "Globalization: A World Adrift." *Alternatives* 22(2): 227–267.

Krasner, Stephen D. 1999. *Sovereignty: Organized Hypocrisy.* Princeton: Princeton University Press.

Kratochwil, Friedrich, and John Gerard Ruggie. 1986. "International Organization: A State of the Art on an Art of the State." *International Organization* 40(4): 753–775.

Kreisberg, Paul H. 1993. "Foreign Policy in 1992: Building Credibility," in Philip Oldenburg, ed., *India Briefing, 1993.* Boulder: Westview, pp. 40–73.

Krishna, Sankaran. 1994. "Inscribing the Nation: Nehru and the Politics of Identity in India," in Stephen Rosow, Naeem Inayatullah, and Mark Rupert, eds. *The Global Economy as Political Space.* Boulder: Lynne Rienner, pp. 189–202.

Kubik, Timothy R.W. 1997a. "Is Machiavelli's Canon Spiked? Practical Reading in Military History Today." *Journal of Military History* 61(1): 1–30.

———. 1997b. "Spiked Canon? The End of Reading in Military Thought." Ph.D. diss., Johns Hopkins University, Baltimore.

Kuper, Leo. 1981. *Genocide: Its Political Use in the Twentieth Century.* New Haven: Yale University Press.

Kux, Dennis. 1992. *India and the United States: Estranged Democracies 1941–1991.* Washington, DC: National Defense University Press.

Kymlicka, Will. 1995. *Multicultural Citizenship.* Oxford: Oxford University Press.

LaFeber, Walter. 1984. *Inevitable Revolutions: The United States and Central America.* New York: W. W. Norton.

Lasswell, Harold K. 1941. "The Garrison State." *American Journal of Sociology* 46(4): 455–468.

Latham, Robert. 1997. *The Liberal Moment: Modernity, Security, and the Making of the Postwar International Order.* New York: Columbia University Press.

Layne, Christopher. 1994. "Kant or Cant: The Myth of the Democratic Peace." *International Security* 19(2): 5–49.

Lee, Namhee. 2000. "Korea's Student Movement." Ph.D. diss., University of Chicago, Chicago.

Lens, Sidney. 1987. *Permanent War: The Militarization of America.* New York: Shocken.

Levy, Jack. 1988. "Domestic Politics and War," in Robert I. Rotberg and Theodore K. Rabb, eds., *The Origin and Prevention of Major War.* Cambridge: Cambridge University Press, pp. 79–99.

Lijphart, Arend. 1977. *Democracy in Plural Societies: A Comparative Exploration.* New Haven: Yale University Press.

———. 1996. "The Puzzle of Indian Democracy: A Consociational Interpretation." *American Political Science Review* 90(2): 258–268.

Limaye, Satu P. 1993. *U.S.-Indian Relations: The Pursuit of Accommodation.* Boulder: Westview.

Lindbloom, Charles. 1977. *Politics and Markets: The World's Political Economic Systems.* New York: Basic.

Linklater, Andrew. 1993. "Liberal Democracy, Constitutionalism, and the New World Order," in Richard Leaver and James L. Richardson, eds., *Charting the Post–Cold War Order.* Boulder: Westview, pp. 29–38.

Lukes, Steven. 1973. *Individualism.* Oxford: Blackwell.

Lustick, Ian S. 1996. "History, Historiography, and Political Science: Multiple Historical Records and the Problem of Historical Bias." *American Political Science Review* 90(3): 83–95.

Lutz-Bachmann, Matthias. 1997. "Kant's Idea of Peace and the Philosophical Conception of a World Republic," in James Bohman and Matthias Lutz-Bachmann, eds., *Perpetual Peace: Essays on Kant's Cosmopolitan Ideal.* Cambridge, MA: MIT Press, pp. 59–78.

Lynn-Jones, Sean. 1996. "Preface," in Michael E. Brown, Sean M. Lynn-Jones, and Steven E. Miller, eds., *Debating the Democratic Peace.* Cambridge, MA: MIT Press, pp. ix–xxxiii.

Machiavelli, Niccolò. 1965. *The Art of War,* trans. E. Farnesworth, with an introduction by Neal Wood. New York: Da Capo.

Macdonald, Donald Stone. 1992. *U.S.-Korean Relations from Liberation to Self-Reliance, the Twenty-Year Record: An Interpretive Summary of the Archives of the U.S. Department of State for the Period 1945 to 1965.* Boulder: Westview.

Maclean, John. 1984. "Interdependence: An Ideological Intervention in International Relations," in R. J. Barry Jones and Peter Willetts, eds., *Interdependence on Trial.* London: St. Martin's, pp. 130–166.

MacMillan, John. 1995. "A Kantian Protest Against the Peculiar Discourse of the Inter-Liberal State Peace." *Millennium* 24(3): 549–562.

———. 1996. "Democracies Don't Fight: A Case of the Wrong Research Agenda." *Review of International Studies* 22(3): 275–299.

Macpherson, C. B. 1973. *Democratic Theory: Essays in Retrieval.* New York: Oxford University Press.

Mann, Michael. 1986. *The Sources of Social Power, Volume I: From the Beginning to 1760 A.D.* Cambridge: Cambridge University Press.

———. 1988. *States, War, and Capitalism.* Oxford: Basil Blackwell.

———. 1993. *Sources of Social Power, Volume 2: The Rise of Classes and Nation States, 1760–1914.* Cambridge: Cambridge University Press.

————. 1996. "Authoritarian and Liberal Militarism: A Contribution from Historical Sociology," in Steve Smith, Ken Booth, and Marysia Zalewski, eds., *International Theory: Positivism and Beyond*. Cambridge: Cambridge University Press, pp. 221–239.

————. 1999. "The Dark Side of Democracy: The Modern Tradition of Ethnic and Political Cleansing." *New Left Review* 235: 18–45.

————. 2001. "The Polymorphous State and Ethnic Cleansing," in John Hobson and Stephen Hobden, eds., *Bringing Historical Sociologies into International Relations*. Cambridge: Cambridge University Press.

Mansfield, Edward D., and Jack Snyder. 1995. "Democratization and the Danger of War." *International Security* 20(1): 5–38.

Mansingh, Surjit. 1984. *India's Search for Power: Indira Gandhi's Foreign Policy 1966–1982*. New Delhi: Sage.

Maoz, Zeev. 1997. "The Controversy Over the Democratic Peace: Rearguard Action or Cracks in the Wall?" *International Security* 22(1): 162–198.

Maoz, Zeev, and Nasrin Abdolali. 1989. "Regime Types and International Conflict, 1816–1976." *Journal of Conflict Resolution* 33(1): 3–36.

Maoz, Zeev, and Bruce Russett. 1992. "Alliances, Contiguity, Wealth, and Political Stability: Is the Lack of Conflict Among Democracies a Statistical Artifact?" *International Interactions* 17(2): 245–267.

————. 1993. "Normative and Structural Causes of the Democratic Peace." *American Political Science Review* 87(3): 624–38.

Marx, Karl. 1977. *Capital,* Vol. I. New York: Vintage.

————. 1978. "The German Ideology, Part I," in Robert C. Tucker, ed., *The Marx-Engels Reader,* 2d ed. New York: W. W. Norton, pp. 146–200.

McCarthy, J. 1995. *Death and Exile: The Ethnic Cleansing of Ottoman Muslims, 1821–1922*. Princeton: Darwin.

McCarthy, Thomas. 1989. "Introduction," in Jurgen Habermas, *The Structural Transformation of the Public Sphere*. Cambridge, MA: MIT Press, pp. xi–xiv.

————. 1997. "On the Idea of a Reasonable Law of Peoples," in James Bohman and Matthias Lutz-Bachmann, eds., *Perpetual Peace: Essays on Kant's Cosmopolitan Ideal*. Cambridge, MA: MIT Press, pp. 201–217.

McClintock, Michael. 1992. *Instruments of Statecraft: U.S. Guerrilla Warfare, Counter-insurgency, and Counter-terrorism, 1940–1990*. New York: Pantheon.

McLellan, David, ed. 1977. *Karl Marx: Selected Readings*. Oxford: Oxford University Press.

McMichael, Philip. 2000. "Globalisation: Trend or Project?" in Ronen Palan, ed., *Global Political Economy: Contemporary Theories*. London: Routledge, pp. 100–113.

McNeill, William H. 1982. *The Pursuit of Power: Technology, Armed Force, and Society Since A.D. 1000*. Chicago: University of Chicago Press.

Mearsheimer, John. 1990a. "Back to the Future: Instability in Europe After the Cold War." *International Security* 15(1): 5–56.

————. 1990b. "Back to the Future: Part II." *International Security* 15(2): 194–199.

Meinecke, Friedrich. 1950. *The German Catastrophe: Reflections and Recollections*. Cambridge, MA: Harvard University Press.

Meyer, John W., John Boli, George M. Thomas, and Francisco O. Ramirez. 1997. "World Society and the Nation-State." *American Journal of Sociology* 103(1): 144–181.

Mills, C. Wright. 1956. *The Power Elite*. New York: Oxford University Press.

————. 1958. *The Causes of World War Three*. London: Secker and Warburg.

Milne, Seamus. 1994. *The Enemy Within: The Secret War Against the Miners*. London: Pan.

Mishel, Lawrence. 1997. "Behind the Numbers: Capital's Gain." *American Prospect* 33 (July-August): 71–73 <http://epn.org/prospect/33/33mishf.html>.

Mishel, Lawrence, Jared Bernstein, and John Schmitt. 1997. *The State of Working America, 1996–97*, Armonck, NY: M. E. Sharpe.

Montville, Joseph V., ed. 1997. *Conflict and Peacemaking in Multiethnic Societies*. Lexington, MA: Lexington.

Moody, Kim. 1997. "Towards an International Social-Movement Unionism." *New Left Review* 225: 52–72.

Moon, J. Donald. 1998. "Engaging Plurality: Reflections on *The Ethos of Pluralization*." *Philosophy and Social Criticism* 24(1): 63–71.

Moore, Barrington, Jr. 1966. *The Social Origins of Dictatorship and Democracy*. Boston: Beacon.

Moravcsik, Andrew. 1997. "Taking Preferences Seriously: A Liberal Theory of International Politics." *International Organization* 51(4): 513–553.

Morgan, T. Clifton. 1993. "Democracy and War: Reflections on the Literature." *International Interactions* 18(3): 197–203.

Morgan, T. Clifton, and Valerie L. Schwebach. 1992. "Take Two Democracies and Call Me in the Morning: A Prescription for Peace?" *International Interactions* 17(4): 305–320.

Morin, Richard. 1991. "Decision to Go to War Given Initial Support." *Washington Post*, January 17: A23.

Morley, David, and Kuan-Hsing Chen, eds. 1996. *Stuart Hall: Critical Dialogues in Cultural Studies*. London: Routledge.

Mouffe, Chantal. 1990. "Rawls: Political Philosophy Without Politics," in David M. Rasmussen, ed., *Universalism vs. Communitarianism: Contemporary Debates in Ethics*. Cambridge, MA: MIT Press, pp. 217–235.

———. 1992. "Preface: Democratic Politics Today," in Chantal Mouffe, ed., *Dimensions of Radical Democracy: Pluralism, Citizenship, Community*. London: Verso, pp. 1–14.

Muppidi, Himadeep. 1999a. "Competitive Economic Restructuring in the Global Economy: A Critical Constructivist Approach." Ph.D. diss., University of Minnesota, Minneapolis.

———. 1999b. "Postcoloniality and the Production of International Insecurity: The Persistent Puzzle of U.S.-Indian Relations," in Jutta Weldes, Mark Laffey, Hugh Gusterson, and Raymond Duvall, eds., *Cultures of Insecurity: States, Communities, and the Production of Danger*. Minneapolis: University of Minnesota Press, pp. 119–146.

Muravchik, Joshua. 1992. *Exporting Democracy*. Washington, DC: American Enterprise Institute.

Nandy, Ashis. 1983. *The Intimate Enemy: Loss and Recovery of Self Under Colonialism*. Delhi: Oxford University Press.

———. 1987. *Traditions, Tyranny and Utopias: Essays in the Politics of Awareness*. Delhi: Oxford University Press.

———. 1990. "The Politics of Secularism and the Recovery of Religious Tolerance," in R.B.J. Walker and Saul H. Mendlovitz, eds., *Contending Sovereignties: Redefining Political Community*. Boulder: Lynne Rienner, pp. 125–144.

———. 1994. *The Illegitimacy of Nationalism*. Delhi: Oxford University Press.

Nehru, Jawaharlal. 1954. *Jawaharlal Nehru's Speeches, Volume Two*. New Delhi: Publications Division, Government of India.

————. 1958. *Jawaharlal Nehru's Speeches, Volume Three.* New Delhi: Publications Division, Government of India.

————. 1961. *India's Foreign Policy: Selected Speeches, September 1946–April 1961.* New Delhi: Publications Division, Government of India.

————. 1964. *Jawaharlal Nehru's Speeches, September 1957–April 1963.* New Delhi: Publications Division, Government of India.

Neuman, Stephanie G. 1986. *Military Assistance in Recent Wars.* New York: Praeger.

Ohmae, Kenichi. 1990. *The Borderless World: Power and Strategy in the International Economy.* Oxford: Clarendon.

Oneal, James, and Bruce Russett. 1997. "The Classical Liberals Were Right: Democracy, Interdependence, and Conflict, 1950–1992," *International Studies Quarterly* 41(2): 267–294.

Onuf, Nicholas G. 1998. *The Republican Legacy in International Thought.* Cambridge: Cambridge University Press.

Onuf, Nicholas G., and Thomas J. Johnson. 1995. "Peace in the Liberal World: Does Democracy Matter?" in Charles W. Kegley, Jr., ed., *Controversies in International Relations Theory: Realism and the Neoliberal Challenge.* New York: St. Martin's, pp. 179–198.

Orden, Geoffrey van. 1991. "The Bundeswehr in Transition." *Survival* 33 (July–August): 352–370.

Oren, Ido. 1995. "The Subjectivity of the 'Democratic Peace': Changing U.S. Perceptions of Imperial Germany." *International Security* 20(2): 147–184.

Owen, John. 1994. "How Liberalism Produces Democratic Peace." *International Security* 19(2): 87–125.

————. 1997. *Liberal Peace, Liberal War: American Politics and International Security.* Ithaca: Cornell University Press.

Panitch, Leo. 1996. "Rethinking the Role of the State," in James H. Mittelman, ed., *Globalization: Critical Reflections.* Boulder: Lynne Rienner, pp. 83–116.

Parekh, Bhikhu. 1992. "The Cultural Particularity of Liberal Democracy." *Political Studies* 40: 160–175.

————. 1997. "The West and Its Others," in Keith Ansell-Pearson, Benita Parry, and Judith Squires, eds., *Cultural Readings of Imperialism: Edward Said and the Gravity of History.* New York: St. Martin's, pp. 173–193.

Pasha, Mustapha K. 1996. "Security as Hegemony." *Alternatives* 21: 283–302.

Pasha, Mustapha K., and David L. Blaney. 1998. "Elusive Paradise: The Promise and Peril of Global Civil Society." *Alternatives* 23(4): 417–450.

Paterson, Thomas G. 1988. *Meeting the Communist Threat: Truman to Reagan.* Oxford: Oxford University Press.

Peck, Jamie, and Adam Tickell. 1994. "Searching for a New Institutional Fix: The *After*-Fordist Crisis and the Global-Local Disorder," in Ash Amin, ed., *Post-Fordism: A Reader.* Oxford: Blackwell, pp. 280–315.

Petras, James F., and Morris H. Morley. 1981. "The U.S. Imperial State," in James F. Petras et al., eds., *Class, State, and Power in the Third World.* Montclair, NJ: Allanheld, Osmun, pp. 1–36.

Pletsch, Carl. 1981. "The Three Worlds, or the Division of Social Scientific Labor, Circa 1950–1975." *Comparative Studies in Society and History* 23(4): 565–590.

Poewe, Karla. 1985. *The Namibia Herero: A History of Their Psychological Disintegration and Survival.* Lewiston, NY: E. Mellen.

Prados, John. 1996. *Presidents' Secret Wars: CIA and Pentagon Covert Operations from World War II Through the Persian Gulf.* Chicago: Elephant Paperbacks.

Przeworski, Adam, and Fernando Limongi. 1995. "Political Regimes and Economic Growth," in Amiya Bagchi, ed., *Democracy and Development*. New York: St. Martin's, pp. 1–23.

Putnam, Robert D. 1993. *Making Democracy Work: Civic Traditions in Modern Italy*. Princeton: Princeton University Press.

———. 2000. *Bowling Alone: The Collapse and Revival of American Community*. New York: Simon and Schuster.

Pye, Lucian W. 1990. "Political Science and the Crisis of Authoritarianism." *American Political Science Review* 84(1): 3–19.

Raghavan, Chakravarthi. 1990. *Recolonization: GATT, the Uruguay Round and the Third World*. London: Zed.

Rawls, John. 1971. *A Theory of Justice*. Cambridge, MA: Harvard University Press.

———. 1988. "The Priority of Right and Ideas of the Good." *Philosophy and Public Affairs* 17(4): 251–277.

———. 1989. "The Domain of the Political and Overlapping Consensus." *New York University Law Review* 64(2): 233–255.

———. 1993. "The Law of Peoples," in Stephen Shute and Susan Hurley, eds., *On Human Rights: The Oxford Amnesty Lectures 1993*. New York: HarperCollins, pp. 41–82.

Ray, James Lee. 1995. *Democracy and International Conflict: An Evaluation of the Democratic Peace Proposition*. Columbia: University of South Carolina Press.

———. 1997. "The Democratic Path to Peace." *Journal of Democracy* 8(2): 49–64.

Reiss, Hans. 1970. "Introduction," in Hans Reiss, ed., *Kant: Political Writings*. Cambridge: Cambridge University Press, pp. 1–40.

Risse-Kappen, Thomas. 1995. *Co-operation Among Democracies: The European Influence on U.S. Foreign Policy*. Princeton: Princeton University Press.

Ritter, Gerhard. 1969–1973. *The Sword and the Scepter: The Problem of Militarism in Germany*, 4 Volumes, trans. Heinz Norden. Coral Gables: University of Miami Press.

Robinson, Ian. 1995. "Globalization and Democracy," *Dissent* (summer): 373–380.

Robinson, William. 1996a. "Globalization, the World System, and 'Democracy Promotion' in U.S. Foreign Policy." *Theory and Society* 25(5): 615–665.

———. 1996b. *Promoting Polyarchy: Globalization, U.S. Intervention and Hegemony*. Cambridge: Cambridge University Press.

Rosenau, James N. 1990. *Turbulence in World Politics*. Princeton: Princeton University Press.

Rosenau, James, and Ernst-Otto Czempiel, eds. 1992. *Governance Without Government: Order and Change in World Politics*. Cambridge: Cambridge University Press.

Rosenberg, David Alan. 1983. "The Origins of Overkill: Nuclear Weapons and American Strategy." *International Security* 7(4): 3–71.

Rosenberg, Hans. 1958. *Bureaucracy, Aristocracy, and Autocracy: The Prussian Experience, 1660–1815*. Cambridge, MA: Beacon.

Ross, Dorothy. 1991. *The Origins of American Social Science*. Cambridge: Cambridge University Press.

Rueschemeyer, Dietrich, Evelyn Huber Stephens, and John D. Stephens. 1992. *Capitalist Development and Democracy*. Chicago: University of Chicago Press.

Ruggie, John Gerard. 1993. "Territoriality and Beyond: Problematizing Modernity in International Relations." *International Organization* 47(1): 139–174.

Rummel R. J. 1994. *Death by Government*. New Brunswick, NJ: Transaction.

Rupert, Mark. 1995. *Producing Hegemony: The Politics of Mass Production and American Global Power*. Cambridge: Cambridge University Press.

———. 2000. *Ideologies of Globalization: Contending Visions of a New World Order*. London: Routledge.

Russett, Bruce. 1990. *Controlling the Sword: The Democratic Governance of National Security*. Cambridge, MA: Harvard University Press.

———. 1993. *Grasping the Democratic Peace: Principles for a Post–Cold War World*. Princeton: Princeton University Press.

———. 1995. "'And Yet It Moves.'" *International Security*, 19(4): 164–175.

Russett, Bruce, John Oneal, and David R. Davis. 1998. "The Third Leg of the Kantian Tripod for Peace: International Organizations and Militarized Disputes, 1950–1985." *International Organization* 52(3): 441–468.

Sagan, Scott. 1993. *The Limits of Safety: Organizations, Accidents and Nuclear Weapons*. Princeton: Princeton University Press.

Sandel, Michael. 1984. "The Procedural Republic and the Unencumbered Self." *Political Theory* 12(1): 81–96.

———. 1996. *Democracy's Discontent: America in Search of a Public Philosophy*. Cambridge, MA: Harvard University Press.

Sanders, Bernie. 1999. "Global Sustainable Development Resolution." Office of Congressional Representative Bernie Sanders, VT <www.house.gov/bernie/legislation/global/index.html>.

Sayer, Derek. 1991. *Capitalism and Modernity*. London: Routledge.

Schaffer, Howard. 1993. *Chester Bowles: New Dealer in the Cold War*. London: Harvard University Press.

Schlesinger, Stephen, and Stephen Kinzer. 1982. *Bitter Fruit*. New York: Anchor.

Schmidt, Brian. 1997. *The Political Discourse of Anarchy: A Disciplinary History of International Relations*. Albany: SUNY Press.

Scholte, Jan Aart. 1993. *International Relations of Social Change*. Buckingham: Open University Press.

———. 1996. "Globalization: Beyond the Buzzword," in Eleonore Kofman and Gillian Youngs, eds., *Globalization: Theory and Practice*. London: Pinter.

———. 2000. *Globalisation: A Critical Introduction*. London: MacMillan.

Shaw, Martin. 1988. *Dialectics of War: An Essay in the Social Theory of Total War and Peace*. London: Pluto.

———. 1989. "War and the Nation-State," in David Held and John B. Thompson, eds., *Social Theory of Modern Societies: Anthony Giddens and His Critics*. Cambridge: Cambridge University Press, pp. 129–146.

———. 1991. *Post-military Society: Militarism, Demilitarization and War at the End of the Twentieth Century*. Philadelphia: Temple University Press.

———. 1994. *Global Society and International Relations*. Cambridge: Polity.

———. 1997a. "Globalization and Post-military Democracy," in Anthony McGrew, ed., *The Transformation of Democracy?* Milton Keynes: Open University Press, pp. 26–48.

———. 1997b. "The State of Globalization." *Review of International Political Economy* 4(3): 497–513.

———. 1999. "War and Globality," in Ho-Won Yeong, ed., *Peace and Conflict*. New York: Dartmouth.

———. 2000a. "Historical Sociology and Global Transformation," in Ronen Palan, ed., *Global Political Economy: Contemporary Theories*. London: Routledge, pp. 229–241.

———. 2000b. *Theory of the Global State: Globality as Unfinished Revolution*. Cambridge: Cambridge University Press.

Shaw, Martin, and Michael Banks, eds. 1991. *State and Society in International Relations*. New York: St. Martin's.

Sheehan, James J. 1978. *German Liberalism in the Nineteenth Century.* Chicago: University of Chicago Press.

Sheehan, Neil. 1988. *A Bright Shining Lie: John Paul Vann and America in Vietnam.* New York: Vintage.

Sheth, D. L., and Ashis Nandy. 1996. "Introduction," in D. L. Sheth and Ashis Nandy, eds., *The Multiverse of Democracy: Essays in Honour of Rajni Kothari.* New Delhi: Sage, pp. 9–26.

Singer, Max, and Aaron Wildavsky. 1996. *The Real World Order: Zones of Peace/ Zones of Turmoil,* rev. ed. Chatham, NJ: Chatham House.

Skocpol, Theda. 1979. *States and Social Revolutions: A Comparative Analysis of France, Russia and China.* Cambridge: Cambridge University Press.

Small, Melvin, and J. David Singer. 1982. *Resort to Arms: International and Civil Wars, 1816–1980.* Beverly Hills, CA: Sage.

Smith, Adam. 1993. *Wealth of Nations,* ed. K. Sutherland. Oxford: Oxford University Press.

Smith, Dan. 1998. "Europe's Suspended Conflicts." *War Report* 58 (February–March): 11–16.

Smith, Paul. 1997. *Millennial Dreams: Contemporary Culture and Capital in the North.* London: Verso.

Smith, R. 1987. "Human Destructiveness and Politics: The Twentieth Century as an Age of Genocide," in Isadore Walliman and Michael N. Dobkowski, eds., *Genocide and the Modern Age: Etiology and Case Studies of Mass Death.* New York: Greenwood, pp. 21–40.

Sparrow, Bartholomew H. 1996. *From the Outside In: World War II and the American State.* Princeton: Princeton University Press.

Spinner, James. 1994. *The Boundaries of Citizenship: Race, Ethnicity, and Nationality in the Liberal State.* Baltimore: Johns Hopkins University Press.

Stannard, David E. 1992. *American Holocaust: Columbus and the Conquest of the New World.* New York: Oxford University Press.

Starr, Harvey. 1997. "Democracy and Integration: Why Democracies Don't Fight Each Other." *Journal of Peace Research* 32(2): 153–162.

Stevenson, Charles A. 1973. *The End of Nowhere: American Policy Toward Laos Since 1954.* Boston: Beacon.

Tambiah, Stanley Jeyaraja. 1996. *Leveling Crowds, Ethnonationalist Conflicts and Collective Violence in South Asia.* Berkeley: University of California Press.

Tanji, Miyume, and Stephanie Lawson. 1997. "'Democratic Peace' and 'Asian Democracy': A Universalist-Particularist Tension." *Alternatives* 22(1): 135–155.

Taylor, Charles. 1985. "Interpretation and the Sciences of Man," in *Philosophy and the Human Sciences: Philosophical Papers 2.* Cambridge: Cambridge University Press.

Theoharis, Athan. 1978. *Spying on Americans: Political Surveillance from Hoover to the Huston Plan.* Philadelphia: Temple University Press.

Thomas, Caroline. 1999. "Where Is the Third World Now?" *Review of International Studies* 25 (special issue): 225–243.

Thomas, Paul. 1994. *Alien Politics: Marxist State Theory Retrieved.* London: Routledge.

Thorne, Christopher. 1988. "Societies, Sociology and the International: Some Contributions and Questions, with Particular Reference to Total War," in Christopher Thorne, *Border Crossings: Studies in International History.* Oxford: Basil Blackwell, pp. 29–58.

Thornton, Thomas Perry. 1988. "India's Foreign Relations: Problems Along the Borders," in Marshall M. Bouton and Philip Oldenburg, eds., *India Briefing, 1988.* Boulder: Westview, pp. 57–83.

Tilly, Charles. 1992. *Coercion, Capital and European States, A.D. 990–1992*. Cambridge, MA: Blackwell.

Todorov, Tzvetan. 1984. *The Conquest of America: The Question of the Other*. New York: Harper and Row.

Tully, James. 1995. *Strange Multiplicity: Constitutionalism in an Age of Diversity*. Cambridge: Cambridge University Press.

Udovicki, Jasminka, and James Ridgeway, eds. 1997. *Burn This House: The Making and Unmaking of Yugoslavia*. Durham, NC: Duke University Press.

United Nations Development Program (UNDP). 1999. *Human Development Report*. New York: UNDP, Oxford University Press.

U.S. Census Bureau. 1996. "A Brief Look at Postwar U.S. Income Inequality." *Current Population Reports* P60-191.

Vagts, Alfred. 1959. *A History of Militarism: The Romance and Realities of a Profession*. New York: W. W. Norton.

Vinod, M. J. 1991. *United States Foreign Policy Towards India: A Diagnosis of the American Approach*. New Delhi: Lancers.

Wachtel, Howard. 1995. "Taming Global Money," *Challenge* (January-February): 36–40.

Walker, R.B.J. 1993. *Inside/Outside: International Relations as Political Theory*. Cambridge: Cambridge University Press.

Walt, Stephen. 1988. "Testing Theories of Alliance Formation: The Case of Southwest Asia." *International Organization* 42(2): 275–316.

Walzer, Michael. 1984. "Liberalism and the Art of Separation." *Political Theory* 12(3): 315–329.

———. 1994. *Thick and Thin: Moral Argument at Home and Abroad*. Notre Dame: University of Notre Dame Press.

Wapner, Paul. 1996. *Environmental Activism in World Civil Politics*. Albany: SUNY Press.

Warner, Roger. 1996. *Shooting the Moon: The Story of America's Clandestine War in Laos*. South Royalton, VT: Steerforth.

Wayman, Frank Whelon, J. David Singer, and Meredith Sarkees. 1996. "Inter-state, Intra-state, and Extra-systemic Wars 1816–1995." Paper presented at the International Studies Association annual meeting, April 16–21, San Diego, CA.

Weart, Spencer. 1998. *Never at War: Why Democracies Will Not Fight One Another*. New Haven: Yale University Press.

Weber, Eugen. 1976. *Peasants into Frenchmen: The Modernization of Rural France, 1870–1914*. Stanford: Stanford University Press.

Weber, Max. 1947. *The Theory of Social and Economic Organization*, trans. A. M. Henderson and Talcott Parsons. New York: Oxford University Press.

———. 1978. *Economy and Society*, Vol. 1. Berkeley: University of California Press.

———. 1981. *General Economic History*, trans. Frank H. Knight, introduction by Ira J. Cohen. New Brunswick, NJ: Transaction.

Wehler, Hans-Ulrich. 1985. *The German Empire: 1871–1918*, trans. Kim Traynor. New York: Berg.

Weldes, Jutta, Mark Laffey, Hugh Gusterson, Raymond Duvall, eds. 1999. *Cultures of Insecurity: States, Communities and the Production of Danger*. Minneapolis: University of Minnesota Press.

Weltman, John J. 1995. *World Politics and the Evolution of War*. Baltimore: Johns Hopkins University Press.

Wendt, Alexander. 1992. "Anarchy Is What States Make of It: The Social Construction of Power Politics." *International Organization* 46(2): 391–425.

————. 1999. *Social Theory of International Politics*. Cambridge: Cambridge University Press.

Wendt, Alexander, and Daniel Friedheim. 1996. "Hierarchy Under Anarchy: Informal Empire and the East German State," in Thomas J. Biersteker and Cynthia Weber, eds., *State Sovereignty as Social Construct*. Cambridge: Cambridge University Press, pp. 240–277.

White, Stephen K. 1995. "Reason, Modernity and Democracy," in Stephen K. White, ed., *The Cambridge Companion to Habermas*. Cambridge: Cambridge University Press, pp. 3–18.

Williams, David. 2000. "Aid and Sovereignty: Quasi-states and the International Financial Institutions," *Review of International Studies* 26(4): 557–573.

Williams, Raymond. 1973. *The Country and the City*. New York: Oxford University Press.

Wimmer, A. 1997. "Who Owns the State? Understanding Ethnic Conflict in Postcolonial Societies." *Nations and Nationalism* 3(4): 631–665.

Wise, David, and Thomas B. Ross. 1974. *The Invisible Government: The CIA and U.S. Intelligence*. New York: Vintage.

Wolf, Charles, Jr., and Katherine Watkins Webb, eds. 1987. *Developing Cooperative Forces in the Third World*. Lexington, MA: Lexington.

Wolferen, Karel van. 1989. *The Enigma of Japanese Power: People and Politics in a Stateless Nation*. New York: Alfred A. Knopf.

Woo, Jung-en. 1991. *Race to the Swift: State and Finance in the Industrialization of Korea*. New York: Columbia University Press.

Wood, Ellen. 1995. *Democracy Against Capitalism*. Cambridge: Cambridge University Press.

Woodward, Susan L. 1997. *Balkan Tragedy: Chaos and Dissolution After the Cold War*. Washington, DC: Brookings Institution.

Wright, Richard. 1956. *The Color Curtain: A Report on the Bandung Conference*. Cleveland: World.

Yiftachel, O. 1999. "'Ethnocracy': The Politics of Judaizing Israel/Palestine." *Constellations: An International Journal of Critical and Democratic Theory*, 6(3): 364–390.

Young, Iris Marion. 1990. *Justice and the Politics of Difference*. Princeton: Princeton University Press.

————. 1996. "Communication and the Other: Beyond Deliberative Democracy," in Seyla Benhabib, ed., *Democracy and Difference: Contesting the Boundaries of the Political*. Princeton: Princeton University Press, pp. 120–135.

Zolo, Daniolo. 1992. *Democracy and Complexity: A Realist Approach*. University Park: Pennsylvania State University Press.

The Contributors

Tarak Barkawi is lecturer in international relations, University of Wales, Aberystwyth.

David L. Blaney is associate professor of political science, Macalester College.

Bruce Cumings is professor of history, University of Chicago.

Raymond Duvall is professor of political science, University of Minnesota.

Timothy R.W. Kubik is instructor in cultural history and assistant director for the high school, Ross Institute and School.

Mark Laffey is lecturer in international relations, School of Oriental and African Studies, University of London.

Michael Mann is professor of sociology, UCLA.

Himadeep Muppidi is assistant professor of political science, Vassar College.

Mark Rupert is associate professor of political science, Syracuse University.

Martin Shaw is professor of international relations, University of Sussex.

Jutta Weldes is lecturer in international relations, University of Bristol.

Index

Albania, 78, 112
Albright, Madeleine, 149
Allende, Salvador, 116
American Friends Service Committee, 125
Annan, Kofi, 191
Aquino, Benigno, 145
Arbenz, Jacobo, 113–114, 118–119
Armas, Castillo, 113
Armenia, 78–79, 189
Army of the Republic of Vietnam (ARVN), 121
Asian values, 131, 150
Australia, 6, 73, 75, 76, 77
Azerbaijan, 79, 189

Balkans, The, 77–81, 176, 188–192
Belgium, 6
Blackbourn, David, 91–92, 96
Bohman, James, 33
Bosnia, 9, 80, 81, 191
Brazil, 113
Brecher, Jeremy, 169–170
Britain, 84, 181, 188; as imperial state, 6; as liberal state, 16, 68–69, 166, 182
British Petroleum, 23
Bulgaria, 78
Burma, 119

California, 73–74, 75
Cambodia, 119, 121
Canada, 170
Capital: internationalization of, 3, 8
Capitalism, 130, 135–137, 153–172,

202–203; as anti-democratic, 165–167; and liberalism, 153–172; and social power, 163–164
Capital strike, 163–164; and citizen sovereignty, 164
Carr, E. H., 207n2
Casey, William, 145
Castro, Fidel, 17
Causal analysis, 2–3, 8, 100–102, 173–177, 196–207; versus constitutive analysis, 22, 199–204; and historiography, 88–99, 102–105; and liberalism, 46, 47–48, 153–155; and realism, 48–49
Ceauşescu, Nicolae, 145
Central Intelligence Agency (CIA), 122–123, 125–126, 139, 145; and Civil Air Transport (CAT), 113, 114; and Correlates of War, 10, 113–115; Korean, 140, 144
Chechnya, 79, 189
Chile, 18, 113, 170
China, 45, 64–65, 66n7, 138, 187–189, 191; relations with India, 53–60, 66n8
Civic culture, 19, 132, 134, 151, 152n6, 152n9
Civil society, 130, 131–135, 188
Class: and class struggle, 15–16; and democracy, 17; and ethnicity, 82, 83; and German militarism, 91–99; and investors, 162–164; and liberal democracy, 15–16, 134–136, 158–172, 199; and South Korean democracy, 146–147

231

About the Book

The connection between liberalism and peace—and the reason why democratic countries appear not to go to war with each other—has become a dominant theme in international relations research. This book argues that scholars need to move beyond the "democratic peace debate" to ask more searching questions about the relationship of democracy, liberalism, and war.

The authors focus on the multiple and often contradictory ways in which liberalism, democracy, war, and peace interrelate. Acknowledging that a "zone of peace" exists, they concentrate on the particular historical and political contexts that make peace possible. This approach allows the redefinition of the "democratic peace" as a particular set of policies and claims to knowledge—a worldview that allows the continuation of violence against "nonliberal" others and the justification of extreme divisions of wealth and power in international society.

Tarak Barkawi is lecturer in international relations at the University of Wales, Aberystwyth. **Mark Laffey** is lecturer in international relations at the School of Oriental and African Studies, University of London. He is coeditor of *Cultures of Insecurity: States, Communities, and the Production of Danger.*